Paradise Lost?

Paradise Lost?

State Failure in Nepal

Ali Riaz and Subho Basu

LEXINGTON BOOKS

A division of
ROWMAN & LITTLEFIELD PUBLISHERS, INC.
Lanham • Boulder • New York • Toronto • Plymouth, UK

LEXINGTON BOOKS

A division of Rowman & Littlefield Publishers, Inc.
A wholly owned subsidiary of The Rowman & Littlefield Publishing Group, Inc.
4501 Forbes Boulevard, Suite 200
Lanham, MD 20706

Estover Road
Plymouth PL6 7PY
United Kingdom

British Library Cataloguing in Publication Information Available

Library of Congress Cataloging-in-Publication Data

The hardback edition of this book was previously catalogued by the Library of
Congress as follows:

Riyaja, Ali.
    Paradise lost? : state failure in Nepal / Ali Riaz and Subho Basu.
        p.   cm.
    Includes bibliographical references and index.
    1. Nepal—Politics and government—21st century. 2. Political stability—Nepal.
    3. Legitimacy of governments—Nepal. 4. Political culture—Nepal. I. Basu,
    Subho. II. Title.
    DS495.6.R59 2007
    954.96—dc22   2006100861

ISBN: 978-0-7391-1426-1 (cloth : alk. paper)
ISBN: 978-0-7391-4664-4 (pbk. : alk. paper)
ISBN: 978-0-7391-5865-4 (electronic)

Printed in the United States of America

Contents

List of Tables

Acknowledgments

We have incurred many debts since we embarked on this venture on Nepali politics more than three years ago. Our friends here in the United States and in Nepal have extended help and support without which this project would have remained a dream forever.

Our colleagues at Illinois State University (ISU) and the University of Syracuse have been enormously supportive. At Syracuse, Bandita Sijapati and Deepak Thapa were instrumental in keeping us on track with new information from their sources and bearing with our provocative arguments. Professor Mahendra Lawoti of Wetsern Michigan University also enlightened us about intricacies of Nepali politics in numerous personal conversations and writings. At ISU, Professor Jamal Nassar not only regularly inquired about the progress but also constantly encouraged us. Craige Champion, Norman Kutcher, T. Y. Wang, and Richard Soderlund had encouraged us in many different ways. Craige had to bear occasional bursts of emails even when the fieldwork of the study was being conducted.

The help we received from our friends, leaders of various political parties, trade union leaders, members of civil society organizations, media personnel, and people at large in Nepal was overwhelming. There are too many of them to be identified individually, but some of them must be acknowledged with deep gratitude. Hari Sharma of Social Science Baha, Laxman Basnet of Nepal Trade Union Congress, and Prakash Raj had been kind enough to spend hours with us despite their busy schedules. Thanks to Kanak Mani Dixit, editor of *Himal Southasia*, for his invaluable suggestions and introducing a number of journalists, including Yubraj Ghimire of Samay, Subel Bhanadari, and Pratyoush Onta. Onta provided us with many contacts. The personal narratives of Bhaskar Gautam and Anubhav Ajit were immensely helpful in understanding various dimensions of the uprising in 2006. Discussions with Dr. Devendra Raj Pandey, Khagendra Sangraulo, Professor Pitamber Sharma, Dr Krishna Hachhethu, and Professor Krishna Khanal helped us understand the role of the civil society in Nepal. Dr. Om Gurung has always been willing to accommodate our odd requests during the field research. Keshavji at Mandala Book Point acted as the contact point for us. Among the political leaders, senior CPN (UML) leader Jahalanath Khanal, CPN (Maoist) leader Sureash Ale Magar and Sadbhavana Party activist Anil Kumar Jha deserve more than our thanks. The Nepal Workers and Peasant Party activists welcomed us in their party offices.

Professor Michael Hutt, one of the most celebrated researchers of Nepali studies, was in Kathmandu in July 2006 when Subho Basu was engaged in gathering new materials for the book. The meeting with him allowed more than an exchange of ideas; it rekindled hope about Nepal. Soura Kumar Basu assisted us enormously by accompanying Subho to Nepal. Without his encouragement and the assistance rendered by Sutapa Basu and Subho's mother Bela Basu, it would have been difficult to conduct the field work.

Some of the arguments of the book were presented at a conference at Cornell University in late 2005. Comments by Dr. Crispin Bates and Professor Sikata Banerjee and others on the paper were very helpful in organizing the book. Dr. Marina Carter went through various drafts of the chapters and provided editorial suggestions and corrected many mistakes. She was, as usual, patient and supportive. Sravani Sarkar, our research assistant, ensured that this manuscript conforms to the Lexington Books style. It was a tedious job, particularly because we come from two different disciplines and are comfortable using two different styles. Two other research assistants, Mina Aitelhadj and Paula Orlando, worked hard to help us meet the deadline. T. J. MacDuff Stewart of Lexington Books was immensely helpful and extremely patient in dealing with us; for her it came naturally. Thanks to our editor Molly Ahearn for taking care of the production process.

Last but not least, it is our families who deserve the most credit. They endured our incoherent ramblings about Nepal for almost three years and shared our hopes and frustrations. They often made suggestions that we would never have thought of. Subho's wife Mallika Banerjee and Ali's wife Shagufta Jabeen were sources of inspirations. They kept us going.

We thank them all. But responsibility for the contents of the book is ours, entirely.

Ali Riaz
Subho Basu

Nepal Timeline

1768–2006

1768–1989: ERA OF MONARCHY AND QUASI-DEMOCRACY

1768–69   Gorkha ruler Prithvi Narayan Shah conquers Kathmandu and lays the foundations for a unified kingdom.

1792   Nepalese expansion is halted by defeat at the hands of the Chinese in Tibet.

1816   Nepal becomes a quasi-British protectorate after the Anglo-Nepalese war.

1846   Hereditary chief ministers known as Ranas usurp power, dominate the monarchy, and cut off the country from the outside world.

1923   Britain formally recognizes Nepal's independence although foreign relations remain under British control.

1950   Anti-Rana forces based in India form an alliance with the monarch.

1951   Sovereignty of the crown is restored and anti-Rana rebels in Nepali Congress Party form a government.

1959   First multiparty election takes place under the monarchical framework of government and the Nepali Congress Party (NCP) wins the elections.

1960   King Mahendra seizes control and suspends parliament and party politics after the NCP wins the elections.

1962   A new constitution provides for a non-party system of councils known as *panchayat* under which the king exercises sole power. Nepal is declared a Hindu state.

1972   King Mahendra dies, succeeded by Birendra.

1980   Constitutional referendum follows upon agitation for reform. A
           small majority favor keeping the existing *panchayat* system.
           The king agrees to allow direct elections to the national as-
           sembly—but on a non-party basis.
1985   The NCP begins a civil disobedience campaign for restoration of
           a multiparty system.
1989   A trade and transit dispute with India leads to a border blockade
           resulting in a worsening economic situation.

1990–2000: THE NEW DEMOCRATIC ERA

1990   April, a pro-democracy movement is coordinated by the NCP
           and leftist groups. Street protests are suppressed by the secu-
           rity forces resulting in deaths and mass arrests. King Biren-
           dra eventually bows to pressure and agrees to a new demo-
           cratic constitution. The new constitution is proclaimed in
           November.
1991   The NCP wins the first democratic elections held on 12 May.
           Girija Prasad Koirala becomes prime minister.
1994   Koirala's government is defeated in a no-confidence motion.
           New elections lead to the formation of a Communist govern-
           ment.
1995   The Communist government is dissolved.
1996   13 February, a radical leftist group, the Nepal Communist Party
           (Maoist), begins an insurrection in rural areas aimed at abol-
           ishing monarchy and establishing a People's Republic.
1997   Continuing political instability as Prime Minister Sher Bahadur
           Deuba is defeated and replaced by Lokendra Bahadur Chand.
           Chand is then forced to resign because of party splits and is
           replaced by Surya Bahadur Thapa.
1998   Thapa resigns because of party splits. G. P. Koirala is returned as
           prime minister heading a coalition government.
1999   Fresh elections give a majority to the NPC. Krishna Prasad Bhat-
           tarai becomes prime minister.

2001–2004: ERA OF REGICIDE AND
THE CRISIS OF DEMOCRACY

2001   1 June, King Birendra and his entire family are killed allegedly
           by Crown Prince Dipendra. On 3 June Dipendra dies and
           King Gyanendra is crowned king of Nepal.

2001	22 July, Sher Bahadur Deuba is appointed as the new prime minister of Nepal. He replaces G. P. Koirala who stepped down under pressure from the opposition political parties and dissidents within his own party.
2001	In the fourth week of August a truce is arranged with Maoists in Nepal followed by a series of talks in September and November—both end in deadlock.
2001	26 November, the government declares an emergency, deploys troops, and classifies Maoists as "terrorists" after severe clashes with the rebels.
2002	Prime Minister Sher Bahadur Deuba calls a special session of parliament to seek approval of an extension of the emergency due to expire on 25 May. Anticipating defeat, Deuba asks the king to dissolve parliament and to call snap general elections on 13 November, two years ahead of schedule.
2002	4 October, the king dismisses the Deuba government and postpones elections. Staunch royalist Lokendra Bahadur Chand is appointed as prime minister to head the new nine-member caretaker government.
2003	29 January, the government and the Maoists announce a ceasefire.
2003	30 May, Chand resigns after months of protests led by political parties demanding that the king appoint a government with their nominees or revive parliament.
2003	4 June, the king appoints Surya Bahadur Thapa as the new prime minister. Major political parties continue to oppose the formation of this government.
2004	7 May, Surya Bahadur Thapa quits as prime minister after weeks of protests.
2004	2 June, Gyanendra reappoints Deuba prime minister.

2005–2006: THE ROYAL COUP AND THE DEMOCRATIC MOVEMENT

2005	1 February, the Deuba government is dismissed, and an emergency declared. The king takes over power.
2005	30 April, the king lifts the state of emergency.
2005	September, Maoists announce a three-month, unilateral ceasefire, the first truce since peace talks broke down in 2003. The truce, later extended to four months, ends in January 2006.
2005	November, Maoist rebels and the main opposition parties agree on a twelve-point program intended to restore democracy.

2006   26 April, the opposition alliance calls off weeks of strikes and protests against the direct rule of the king after the monarch agrees to reinstate parliament. G. P. Koirala is appointed prime minister. Maoist rebels call a three-month ceasefire.

2006   May, parliament votes unanimously to curtail the king's political powers, and declares the state to be secular, scrapping the constitutional clause recognizing a Hindu state. The government and Maoist rebels begin peace talks, the first in nearly three years.

2006   16 June, rebel leader Prachanda and Prime Minister Koirala hold talks—the first such meeting between the two sides—and agree that the Maoists should be brought into an interim government.

Introduction

Understanding the Crisis in Nepal and State Failure

Nepal, a small country located at the foot of the snowcapped Himalayas, often referred to as *Shangri La*—a place of complete bliss and delight—has been in the throes of political crisis for more than a decade. During this period, this country not only experienced the gradual erosion of the state's capacity to deliver to its citizens, but also the rise of an insurgency, and the failure of constitutional political parties to offer a sustainable solution to the problems faced by the nation. The king's repeated attempts, including a violent and unpopular royal coup, to reestablish an absolute monarchy of a bygone era made the situation worse. These events in Nepal left more than twelve thousand dead, thousands injured, and two hundred thousand displaced.

This book is an examination of the causes of and the conditions for these crises, an attempt to trace the factors leading to the rise of the Maoist insurgency that has engulfed the country and to map the future trajectories of the Nepali polity. The central questions this book intends to answer are: Why is Nepal caught in this crisis? Why have violence and political maelstrom so deeply destabilized this picturesque kingdom? Has the state in Nepal failed? What does the future hold for this tiny kingdom?

Despite the geo-strategic importance of this landlocked country sandwiched between China and India, barring a few exceptional moments, Nepal has not featured significantly in the international media. The exceptional moments such as the pro-democracy movement in 1990, the massacre of the royal family in 2001, royal coups in 2001 and 2005, the intensification of the Maoist insurgency in 2004, and the popular uprising in April 2006 brought media attention. But the media coverage was episodic in nature and often driven by events, and consequently has lacked longitudinal perspectives. Our object is to situate the events in historical context and provide background for a better understanding of the present and future of this nation of about twenty-eight million people.

This book is also about the state in developing societies: an investigation into the formation and transformation processes of states, and the nature and consequences of state failure. The latter issue is being debated in academic and policy-making circles both passionately and vigorously since the announcement of "the National Security Strategy of the United States of America" in 2002.[1] This study is empirical in nature and focuses on one country, but it has conceptual implications for the debate on the state in general. We expect to insert the issue of the state-society relationship into the debate on the state at a time when discussions, particularly at the policy-making levels, are intense, and when states are erroneously perceived by some as ahistorical structures divorced from their social contexts and which therefore can be reshaped by exogenous forces at will.

The central argument of this study is that the Nepali state, founded in the eighteenth century, characterized by its extractive patrimonial nature and dependent on a monarchical political order, has failed; and the nation is standing at crossroads with a catastrophic past behind and an uncertain future ahead of it. Our contention is that the crisis in Nepal was a long time in the making, and that state formation in Nepal, especially the tendency toward the centralization of power, and a disjuncture between the state and society have contributed to the making of this crisis. Simply stated, the unrepresentative process of state formation and the tradition of governance have contributed to the alienation of the citizens from the state and engendered the crises. Despite the lack of "embeddedness,"[2] the Nepali state had succeeded in maintaining its hold over the population through a constructed Hindu identity and a complex connection between this identity and the cultural legitimacy of the social order. This constructed identity was designed to subsume ethnic and regional differences. This hegemonic ideology was ruptured in the 1990s, especially after the mass upsurge of 1990. The ideological vacuum left by the demise of the Hindu absolute monarchical system could not be entirely filled by constitutional alternatives and thus created a political space for violent rebellion and state terrorism. The rise of the Maoist insurgency resulting in the deaths of thousands at the hands of the state security forces and the rebels bears testimony to this phenomenon.

In arguing the case we will use three analytical tools: patrimonial state, state failure, and hegemony. In this chapter we will discuss these concepts, their meanings within this study, and their relevance in understanding the Nepali state and society. This chapter begins with a recap of the political history of Nepal, followed by discussions on the above-mentioned concepts and their significance to our study. The final section presents an outline of the book.

HISTORY IN BRIEF

Nepal has been an independent kingdom in its current geographical shape since 1768. The country was virtually isolated from outside influence throughout the eighteenth and nineteenth centuries, although it remained a de facto British protectorate between 1816 and 1923. After 1846, the Rana family gained power as hereditary prime ministers and reduced the monarch to a figurehead.[3] This continued until 1950, when the Nepali Congress Party formally decided to wage an armed struggle against the Rana regime. They were assisted in no uncertain terms by the reigning monarch, King Tribhuvan. The Rana regime capitulated as the insurgency gained momentum in November 1950 and the Indian government put pressure on the Ranas. On 8 January 1951, Mohan Shamsher Rana, the hereditary prime minister, promised the restoration of the monarchy, amnesty for all political prisoners, and elections based on adult suffrage no later than 1952. This accord revived the power of the king and launched the era of a quasi-constitutional monarchy. However, it took about eight years for King Mahendra to promulgate a new constitution followed by the country's first democratic elections. But the democratic experiment was short-lived. Eighteen months later the king dismissed the elected government, suspended the constitution, and declared the parliamentary system a failure.

The king promulgated a new constitution in 1962. The new constitution established a "partyless" system of *panchayats* (councils). Political parties were banned but continued to exist with the tacit support of neighboring India, and Nepal witnessed periodic movements for the reintroduction of constitutional democracy. The situation did not witness any radical change when King Birendra, the Harvard-educated son of Mahendra, assumed the throne in 1972. Contrary to the popular expectation of reform, King Birendra in 1975 introduced an amendment of the constitution that resulted in further centralization of power and stricter control of political parties. However, simmering political tension exploded in 1979 when student agitation escalated into a wider movement against the Nepali *panchayat* system. The government called in the army to restore order but King Birendra also promised a referendum on the future of the partyless *panchayat* system. The referendum took place in 1980. The results favored the government, but the process was thoroughly rigged. Not only did the opposition face stringent conditions in their campaign for a negative vote, but activists were also blatantly intimidated. Yet almost 45 percent of people voted against the *panchayat* system. Realizing the intensity of the opposition, King Birendra introduced three constitutional amendments: direct elections to the *Rashtriya Panchayat* would be held every five years on the basis of universal franchise; the prime minister would be elected by the *Rashtriya Panchayat*; and the cabinet would be appointed by the king on the recommendation of the prime minister and would be accountable to the *Rashtriya Panchayat*. Thus Nepal limped toward formal democracy, but the government reformed only in response to mass movements at the grassroots level. Since 1980 the *panchayat* system continued to exist but in much changed form, as did quasi-clandestine opposition to the system. Yet external factors impinged on Nepali politics in 1989 again when India arbitrarily closed all but two trading points with Nepal. As economic hardship increased, the movement against autocratic rule slowly resurfaced. Indeed, the news of the collapse of the Communist regimes in the eastern European nations triggered the mass upsurge of 1990 called *Jana Andolan* (People's Movement). This brought about a return to the multiparty system and rule by elected governments.

The new era of democracy has been marked by political turbulence and a high degree of instability. Over the following fourteen years, three parliamentary elections were held and thirteen governments came to power. After February 2005, with the king's intervention in the political system, the country was ruled by various appointees of the king rather than elected by the parliament until the mass upsurge of March–April 2006.

During this period a Maoist insurgency swept through the rural areas of the country. The parliamentary Communists, who gained power through the second general election in 1994, were forced out of power within a year as other political parties refused to extend support to the minority Communist government. However, parliamentary Communists elected to operate within the institutional structure of the state provided by the constitution of 1990 and thus remained part of the newly emerging party political establishment. In contrast to the parliamentary Communists, Maoists faced concerted repression of the state as they were seeking to consolidate their position in the remote western region of rural Nepal where they had a powerful base. Their anger at the concerted repression of their activities by the state and the plight of the rural poor prompted them to take up arms. From a group of less than a dozen in 1996 the rebels grew to an army of four thousand fighters and established influence over two-thirds of the rural areas, rendering the state virtually ineffective. Negotiations between the government and the Maoists failed. In addition to continuing military support from India, the Nepali government received enormous military aid since 9/11 from the United States and Britain, yet it was not successful in containing the insurgents.

It was in this context that the "royal coup" was orchestrated in February 2005. Alleging that the cabinet had failed to quash the Maoist rebellion, the king suspended the cabinet and clamped down on democratic procedures. Political leaders, journalists, and human rights activists were incarcerated and a massive security operation was launched. A handpicked cabinet, whose primarily role was to provide a democratic façade, received very lit-

tle support from the populace and an attempt to organize a local-level election in February 2006 was foiled by the opposition.

But the most dramatic development took place behind the scenes in November 2005 when the seven-party opposition alliance (SPA) signed a
twelve-point accord with the Maoists to launch a movement for the restoration of parliament, election to a constituent assembly (CA), and rewriting
of the constitution. This resulted in the weeks of agitation beginning in late
March, and forced the king to capitulate on 24 April as he agreed to reinstate the parliament. The coalition elected Girija Prasad Koirala as the prime
minister and later the parliament voted unanimously to curtail the
monarch's political powers rendering him a ceremonial figure. Election to
the CA is expected in early 2007.

STATE FORMATION AND PATRIMONIAL STATE IN NEPAL

As one of the most problematic concepts in political science, the state has
been variously conceptualized in the fields of political theory and international relations. One of the consequences of these discussions is the rise of
various schools of thought in regard to state formation.

A closer examination of the theories related to the state reveals that con-
ceptualizations of the state are based upon some combinations of its functions, purposes, activities, personnel, organizational contours, legitimacy,
legal norms, rules and machinery, sovereignty, coercive monopoly, and territorial control. In this study, the concept of the "state" is meant to convey
a differentiated set of institutions and personnel which have a legitimate
monopoly on authoritative rule-making, backed up by a monopoly on the
means of physical violence, within a territorially demarcated area.[4] The concept implicitly incorporates three aspects of the state: apparatus, power, and
authority. State apparatus, in this context, means the complex set of institutions staffed by a professional bureaucracy and armed forces, specialized
to some degree or other, which together ensure the formulation and execution of policies. Secondly, the state represents a concentration of economic
and political power. In most cases, it is the biggest single such concentration in a particular social formation. Thirdly, it also represents a concentration of authority. Which means, in the ideological sense, it is able to give legitimacy to the actions of those who act in its name, or at least claim such.

One important aspect of the state left out in the aforementioned concep-
tualization is the functional aspect: What does the state do? One can approach the issue from the normative perspective as well: What is the state
supposed to do? For decades the question has remained central to policy
debates in connection with development issues in the Third World and has
influenced the policy undertakings of governments, international agencies,

and nongovernmental organizations. Two different views in this regard are discernable according to Khan.[5] The first insists that the primary role of the state is to provide a range of services, in particular law and order, public goods, social security, welfarist redistributions, and market regulation, while the second contends that the state has a more critical and problematic role—transformation of the pre-capitalist and pre-industrial societies into dynamic and essentially industrial capitalist models. The first is identified as the "service delivery model" and the second is called the "social transformation model." Importantly, these two are not mutually exclusive: "historically, success in service delivery has depended in most cases on the success of states in pushing social transformation rapidly in the direction of viable capitalist economies."[6]

In terms of the constitutive elements of the state, we can broadly group them into three sets: the regime (mostly armed with legislative power, and having limited capacity for implementation); the executives (or, in other words, the bureaucracy and attendant organizations which have immense control over the implementation process); and the military (along with other paramilitary forces that have a monopoly over legitimate coercion). However, the state should not be viewed as only the conglomeration of these elements. Rather, it should be understood as the balance between them. At a given moment of time and in a given social formation, it is the relationship and balance among these elements that determines the nature of the state.

As regards state formation, one can recognize a general agreement among theorists that state formation, interchangeable with "state-building" and "state-making," refers to the processes that lead to the centralization of political power over a well-defined territory, and with a monopoly of the means of coercion.[7] However, theorists differ whether conflicts or integration was the primary causal agent in state formation. Charles Tilly, who argues for the primacy of warfare as a causal agent in state formation, combined these two orientations. Drawing on the European experience, Tilly[8] has noted that "war made states." According to the Tillyian model, state formation involves four stages: state-making by war-making (that is, to neutralize rivals outside the territory); state-making by elimination (that is, to eliminate potential challengers within the territory); providing protection to the supporters (that is, to create an environment for continued existence of the new structure); and, finally, extraction of resources (that is, to subject the population and territory to continuous taxation for the maintenance and/or expansion of the territory).[9]

While the classical pattern of state-making delineated by Tilly is scarce, if not nonexistent, in peripheral societies, the Nepali state bears all the hallmark of these processes, including their violent nature. Thus, both the process of state-making and the location of the state represent exceptionalism in regard to the Nepali state. The genesis of the Nepali state lies in the war-making of Prithvi Narayan Shah (1723–1775), ruler of the tiny Gorkha principality in the eighteenth century. He conquered sixty local kingdoms through a series of wars that took more than a quarter of a century. Additionally, Prithvi Narayan and his successors continued the annexation and expansions to incorporate the regions that established the country now known as Nepal and the rudimentary form of the Nepali state. We would like to emphasize the point that we are identifying this as a "rudimentary" form of the state, for we are aware of the limitations of applying the idea of territorial sovereignty to the pre-capitalist polity of Nepal. In most pre-capitalist polities, political power was parceled out among various actors. In the context of Nepal, the very idea of territorial sovereignty was contingent upon British assistance in mapping territories. Even the idea of Nepal as a signifier of a country primarily applied to the Kathmandu valley in the minds of the inhabitants of the Shah kingdom. Yet the Nepali state that came into existence in the late eighteenth century survived into the twentieth century and initiated a process to convert the Nepali kingdom into a nation-state. Hence, the significance of the term *rudimentary* in this context.

Therefore it is our contention that the formation of the Nepali state, at least in its rudimentary form, followed a classical pattern, which, as we have seen, is very unusual for a peripheral society. The Nepali state is an exception in another count: it sustained itself in an adverse external political environment. In South Asia, the eighteenth century brought the decline and the eventual demise of the Mughal Empire on the one hand and the rise of an array of new principalities on the other. But a large number of these principalities soon collapsed under the weight of British colonial expansion and imperial rule. Those that managed to avoid direct annexation and colonization stagnated because of the indirect colonial rule imposed on them.

Generally speaking, in peripheral societies, states are mostly imported entities, at least on two counts. First, the material basis upon which they rest is not a product of indigenous evolution, and secondly, the structures of the state have been (largely) imported through colonial expansion. There is no denying that capitalism serves as the material basis of states in peripheral societies and that the present form of capitalism has been implanted in the periphery due to Western capitalism's need to expand its geographical sphere and the scale of its accumulation as well as indigenous incipient entrepreneurs' ability to negotiate with such expansion. Additionally, historical accounts show that the origins of the state in peripheral societies are either colonial, or, where they are not (for example, Thailand, China, Russia, or Turkey), they are engaged in a conscious attempt to modernize based on the European model. Notwithstanding the fact that these states have their own local peculiarities, "they have been 'parachuted' by colonial rule and then taken over, lock, stock, and barrel, i.e., in their territorial claims, administration, and legal structures, by 'independence movements.'"[10] The Nepali state does not conform to this generalization despite the fact that the British Empire in India has influenced its contours. The Treaty of Sagauli signed by the Gorkha monarch with the East India Company in 1816, after a brief Anglo-Gorkha War (1814–1816), defined the outer parameters of the monarchical polity. This treaty stopped the process of expansion of the Gorkha kingdom, therefore limiting the war-making aspect of state formation. However, this has not made the Nepali state a "colonial state."[11]

This twin-exceptionalism of the Nepali state (i.e., the classical pattern and its location) has not wiped out one of its fundamental characteristics: extraction from a larger population as an agent of the rulers to perpetuate other activities of the state. "The relationship between the state and extraction has been clear since the beginning of European state formation"[12] and has remained unchanged throughout the centuries. "Taxation, or extraction, is thus a central task for the state to master before pursuing any other goals."[13] Although extraction remains a fundamental and perhaps a universal character of the state, not all states can be characterized as "extractive states"; in an ideal situation, the extraction also produces a contract between the rulers and the ruled. In the early phase of state-making that contract involves protection from external rivals, and where external rivals are absent, the maintenance of law and order in the face of potential or real internal contenders for power. In modern times, the state is expected to provide, in addition to human security, "positive political goods" such as an independent judicial system to adjudicate disputes, enforce the rule of law, and protect the most fundamental civil and political rights; a functioning educational and healthcare system; and transportation infrastructure.[14] In the absence of all or any of these, the extraction of resources can be described as "banditry" and the state can be characterized as an "extractive state." The Nepali state, since 1816, has assumed this role; very few changes have taken place in almost a century up to 1951, and even after that it retained many features of the earlier state. This point has been emphasized by Regmi in a study that covered the period between 1768 and 1846.[15] Similarly, Devkota has noted that the Ranas "spent little on public welfare during their 104 years of rule. . . . Whatever they got from the people or other taxable sources was their own private property, which they enjoyed at home and abroad."[16] Furthermore, Devkota insists that the economic crisis in the 1960s was "a crisis of structural underdevelopment of the economy which is spatial and chronic" and this was due to "the state's revenue generation attitude rather than stimulating the production and expansion of the economic base."[17]

Here Mancur Olson's[18] explanation of how the state emerges out of anarchy, especially the tale of roving and sedentary/stationary banditry, is instructive in understanding the Nepali state. Olson insisted that under anarchy, what happens is "uncoordinated competitive theft" by groups of "roving bandits." This destroys the incentive to invest and produce. It makes sense for one of these roving bandits to destroy the competition, set himself up as dictator, and "rationalize theft in the form of taxes." The state, therefore, is the "stationary bandit." But the Nepali state has never gone through this dramatic, yet necessary, transformation. It essentially remained the "roving bandit."

Having arrived at this point of our analytical journey we must investigate the causes as well as consequences of the avoidance of this transformative phase. Or, in other words, we need to ask: Why has the Nepali state evaded this phase of state formation? How has this impacted upon the politics of Nepal, especially on recent developments?

The fundamental reason for the absence of this transformation is due to the lack of embeddedness of the Nepali state. The configuration of the society where the state is located is seen as one of the predicating factors of the nature of the state. The state, in general, is understood to be "a historically contingent creation" whose properties depend on, among other things, "the character of the surrounding social structure."[19] But the Nepali state remains a striking anomaly, for it has not reflected the social structure on which it is based. While Nepali society is divided along various caste, linguistic, and geographical residency lines, the ruling bloc has been comprised of a small segment. At its formation, the ruling class was composed of the military hierarchy of Gorkhas (*Thakuri* and *Chetri*) and Brahmin attendants and advisors. During the conquest, Gurungs and Magars, indigenous nationalities from the mid-west were involved to some degree in the Gorkha military conquests but they were marginalized gradually with the conquest of the Gorkha kingdom. Lacking the skills to control the expanding kingdom, these rulers became dependent on the administrative and financial skills of the *Newars*, who became members of the new ruling bloc. These high castes supervised the political system and extracted surplus both in kind and labor from low caste artisans.[20] Therefore from the outset the ruling class has been narrowly based. Mahendra Lawoti shows that to date it has remained unchanged:

> High caste Hindu elite males from the hills (Caste Hill Hindu Elite—CHHE) overwhelmingly dominate power positions in politics, administration, the judiciary, parliament, academia, civil society, industry/commerce, local government, and education. Jointly the CHHE and Newar constitute 37.2 percent of the population, but in 1999 they held more than 80 percent of leadership positions in the important arenas of governance.[21]

The disjuncture between the state and society is also reflected in the political economy of governance and reproduced through the patrimonial nature of the state. The complex tenurial system, often described as "state landlordism," allowed the ruling class to usurp the territorial domains of the indigenous population and reapportion them as private entitlements to the army and loyal government functionaries. Despite variations, the tenurial system in general supported the upper caste elites, but the elites were essentially a class of *rent-receiving* functionaries because the state remained the possessor of the land and these "land grants" were temporary and alienable entitlements. Another significant impact of this system has been that most of the peasants throughout the kingdom were reduced to the status of tenants without legally defined rights, which furthered their alienation from the state.

The tenurial system has been consistent with the predominant patron-client relationship between the state and its functionaries. As we know, the "patron-client relationship means a mutually obligatory arrangement between an individual who has authority, social status, wealth, or some other personal resource (the patron) and another person who benefits from his or her support or influence (the client)." Following Weber, we underscore the point that loyalty and relationships are important to an understanding of the relationship between state and society.[22] In the absence of structured institutions, the political leader plays a critical role in structuring the modes of governance and the nature of fiscal management. Weber described this as patrimonialism.

Under such circumstances, the political leader selects administrative personnel based on personal loyalty. In such a polity, political rights and economic rights converge, in the sense that political power claims ownership of all resources. Property rights or political rights for any group independent of the leader (or state authority) do not exist. In such a system, the "chief executive maintains authority through personal patronage . . . (and) relationships of loyalty and dependence pervade a formal political and administrative system."[23]

In the case of Nepal, the political system has always evolved around the Royal palace apart from a period of Rana rule (i.e., between 1846 and 1951), when self-appointed hereditary prime ministers (or Ranas) were predominant. During Rana rule the political system revolved around Rana rulers who distributed resources among a hierarchy of political elites through a strong patron-client network extending from the palace to remote villages. The political culture evolved in such a manner that fierce factional competition for resources among elites simply served to bolster the palace's hold over them. In a society where the patron-client relationship is the dominant mode of interaction the system is organized along a vertical line of subordination. It is also prone to corruption and subject to the personal whim of the patron(s), as reflected in post-1990 Nepal when the country experienced the exuberant growth of patron-client relationships:

The political leaders, especially the top leadership, can exercise unrestrained power, appointing sycophants to administrative posts, ignoring party rules and procedures, and often governing on their personal whims. The leaders nominate at least half of the central committee members, often relatives (such as the NC), friends, and/or caste brethrens (as in the CPN-UML). The appointees, in turn, remain personally loyal to the leaders. Leaders also appoint party candidates for parliamentary, local, and organization[al] elections.[24]

But the political leaders themselves are also subject to this unequal relationship, as clients of the palace, because the palace has been the only "fountain of privileges." This mode of state formation and associated political culture encountered a great deal of resistance and faced periodic revolutionary upsurges but on each occasion the changes produced compromises, either externally induced or internally worked out, that posited the palace as a natural ruling authority and a symbol of unity. In so doing, it perpetuated the patrimonial state.

A patrimonial state with limited resources and an extractive agenda akin to roving banditry is bound to create inequality within the society.

Where governments behave like roving bandits, they are unlikely to have a development agenda that can be shared with those that they seek to govern. Improvement in the citizen's [*sic*] quality of life would therefore be accidental. Under the roving bandit form of government, the evolution of development policies is also unlikely, considering the absence of clear goals for the future. Such forms of government cannot encourage the evolution of clear rules and enforcement mechanisms through which private interests for the benefit of the community can be encouraged. On the contrary, self-seeking governments tend to stifle the developmental outcomes of atomistic behaviour [*sic*]. Such governments also encourage the birth of parallel systems of micro-governance that find expression in parallel activities which undermine broader development efforts.[25]

Nepal is an embodiment of this phenomenon. With close to half of its population living below the poverty line, Nepal is among the poorest and least developed countries in the world. This raises the question: How have the ruling elites maintained their hold over the socially and economically deprived population without any challenges? What has provided legitimacy to this blatantly unequal social order? Answers to these questions require an understanding of the role of ideological hegemony of the ruling classes.

HEGEMONY, IDEOLOGY, AND MONARCHICAL SYSTEM

Hegemony, according to Gramsci, is characterized by "the 'spontaneous' consent given by the great masses of the population to the general direction imposed on social life by the dominant fundamental group; the consent is 'historically' caused by the prestige (and consequent confidence) which the dominant group enjoys because of its position and function in the world of production."[26] The question of hegemony, however, is not merely material; it is also a politics of moral and intellectual leadership. To assert its hegemony, the ruling class must be able to defend its own corporate interests by universalizing them, by ensuring that these interests can at least apparently "become the interests of the . . . subordinate groups."[27] To this extent, hegemony implies consent rather than domination, integration rather than exclusion, and co-optation rather than suppression. Gramsci further reminds us that consent and coercion coexist in all societies. The coercive elements inherent in a hegemonic system are laid bare if, and when, the ability of the ruling classes to organize consent weakens. Under normal circumstances, the elements of coercion are kept latent, concealed. The ruling classes seek and, of course, prefer the active and voluntary consent of the subordinate masses. But when the masses "do not 'consent' actively or passively" or the consent is not sufficient to reproduce capitalist relations, the apparatus of state coercive power "legally enforces discipline on those . . . who do not consent."[28] That is why the ruling classes, in any society, attempt to impose a general direction on social life through their ideology and ensure social conformity to that ideology. If that fails, coercion becomes the principal tool to rule the masses.

In the Nepali context, the ruling class universalized their interest through careful creation of various layers of myths that present the monarch as the descendant of the Hindu god Vishnu and the true protector of the Hindu religion. The divine lineage provides the monarchy with the divine right to rule, which has been sanctified and legitimized through complex religious rituals. The blessing of the king by the "living goddess" Kumari, is a case in point. Prithvi Narayan Shah used the latter to gain instant legitimacy when he sealed his conquest of Kathmandu during the *Indra Jatra*, a royal festival of the indigenous Newar population of the Kathmandu Valley, and placed himself before the Kumari to receive immediate sanctification as the ruler of Nepal. The Hinduization of the culture was further consolidated during the Rana regime, especially through the *Muluki Ain* (law of the land) which established a legally sanctioned hierarchical social order based on Hindu caste ranking.[29]

Indeed, religious rituals and practices among subjugated ethnic minorities did indicate organized resistance to this construction of hierarchy.[30] More importantly, from an empirical perspective it could be further asserted that many clauses of *Muluki Ain* had never been implemented in practice. The state also accommodated various regional and local authorities into the power structure through selective provisions of autonomy for local elites and the distribution of patronage to powerful entrepreneurs. Yet it is undeniable that this projection of political authority was articulated through an ideological framework of caste hierarchy codified in *Muluki Ain*, if not always implemented in terms of details of its prescriptions. Indeed, the concept of hegemony does not preclude the possibility of resistance. Rather, resistance could always be part of the function of hegemonic political ideology. Thus the hierarchy of caste provided an ideological legitimacy to the process of extraction of revenues and labor by the state and elite groups in the eyes of many despite resistance from below.

However, this hegemony of the ruling class, particularly of the monarchy, faced a series of challenges throughout the 1970s and the 1980s. The popular uprising of 1990 signaled the rupture of this ideological hegemony. This is not to say that the *Jana Andolan* of 1990 brought revolutionary changes in the Nepali state structure; on the contrary it maintained a hierarchical and centralized political system that is riddled with conspiracies and dominated by a patron-client nexus.[31] Although negotiations, especially compromises, had taken away most of the achievements of the street agitations, one thing that could not be taken away was the emergence of democratic pluralism and new space for political activism. The democratic pluralism, in the limited sense of participation of mainstream parties in political processes and elections, didn't pose any major challenges to the legitimacy of the monarch. This was because the constitution of Nepal enacted in 1990 remained a quasi-monarchical democratic document as it allowed the monarch to retain a substantial degree of power. The regime based on this constitution could hardly transform the palace into a ceremonial entity as demanded by democratic activists on the street and as is the case in most constitutional democracies. But this democratic pluralism opened the possibility of a threat from marginalized segments of the society. This possibility wasn't anticipated by many. It came via the activism and mobilization of the lower castes, which demonstrated new assertiveness against the constructed Hindu ethno-religious order. As the monarchical system of governance and the legitimacy of the monarch rested on this constructed social order, the challenge was more than a political battle or power game. It took various forms including social activism by *Dalits*, or occupational castes who were officially declared untouchable some six centuries ago. More importantly, a new social movement/organization emerged in the form of the Janajati movement. *Janajatis*, or those "ethnic groups" who are conscious of their common ethno-communal culture and have their own myths and languages separate from high caste Hindu values, claimed the status of *adivasi* or original inhabitants of the land. With the intensification of ethnic activism Janajati movements evolved into a mass movement and opened up new debates concerning their status in Nepali society. As religion had been integrally related to a cultural linguistic identity, these debates also brought the issue of language and the cultural heritage of ethnic groups to the fore.

The discourses of ethnic identities, which previously remained outside political discourses of all kinds, suddenly burst onto the scene and initially caught most of the politicians off-guard. But soon the mainstream political parties realized the need for the incorporation of ethnicity in their discussions and co-opted the vocabulary of ethnicity-based activism. Perhaps the Marxists and the Maoists went the furthest, although it was far more challenging for them. Historically, orthodox Marxists always had difficulties in addressing issues outside the realm of class, for example nationalism. Yet the Nepali leftists—both parliamentary Marxists and Maoists—blended ethnic and class issues together. The quasi-monarchical democratic Nepal experimented with an ethnic pluralism that sought to address the historical wrongs committed by the Hindu patrimonial state. The rupture of the dominant ideology of Hinduism (or in true terms, the monarchical interpretation of Hinduism), and the dawning of the quasi-monarchical democratic era in 1991 also heralded a period of factional wrangling among the political parties, acrimony between various factions of the parties, and political instability.

While the quasi-monarchical democratic era brought limited changes to economic and social systems, it added new claimants to the limited resources of the state contributing to the further deprivation of the already marginalized ethnic and caste groups. More importantly, experiments with an open democratic political structure also made such transactions visible to the broader society. What is of further significance is that it started to take a heavy toll on certain geographical areas. The economic policies of the government had already impacted adversely on the mid- and far western regions of the country; resource constraints now worsened the situation. For centuries these regions had been neglected. With rapid population growth, massive migration to Terai, over-extraction of natural resources, land degradation, and stagnant land productivity the Nepali economy in general had been facing bleak prospects, but the situation was far worse in the mid- and far western regions. These regions, mostly inhabited by the members of marginalized ethnic and caste groups, bore the brunt of the unequal economic system for quite some time.

In the 1990s, while the high politics of Nepal was revealing its fractious nature, the political leaders in Kathmandu were engaged in intra- and inter-party squabbles, and King Birendra, the monarch, was acting as a distant spectator except for his controversial decision of not deploying the army against Maoists despite a request from the prime minister. The king gained a certain degree of popularity for his studied aloofness from politics while political parties also gained a quasi-autonomous standing. His successor, King Gyanendra, assumed a more direct role from October 2002 and soon indulged in hiring and firing prime ministers, contributing further to the growing political instability. The Nepali people became disenchanted and hopelessness took hold over these regions. The distress of these regions on the one hand highlights the fact that inequality in Nepal is not only social but also spatial[32] while on the other hand demonstrates that the Nepali state is weak, limited, and absent in certain geographical areas. The state is not only absent in remote areas but also in various other sectors as noted by Lawoti: "the state's reach and influence in development, service delivery, administration, and security is severely limited. The state does not have any effective presence in many sectors and regions."[33] This is truer in the far western region of Nepal with a higher concentration of Dalits, and the mid-western region, where there is a substantial presence of indigenous peoples.

The absence of the state is one of the keys to understanding the rise of the Maoist movement, especially their success in establishing control over various rural areas in a short span of time. The absence of the state, either in certain geographical areas (e.g., rural areas) or in regard to certain social services (e.g., security), obviously accentuates the crisis of governance, and is bound to create a void, which, in turn, leads to the establishment of a parallel structure of authority. In Nepal, a parallel structure of authority came from the Maoist movement, while elsewhere it has given rise to warlords or vigilante groups.[34] It is no surprise that the Maoists chose the mid-western hills of Rukum, Rolpa, Salyan, and Jajarkot, where the state was absent—both as the facilitator of development (reflected in the low per-capita income of these districts) and as an administrative unit, as their first points of insurgency. Murshed and Gates mention that "mid-western districts such as Rolpa, Jajarkot, and Salyan had 25, 19, and 17 percent respectively of the average income of Kathmandu. . . . [T]he HDI for Rolpa, Jajarkot, and Salyan were only 45, 44, and 35 per cent respectively of the Kathmandu level in 1996."[35] As noted before, the mid- and far western regions, in general, have been impoverished regions compared to the other four administrative regions. The Human Development Report 2004 notes that "the far western and mid-western regions lag far behind the others; most of the districts where HDI falls below 0.4 lies in these two regions."[36] Government documents have also acknowledged the geographical dimension of poverty. For example, the National Planning Commission's Poverty Reduction Strategy Paper, commonly referred to as the tenth plan (2002–2007), states, "the Mid-Western and Far Western regions, far from the center of power, have been traditionally neglected."[37]

Bhurtel and Ali, in their exploration of the environmental roots of the Maoist movement, concluded that, "the ecological degradation widened resource scarcity especially in the form [of] people's access to sufficient fertile lands in the Mid- and Far Western regions. When the resource is limited and widespread deprivation is prevalent, other socio-economic variables—such as land tenure issues, resource capture by local privileged few, gender, caste, and ethnic equations—intervene. Such gradual loss of livelihood made people vulnerable to the exploits and rhetoric of Maoists, who offered an alternative (albeit violent)."[38]

The spatial and environmental dimension of the conflict in Nepal, long overlooked, has recently drawn some attention. For example, Fiona Rotberg has identified "environmental scarcity" as one of the indirect causes of the Nepali crisis. Environmental scarcity, defined as "natural resource scarcity; population growth (which leads to a reduction in per capita availability of a resource); and unequal resource distribution (such as unequal land holdings, with more in the hands of elites, for example)," is an issue one should not be ignoring in assessing the causes of the crisis in Nepal, insists Rotberg.[39] She draws a causal relationship between environmental scarcity and the crisis of the state: "environmental scarcity causes economic deprivation, it in turn causes institutional disruption, and civil strife; and an eventual breakdown of the state is likely to follow."[40] Similarly, Matthew and Upreti have stressed the significance of the environment: "environmental stress and population factors have played significant roles in creating the underlying conditions for acute insecurity and instability."[41]

The spatial and environmental dimensions of Nepali crisis, while important on their own merit, also reinforce the point we made earlier that the state has been absent on various fronts (geographically and as development agent). The absence of the state and the rise of Maoist militancy are symptomatic of a larger problem: the failure of the Nepali state.

STATE FAILURE IN NEPAL

Introducing the concept of state failure in a discussion often evokes emotional reactions from various quarters, especially in the context of the post-9/11 international environment. This is due to largely to the fact that in recent years the term has been widely used in policy-making circles and seen by many, particularly in the global south, as a precursor to the vilification of certain regimes and creating a pretext to pursue a military solution, and perhaps external intervention, to solve complex problems.[42] Also there is a tendency on the part of some scholars of international relations to attribute all ills to state failure. Francis Fukuyama represents this tendency in the clearest terms when he states "the chief threats to us and to world order come today from weak, collapsed, or failed states."[43] It is not too difficult to understand that Fukuyama is looking at the world through the prism of security—articulated as global security but essentially the security of the United States. Such a skewed approach makes many wary, to say the least.

Emotive reactions notwithstanding, the disquiet about the concept is shared by many, as Susan Woodward has noted in her introductory remarks in a workshop in 2005 on state failure. Woodward notes that the disquiet reflects two other concerns:

> the implicit assumption that the range of concrete threats attributed to state failure are the sole responsibility of states and their leaders, not equally a consequence of the international economic or political order and the responsibility of major political and economic powers or their international institutions; this applies to the causal analysis and the proposed remedies of domestic reforms; and related to this, the focus on state failure as a threat to the security of wealthy states (the United States, the EU member states), not the security of the citizens and residents of such a country; also the extent to which that security agenda in practice may actually be increasing the insecurity of targeted states or their populations. The attempt to restore attention to the concept of human security as an antidote neither addresses the new security focus of the first group (above all the United States) nor resolves its own deep ambivalence about the state.[44]

We understand the uneasiness with the concept and are cognizant of the potential pitfall of its unqualified acceptance, but it is also our contention that the concept and consequently the framework of analysis provide helpful tools in analyzing the situation in Nepal. In this context, a reassessment and reformulation of the concept to better reflect the complexities of the societies in question is called for. In so doing, we are opposed to privileging any solutions, military or otherwise, as a panacea of state failure. It is not our intention to label Nepal as a failed state to drive a policy agenda. Instead, our object is to understand the underlying causes of the crisis Nepal has been facing for decades. We employ the concept of state failure as the "basis for investigations into human security—that is, a state's ability or willingness to function in a manner conducive to the welfare of the majority of its citizens."[45] Therefore, for us the central question is for whom the Nepali state failed, and how?

The publication of Helman and Ratner's article in *Foreign Policy* in 1993[46] is seen as the beginning of the discussions on the failed state. However, one can also trace the genesis of the term in the efforts to understand the regional dynamics of Eastern Europe and the former Soviet Union in the early 1990s,[47] and the concept behind Kaplan's 1994 essay titled "The Coming Anarchy," which suggested that fast-growing populations, demographic change, and weakening state capacities are bound to generate an anarchic Africa with state failures as natural consequences.[48] The impact of these discussions on policy-makers became obvious in 1994, as the Central Intelligence Agency (CIA) appointed a task force comprised of academics, called the "State Failure Task Force" (later named Political Instability Task Force—PITF) at the request of Vice President Al Gore. Concurrently, U.S. officials began to point to the "failed state" as a cause of global problems. A comment of Brian Atwood, the administrator of the U.S. Agency for International Development (U.S.AID), in early 1994 is a case in point. Atwood insisted that "disintegrating societies and failed states with their civil conflicts and destabilizing refugee flows have emerged as the greatest menace to global security."[49] The focus on security has been amplified after 11 September 2001, indicating the securitization of the concept of state failure.[50] The National Security Strategy of the United States in 2002 exemplified this move.[51] Contemporaneously discussions began highlighting the symptoms rather than causes of the state failure, and were notably geared toward policy recommendations.

In these discourses a direct link between the events of 9/11 and the failed states was made in unambiguous terms. This is reflected in the report of the Bi-partisan Commission on Post-Conflict Reconstruction published in 2003:

> One of the principal lessons of the events of September 11 is that failed states matter—for national security as well as for humanitarian reasons. If left to their own devices, such states can become sanctuaries for terrorist networks, organized crimes, and drug traffickers as well as posing grave humanitarian challenges and threats to regional stability.[52]

The candor of the report is noteworthy as it stated "not all failed states are created equal. Not all will be equally important to the United States and the international community."[53] Obviously the importance of a "failed state" to the United States would be determined by its strategic interests. But the question remains: How can a state be identified as a failed state?

Here we face the fundamental problem with the concept of state failure: the absence of a commonly accepted meaning of the term. In other words, although the term is in vogue, it is also vague. To date, different approaches have been employed in explaining the phenomenon and in identifying states to be classified as a "failed state." These exercises have generated a host of lists in academic and policy-making circles.[54] However, there is a clear difference between the approaches taken by academics and those of policy-makers, especially development practitioners.[55] Political scientists and scholars of international relations incorporate and privilege political data into the classification, while for development agencies classification proceeds from development indicators and then social, economic, and political criteria are inserted into it. Related to the second strand is the emerging definition proposed by Picciotto, et al. Drawing on the Country Policies and Institutional Performance Assessment (CPIA) list generated by the World Bank, Picciotto, et al., have applied capacity (to deliver public goods) and resilience (ratings of voice and accountability and political freedom) as key indicators of state fragility.[56]

Analysts and policy-makers have circumvented the definitional problem by favoring characterization of the states using a four-fold categorization suggested by Rotberg:[57] weak, failing, failed, and collapsed.[58] Distinctions between these four categories of states are made "according to the levels of their effective delivery of the most crucial political goods."[59] Within this framework, weak states are those plagued with problems limiting their ability to function properly. These problems can be inherent due to geography or can be a product of management flaws or despotism.[60] Failing states are weak states that have begun to fail, but have yet to reach a level where they have lost the ability to deliver. Failed states, according to Rotberg,

> [are] tense, deeply conflicted, dangerous, and contested bitterly by warring factions. In most failed states, government troops battle armed revolts led by one or more rivals. Occasionally, the official authorities in a failed state face two or more insurgencies, varieties of civil unrest, different degrees of communal discontent, and a plethora of dissent directed at the state and at groups within the state.[61]

The fourth and the last in the continuum is the collapsed state, "a rare and extreme version of a failed state," according to Rotberg.[62] One important point should be underscored in regard to the failed and collapsed state: the former points to the functional dimension of the state while the latter delineates the functional as well as structural aspect of the state. But they have one thing in common: they are the end product of the process. Therefore although policy discussions refer more often to the failed (and occasionally to the collapsed) states, the earlier stages and the processes leading to the end stage deserve more attention.

Drawing on the above discussion and available literature we can summarize the essential features of the state failure and examine the process of the state failure.

The most conspicuous features of the failed states are: the presence of enduring violence—often in the form of civil war directed against the state; the predatory and oppressive nature of the state resulting in persecution of its own citizens; inability of the state to control its own territory; growth of criminal violence and lawlessness posing a threat to the security of the people; deterioration and/or destruction of physical infrastructure; the decaying state of social services (including education and health); and providing economic opportunity for a few at the expense of the majority of the population.[63] An equally important element of the failed state is the loss of legitimacy.

One of the sources of the state's legitimacy is external, meaning the legitimacy of a state depends on its ability to project its sovereignty vis-à-vis other states. Protection of its territory and establishing its command over the recognized territory are necessary to claim this kind of legitimacy. The other source of legitimacy is internal, which means that the legitimacy is dependent upon its internal capability: to command and conduct public affairs, and give meaning to its social action. The internal aspect of legitimacy rests on the ideological hegemony of the state and its ability to deliver. Should the ideological hegemony of the state dissipate and its actions become questionable and illegitimate in the hearts and minds of its citizens, the dominance of the state soon fades.

The examination of the state-society relationship in Nepal reveals that the disjuncture between the state and the society increased dramatically over time, particularly after 1950. Additionally, throughout the 1990s the Nepali state lost its hegemonic hold over its citizens creating a void in the ideological realm, and thus paved the way for the rise of a counter hegemonic ideology. This is what can be described as "dominance without hegemony"[64] leading to a crisis and eventually the failure of the state. We believe that the absence of the Nepali state—in various geographic areas and on various issues—was both an indication and the cause of the state failure. From this perspective, the failure of the Nepali state consists of both "errors of omission" (the state failed to do things that could have improved the situation) and "errors of commission" (the state did things that worsened the situation).

There is also an intrinsic relationship between the performance of the state and its legitimacy. Simply stated, if the state functions well, its citizens view it as legitimate. We can call this "the performance legitimacy" of the state. Performance legitimacy serves to increase the state's ability to gain the consent from the people it governs, and consequently the state becomes strong. Marginalization of ethnic groups and limitation of the participation of citizens, which continued even after the pro-democracy movement in 1990, undermined the legitimacy of the Nepali state. However, the Nepali state was no exception. Generally speaking, exclusionary policies contribute to the erosion of state's legitimacy and limit the ability of the state to function. Lemarchand's study on Central Africa bears out this point.[65] In an ethnically heterogeneous society, the issue assumes greater significance, because the ethnic policies the state pursues—whether it favors one group or follows a distributive principle—are fundamental in attaining and maintaining its legitimacy.[66] The picture that emerges from Nepal on this count is not positive. The narrow ethnic base of the dominant group has been maintained since its inception and strengthened in the post-1990 democratic era.

The failings of the Nepali state both as the agency of delivery and in upholding their end of the bargain of the unwritten "social contract" was narrated in a passionate manner in an editorial of a Nepali weekly newspaper in February 2004:

What makes a failed state then? What factors lead to the collapse of a state? What elements put together make a failed state?

To the best of our knowledge backed by what Nepali academics have to say in this regard is that when a state is in a state of continued political vacuum; when a state is close to economic collapse; when the men governing the state lack the required credibility in the eyes of those being governed and those who mean much in a democratic system; when the political actors either fail to perform or are not allowed to do so; when the political actors eye chairs instead of development of the nation; when the security apparatuses either fail to provide needed security to its citizens or are projected by some interested quarters to be so; when the state fails to deliver goods to the people; when the state's bread-earning sectors, such as agriculture, tourism, and industries, either by the lack of proper security arrangements do not yield results or become the targets of uninterrupted *chakka* jams and *bandhs*; when a state itself becomes directionless and fails to assure the governed ones that not everything had gone worse; when cases of the abuse of HR continue unabated from both the warring sides and both not converging to sign the Rights accord as suggested and demanded by academics and HR activists within and without; when the state remains not in a position to enjoy confidence from the opposition forces which is a must; and when the constitutional crisis of the sort of the one that has gripped the country lingers for all along sixteen months with no signs at the end of the tunnel for its correction; and above all when the governed ones remain perpetually disillusioned as to what disaster was next awaiting them in the impending future. Add to this, when a situation wherein the political actors suspect each and every action[s] of the Head of the State for long and the latter in turn too suspects the very credentials of the former, the state is certainly close to collapse if not a total one.

In our opinion, all these elements if put together were sufficient to make any state a failed one. Unfortunately, we have all these basics here. We would strongly wish that the elements listed above proved to be incorrect. But the fact is that they are there very much kicking and alive.[67]

In the Nepali context, the weak performance of the state was not only limited to its delivery functions, but also affected its transformative functions. The function of the state, particularly in developing societies, as we discussed before, is both to be the agency of delivery and the agency of transformation. While Nepal experienced periodic changes in politics and in the social arena, the socioeconomic structure remained unmoved. The inability of the Nepali state to act as the agency of transformation is deeply tied to the mode of extraction it pursues on the one hand and its dependence on external assistance, on the other. The patrimonial character of the state has given rise to a rent-seeking class, a small coterie close to the monarchy that is engaged in plundering rather than reproducing the nation's wealth. Add to this the various functionaries of the state who have provided Nepal with a semblance of modern state but also became the basis for further extraction. The extracted resources are not ploughed back to the society through social services, welfarist redistributions, developmental efforts, or productive mechanisms.

These two levels of inability (as delivery agency and as transformative agency) reinforce each other and place the state in a downward spiral toward state failure and perhaps collapse. It is well to bear in mind that state failure is not an overnight spectacular event, nor a short-term phenomenon. Instead it is a long-term process, comparable to degenerative diseases. In agreement with David Carment, we can say that "state failure is a nonlinear process of relative decay."[68] Thus the process is not unidirectional and it is not path-dependent. State failure is not a result of state weakness. It should be borne in mind that although state failure begins with the weakening of state institutions, weak states are not destined to be failed states, and not all failed states collapse.

However, steps marking the progression in the direction of state failure are identifiable. There are at least three stages: first, institutions fail as delivery agencies; second, ethnic, social, and ideological competition further weakens the ability of the institutions entrusted with service delivery; and third, various sources of pressures (such as poverty, urbanization, environmental degradation) overwhelm the state, leading to failure.[69] Often the first sign—the failure of the delivery institutions—triggers the whole process. That is why we insisted that this should be considered as the cause of the state failure as much as the first indication of the process. The economic and political processes of Nepal assessed over a century, particularly since 1951, not only vindicate this path of progression, but in many ways make it a paradigmatic case of state failure.

The Nepal case also underscores the need for a longitudinal perspective as opposed to the "static, ahistoric, technical, and functionalistic" approach predominant in current explanations of state failure.[70] In our understanding this is more than necessary—it is an imperative, because the structure as well as the legitimacy, capacity, and authority of the state change over time. They can increase as much as they can recede. State failure implies a recession in the capacity of the state which can be due to "bad governance, lack of social and political space for minorities, debts, poor ecological situations, and scarcity of land and water," to name a few. But in any case the recession is bound to take time. The second point that emerges from the discussion on the relevance of the state failure thesis in understanding the Nepali state is that a judicious balance between three levels of analysis is important. These three levels are macro, intermediate, and micro. The macro level involves state formation processes, the intermediate level involves state-society relationships and the functions of state institutions, and the micro level involves time and the actors, their preferences for particular modes of activism, or, in other words, the triggering mechanisms. Throughout this study the combination of these three levels is used as the guiding framework.

ORGANIZATION OF THE BOOK

The book comprises six chapters. In the first chapter we trace the formation processes of the Nepali state since 1769. The Nepali state, while simultaneously representing the classical features of state building and uniqueness due to its location, needs to be examined in the context of Nepali society, particularly within the framework of state-society relationships. In the case of Nepal, we argue, the relationship is highly problematic. The historical narrative shows a colossal disjuncture between the state and the society upon which the state edifice has been built. This disjuncture is both structural and ideological. Structurally all the hallmarks of a patrimonial state are deeply inscribed in the institutions and its modes of performance, while ideologically the social order is based on a carefully stipulated caste hierarchy stemming from a Hindu ethno-religious creed. The complex connections between the constructed Hindu identity and the cultural legitimacy of social order, which have existed since the inception of the state in the eighteenth century, essentially ruptured after the democratic uprising in 1990. At another level this cultural phenomenon is manifested in the deep-seated *Chakari* system. The system stipulates that the nobles at court would attend to the rulers' needs at a particular time period and had to sublimate his desires. This system was replicated by the nobles themselves. The monarchical system thus set up a clientelist structure of distribution of resources. Within this structure, powerful individuals looking for favor from the court competed with each other, and powerful social and political entrepreneurs were provided with material resources so that they did not rebel. It was only with the crisis of legitimacy of the system that opposition to the regime strengthened. The uprising, dramatic as it may be, was a long time in the making—the result of urbanization, partial economic modernization, and expansion of educational opportunities from the 1950s. All of these changes brought into existence social classes who could challenge the monarchical system and had the potential to become its "gravediggers."

The uprising opened the democratic space for the activism of these new social classes as much as for other marginalized sections of the society, but neither the social structure nor state institutions reflected the much-needed transformation. On the contrary, an unending battle between the monarchy and party political establishments ensued. In a way, by agreeing to operate in a quasi-monarchical set up, political parties, particularly the Nepali Congress, imbibed and emulated a similar clientelist framework of operations and thus engaged in a self-annihilating competition for power among themselves. They remained engaged in a debilitating game of undermining and fragmenting existing institutional frameworks creating a crisis of governance and in turn causing political instability which became the defining characteristic of Nepali politics following the first freely held election in

April 1990. Thus, the nature of the Nepali state, we argue in this chapter, remained unchanged although it had plunged into an unassailable crisis and consequently its ability to govern was significantly weakened.

The presence of a variety of ethnic groups has not only made Nepal a heterogeneous society but has also impacted upon the nature of the state, and, consequently, on the ongoing crises of the state. In Nepal, ethnicity and caste intersect in many ways adding complexity to identity formation, party politics, ideological hegemony, and socio-political institutions. The structure of Hindu upper-class domination has been maintained and reproduced by the monarchy and through the state structure for centuries. Evidently, the ideology of the pre-1990 Nepali state was to preserve social, economic, and political domination of upper-caste Hindus associated with the court located in the Kathmandu valley. The two most evident results of this have been the subjection of certain groups of people along caste lines, and secondly a development process that is elitist in orientation and biased towards certain castes. Concomitant to these is the spatial aspect of these policies, breeding higher inequality in some regions than others. Simmering discontent due to this deliberate policy of marginalization engendered political activism along ethnic lines. The question is: Did the new ethnic movements, particularly in the 1990s, pose challenges to the existing exclusionary socio-political structure? In the second chapter we demonstrate that with the rise of democracy, peripheral Janajati, or marginalized social groups, under the leadership of various ethnic movements, Marxist organizations, and NGOs challenged the social order and demanded the recognition of a pluralist identity that further de-legitimized the existing social structure. These movements brought into sharp focus the issue of material and cultural liberation from the stranglehold of a Brahminical Hindu social order.

The third chapter of the book looks at the causes of and conditions for the weak "performance legitimacy" of the government. We argue that a number of factors contributed to the crisis of performance legitimacy: dependence on foreign aid, failure to implement fundamental redistributive reforms, lopsided urban centric development, the fragile ecology, and massive inequality along class, caste, and gender lines, to name but a few. Nepal's geo-formation has provided little opportunity for resource augmentation through agriculture. The country's most critical economic zone is located in the southern Terai region—an extension of the Indo-Gangetic plain. In the twentieth century with growing population pressure, people from the hill regions increasingly moved and colonized the densely forested southern plain where earlier only settlers of north Indian origin had lived. This meant a radical transformation in the demographic composition of the country. In these circumstances Nepal experienced an economic growth centered on the Kathmandu valley. Regional lopsidedness was obviously accompanied by wider deprivation in Janajati communities of the east or peripheral communities. Women also felt the burden of deprivation. The political economy of deprivation in a new democratic environment has varying degrees of significance for its people. Through the agency of democratic political parties and NGOs they registered their protests against the system. Thus, this chapter will not only discuss the perpetual economic crisis of Nepal's fragile ecology and dependent capitalistic development, but will also explain how this crisis of economy impacted its citizens.

States in the developing world, particularly on the periphery, are beset by perennial crises—both political and economic. Masquerading as strong and behaving in predatory and interventionist fashions masks the weaknesses but surely does not remove the structural causes of the crises. The Nepali state is no exception, as the political history of the country discussed in the first chapter and the economic policies discussed in the third chapter will clearly demonstrate. But the existence of crises, even in severe forms, is not sufficient to provoke an insurrection against the system. Any sustained challenge to the system requires participation by the masses beyond spontaneity, strong organization to enable them to withstand the state's assault, and above all, the capacity of a party/group to mobilize the masses for a definite objective. In other words, structural causes do not produce rebellion without human agency to move beyond structure limitations in order to seek changes. In the case of Nepal, the Maoists have demonstrated, to a great extent, all of these features. In the fourth chapter, we examine the causes of and conditions for the successes of the Maoists. Begun with a very small band of rebels, the Maoist movement has experienced a meteoric rise in the last decade, in terms of influence over politics even if not in terms of numbers of followers. In answering crucial questions, such as why are Maoists so successful in establishing their political presence and what strategies have assisted them in spreading their influence and popularizing their political goals, we look at their political agenda and the locations of the left movement in Nepal within the broader political landscape. Undoubtedly the plight of the poor helped Maoists gain support in rural areas, but it is our contention that the power game in the capital and the monarchy's hidden agenda to de-legitimize democratic politics also played pivotal parts. As Maoists became more powerful, the monarchy hoped to cash in on an increasing polarization of society and the patronage offered by India and the United States to defeat insurgency. In other words, Maoist successes are also products of the institutional crisis of the state and the fragmentation of elite response to the crisis.

The political crisis in Nepal reached its zenith in April 2006 when the seven-party alliance of the mainstream political parties, emboldened by their understanding with the Maoists in November 2005, called for demonstrations demanding the reinstatement of parliament and the restoration of civil liberties. Their movement received a new strength when civil society activists also joined the movement. This three-prong movement besieged the Nepali state. While Maoists undermined the regulatory power of the state, the civil society activists problematized normative acceptance of the state's claim to be acting in the people's interests. Civil society activists maintained that they were not seeking power for themselves but fighting for the greater good of the society and to achieve goals such as preservation of democratic rights. Thus, the alliance became a formidable challenge to the palace establishment. On a daily basis the alliance drew strength from the fact that political parties across the spectrum joined together based on specific objectives and clearly delineated goals articulated in the twelve-point understanding of November 2005. Reminiscent of the uprising of 1990, for weeks the streets of Kathmandu turned into battlegrounds between the security forces and unarmed civilians. However, unlike 1990, the protesters were ahead of their leaders in demanding change and making it happen. Spontaneity and the preponderance of grassroots activists in demonstrations were the defining characteristics of the early, and perhaps the most crucial, days of the uprising. Despite brutal repressions and scores of deaths, the Nepali people forced the king to capitulate. On 24 April, the curtain dropped on King Gyanendra, who not only reinstated parliament, acknowledging the "spirit of the people's movement," but also agreed to implement the roadmap of the alliance, which includes the election of a constituent assembly and rewriting the constitution. In the fifth chapter, we revisit the uprising through the narratives of the participants and organizers, looking at the tactics of popular mobilization and the immediate achievements of this bloody episode.

In the concluding chapter we address the immediate challenges faced by the nation and the long-term questions that need to be addressed. The uprising of 2006 on the one hand has vindicated the fact that the Nepali state, characterized by its patrimonial nature and repressive feature, has failed and that the transformation of the Nepali state is well overdue; but on the other hand, it has also laid bare the uncertain future of the country. The Maoists are out from the cold, the election for a constituent assembly is to be held, and a new constitution to be written, which would deal with the fate of the monarchy, among others—these are all that we know, but what we don't know can be more significant. There is obviously a significant curtailment of the power of the monarch. Nepali society is now being gradually polarized on the question of the fate of the monarchy as an institution: Will Nepal retain a ceremonial monarchy or will it become a republic? Will the king and the powerful networks around him accept defeat and be thrown into oblivion so easily? There are also urgent questions involving the roles of the Maoist army, and the Nepali army during the transition period. What will be the nature of the new constitution and how will the new constitution address the related issues of ethnicity, caste, and gender? Equally important is the long-term question related to the nature of the state—will a new Nepali state emerge?

NOTES

1. George W. Bush, *The National Security Strategy of the United States of America*, Washington, DC: White House, September 2002, http://www.whitehouse.gov/nsc/nss.html (22 January 2003).

2. Peter Evans, *Embedded Autonomy: States and Industrial Transformation* (Princeton: Princeton University Press, 2005), 35.

3. An ambitious nobleman named Jang Bahadur Kunwar Rana usurped political power through palace coups in 1846. He became de facto ruler of the country and appointed himself as the self-styled ruler of the kingdom. However, this was not new in Asian history. In the Maratha confederacy of eighteenth-century Peshwa, the Brahmin prime minister became the most powerful person while the king faded from power. In Japan during the Tokugawa period, the shogun became the real ruler and the emperor remained a mere figurehead. A similar situation developed in Nepal under the Rana family, whereby prime ministers were appointed from among male descendants of Jang Bahadur. The Rana family continued to rule Nepal by virtually imprisoning the royal family within the palace. In this book we have referred to Rana in singular form when we imply the hereditary prime minister in person and in plural when we refer to the entire Rana clan.

4. Michael Mann, "The Autonomous Power of the State," in *States in History*, ed. John A. Hall (Oxford: Basil Blackwell, 1986), 109–36; Dietrich Reuschmeyer and Peter Evans, "Transnational Linkages and the Economic Role of the State: An Analysis of Developing and Industrial States in the Post-World War II Period," in *Bringing the State Back In*, ed. Peter Evans, Dietrich Reuschmeyer, and Theda Skocpol (Cambridge: Cambridge University Press, 1986), 45–46.

5. Mushtaq H. Khan, "State Failure in Developing Countries and Strategies of Institutional Reform" (paper presented at the Annual Bank Conference on Development Economies, Oslo, 24–26 June 2002).

6. Khan, "State Failure," 1.

7. Rolf Schwarz, "State Formation Processes in Rentier States: The Middle Eastern Case" (paper presented at the fifth Pan-European Conference on International Relations, ECPR Standing Group on International Relations, Hague, 9–11 September, 2004).

8. Charles Tilly, "Reflections on the History of European State-Making," in *The Formation of National States in Western Europe*, ed. Charles Tilly (Princeton, NJ: Princeton University Press, 1975); Charles Tilly, "War Making and State Making as Organized Crime," in *Bringing the State Back In*, ed. Peter Evans, Dietrich Reuschmeyer, and Theda Skocpol (Cambridge: Cambridge University Press, 1985); Charles Tilly, *Coercion, Capital and European States, AD 990–1990* (Oxford: Basil Blackwell, 1990); Charles Tilly, "Entanglements of European City States," in *Cities and the Rise of the State in Europe, AD 1000–1800*, ed. Charles Tilly (Boulder, CO: Westview, 1994).

9. Tilly, "War Making,"181.

10. Teodor Shanin, "Class, State and Revolutions: Substitutes and Realities," in *Introduction to the Sociology of the "Developing Societies,"* ed. Hamza Alavi and Teodor Shanin (New York: Monthly Review Press, 1982), 315.

11. The treaty allowed a British resident to be placed in the royal court of Kathmandu to supervise the process of governance. The resident played a crucial role in local politics. In a situation of externally imposed restrictions on political dynamism for an expanding princely polity, the very power of the monarch as a military leader had been curbed; this substantially contributed to the weakening of the monarch's hold over the court. The monarchical crisis deepened as a series of minors succeeded to the throne. Many of these new rulers had little ability or desire to rule. Not being able to engage in wider military conquests, courtiers now concentrated on orchestrating intrigues, factional fighting, and coups. Not surprisingly, after 1816 the monarchy as an institution was gradually weakened by internal squabbles. As elsewhere in South Asia, the British resident's presence and his occasional dabbling in court politics further contributed to growing factional squabbles among courtly elites.

12. Cameron Theis, "State Building, Interstate and Intrastate Rivalry: A Study of Post-Colonial Developing Country Extractive Efforts, 1974–1993" (paper presented at the annual meeting of the International Studies Association, New Orleans, 24–27 March 2002), 4.

13. Theis, "State Building," 4.

14. Robert Rotberg, *State Failure and State Weakness in a Time of Terror*, Washington, DC: Brookings Institution Press, 2003.

15. M. C. Regmi, *A Study of Nepali Economic History 1768–1846* (New Delhi: Manjushree Publishing House, 1971).

16. Surendra R. Devkota, "The Politics of Poverty in Nepal: Structural Analysis of Socioeconomic Development from the Past Five Decades," Heidelberg Papers in South Asian and Comparative Politics, Working Paper no. 25 (Heidelberg: South Asia Institute, Department of Political Science, University of Heidelberg, February 2005): 3.

17. Devkota, "The Politics of Poverty," 5.

18. Mancur Olson, *Power and Prosperity* (New York: Basic Books, 2000); "Dictatorship, Democracy, and Development," *American Political Science Review* 87 (1993), 567–76.

19. Peter Evans, *Embedded Autonomy: States and Industrial Transformation* (Princeton: Princeton University Press, 1995), 35.

20. David N. Gellner, "Introduction," in *Nationalism and Ethnicity in a Hindu Kingdom: The Politics of Culture in Contemporary Nepal*, ed. David Gellner, N. Joanna Pfaff-Czarnecka, and John Whelpton (Amsterdam: Hardwood Academic Publishers, 1997), 8.

21. Mahendra Lawoti, "Centralizing Politics and the Growth of the Maoist Insurgency in Nepal," *Himalaya* 13, no. 1 (2003): 49–58.

22. Max Weber, *The Theory of Social and Economic Organization*, ed. Talcott Parsons (London: Collier-Macmillan Ltd., 1947), 347–58.

23. Michael Bratton and Nicolas van de Walle. "Neo-Patrimonial Regimes and Political Transitions in Africa," *World Politics* 46 (July 1994): 453–89.

24. Lawoti, "Centralizing Politics," 49–58.

25. Peter Kimyu, "Development Policy In Kenya: Which Way Forward?" *Wajibu* 15, no. 2, 1999, http://web.peacelink.it/wajibu/7_issue/p1.html (1 September 2005).

26. Antonio Gramsci, *Selections from Prison Notebooks* (New York: International General, 1971), 12.

27. Gramsci, *Selections*, 181.

28. Gramsci, *Selections*, 12.

29. András Höfer, *The Caste Hierarchy and the State in Nepal—A Study of the Muluki Ain of 1854* (Innsbruck: Universitatsverlag Wagner, 1979).

30. Mary M. Cameron, *On the Edge of the Auspicious: Gender and Caste in Nepal* (Urbana and Chicago: University of Illinois Press, 1998).

31. Hari Shrama, "Political Conflict in Nepal and Quest for Autonomy," *Calcutta Research Group Seminar* (July 2005), 4.

32. Mansoob S. Murshed and Scott Gates, "Spatial-Horizontal Inequality and the Maoist Insurgency in Nepal," 2003, www.worldbank.org/research/inequality/June18Papers/NepalConflict.pdf (2 October 2005); Jugal Bhurtel and Saleem H. Ali, eds., "The Green Roots of Red Rebellion: Environmental Degradation and the Rise of the Maoist Movement in Nepal," n.d., www.uvm.edu/~shali/Maoist.pdf (29 September 2005).

33. Lawoti, "Centralizing Politics," 49–58.

34. Ali Riaz, *Unfolding State: The Transformation of Bangladesh* (Ontario: de Sitter Publications, 2005), 263–70.

35. Murshed and Gates, "Spatial-Horizontal Inequality."

36. UNDP, *Nepal Human Development Report 2004: Empowerment and Poverty Reduction.* (Kathmandu: UNDP, 2004), 2–3.

37. National Planning Commission (NPC), *The Tenth Plan (Poverty Reduction Strategy Plan) 2002–2007* (Kathmandu: NPC, 2003), 26–27.

38. Bhurtel and Ali, "The Green Roots," 18.

39. Fiona Rotberg, "Nepal: Environmental Scarcity and State Failure," 2006, http://www.worldsecuritynetwork.com/showArticle3.cfm?article_id=12984 (31 July 2006).

40. Rotberg, "Nepal: Environmental Scarcity."

41. Richard Matthew and Bishnu Raj Upreti, "Environmental Stress and Demographic Change in Nepal: Underlying Conditions Contributing to a Decade of Insurgency," *Environmental Change and Security Program Report* 11 (Washington, DC: The Woodrow Wilson Center for International Scholars, 2005), 29–39.

42. This perception is also informed by the historical development of colonialism, particularly in the Pacific. Drawing on Robert Dorff's presentation at the Failed and Failing States Conference held in Florence, Italy, 7–10 April 2000 (Robert H. Dorff, "Addressing the Challenges of State Failure"), Minh Nguyen argued that "at the zenith of European expansion, the failure of Pacific indigenous efforts at self-government had frequently provided the opportunity and justification for great power interventions. Powerful states often intervened in weaker states to quell social disorder that threatened their security and trade interests" (Ming Nguyen, "The Question of 'State Failure,'" *JRS Occasional Paper*, no. 8 [Sydney, Australia: March 2005]).

43. Francis Fukuyama, "Nation Building 101," *Atlantic Monthly* (January/February 2004), http://www.theatlantic.com/doc/200401/fukuyama (25 January 2005).

44. Introduction to the "Workshop on State Failure: Reframing the International Economic and Political Agenda" organized by the Program on States and Security, Ralph Bunche Institute, the Graduate Center, City University of New York, 9–10 May 2005. This was the first of a series of workshops of the program which intends to apply "a critical lens on the concept of state failure and on the models of the state on which it is based, and to do serious empirical research on state failure and international response with the aim of proposing policy alternatives."

45. Morten Bøås and Kathleen Jennings, "Insecurity and Development: The Rhetoric of the Failed State," *European Journal of Development Research* (September 2005).

46. Gerald Helman, and Steven Ratner, "Saving Failed States," *Foreign Policy* 89, (Winter 1993), 3–20.

47. Robert Dorff, "Failed States after 9/11: What Did We Know and What Have We Learned," *International Studies Perspectives* 6, no. 1 (2005): 20–34.

48. Robert D. Kaplan, "The Coming Anarchy," *Atlantic Monthly* (February 1994): 44–76.

49. Quoted in Rachel Stahl and Michael Stahl, "The Failed and Failing State and the Bush Administration: Paradoxes and Perils" (paper prepared for the workshop on "Failed and Failing States," Florence, Italy, 10–14 April 2001), http://www.cdi .org/issues/failedstates/Bush.htm (10 March 2004).

50. Securitization means framing and handling an issue in a manner that it is presented as an imminent threat, requiring immediate actions and thus allowing the agent of the securitization to gain unusual emergency powers.

51. Bush, *The National Security*.

52. Center for Strategic and International Studies (CSIS) and the Association of the United States Army (AUSA), *Play to Win: Bi-partisan Commission on Post-Conflict Reconstruction* (Washington, DC: CSIS and Arlington: AUSA, 2003), 1.

53. CSIS and AUSA, *Play to Win*, 2.

54. For a list of these classifications and the results, see Stefan Wolf, "State Failure in A Regional Context," 2005, www.stefanwolff.com/working-papers/state-failure.pdf (25 March 2006).

55. David Carment, "Assessing State Failure: Implications for Theory and Policy," *Third World Quarterly* 24, no. 3 (2003): 407–27.

56. Wolf, "State Failure."

57. Robert Rotberg, "Failed States, Collapsed States, Weak States: Causes and Indicators," in *State Failure and State Weakness in a Time of Terror*, ed. Robert Rotberg (Washington, DC: Brookings Institution Press, 2003), and *When States Fail: Causes and Consequences* (Princeton: Princeton University Press, 2004).

58. While these four categories have been used by most of the analysts in recent years, there are other categories in use too. In the 1990s in African context, scholars had used the terms "fragmented" and "archipelago" state in describing the states characterized with weak capacity to extract revenues and loss of control over and fragmentation of the instruments of physical coercion.

59. Rotberg, "Failed States," 4.

60. Robert Rotberg, "The Failure and Collapse of Nation States: Breakdown, Prevention and Repair," in *When States Fail: Causes and Consequences*, ed. Robert Rotberg (Princeton: Princeton University Press, 2004), 3.

61. Rotberg, "The Failure and Collapse," 4.

62. Rotberg, "The Failure and Collapse," 7.

63. Rotberg writes, "Failed states offer unparalleled economic opportunity—but only for a privileged few. Those clustered around the ruler or the ruling oligarchy grow richer while their less fortunate brethren starve." Rotberg, "The Failure and Collapse," 12.

64. Ranajit Guha, *Dominance Without Hegemony: History and Power in Colonial India* (Cambridge, MA: Harvard University Press, 1998).

65. René Lemarchand, "Patterns of State Collapse and Reconstruction in Central Africa: Reflections on the Crisis in the Great Lakes Region," *afrika spectrum* 32, no. 2, (1997): 173–93.

66. Nirvikar Singh, "Cultural Conflicts in India: Punjab and Kashmir," in *The Myth of Ethnic Conflict*, Ronnie Lipschutz and Beverly Crawford, eds. (Berkley, CA: University of Berkley Press, 1999), 352–60.

67. Editorial, "Failed State?" *Weekly Telegraph (Kathmandu)*, 19 February 2004, http://www.nepalnews.com.np/contents/englishweekly/telegraph/2004/feb/feb18/editorial.htm (14 January 2006).

68. Carment, "Assessing State Failure," 409.

69. Douglas H. Dearth, "Failed States: An International Conundrum," *Defense Intelligence Journal* 5 (1996): 119–30. Quoted in Carment, "Assessing State Failure," 414.

70. The point is highlighted by Jan Ruyssenaars, an official of Netherlands chapter of the international aid agency Novib-Oxfam. For his comments, see: "On Failed, Failing, Weak and Collapsed States," http://www.realityofaid.org/themeshow.php?id=22 (15 July 2006).

1

State Formation and Political Transition in Nepal (1768–2005)

States are not natural entities; they are the products of complex social and historical processes. The capacity, authority, structures, legitimacy, and sovereignty of states depend on the forces that participate in the process of state-making. Factors that contribute to these processes constantly change, causing new dynamics at different times under different circumstances. Structural as well as conjunctural developments, individuals, and time affect these multifaceted processes.[1] Therefore, there is no linear, step-wise process with a clearly identifiable end in the state formation process. There is no finality to the process—states remain open to potential changes all the time. State formation processes not only create and consolidate the structures, provide mechanisms for social integration, and construct a new identity, but also cause conflicts, contradictions, and frictions, and create disruptive forces. They are integral parts of the very same processes. Nepal is no exception.

For more than one and a quarter century, the Nepali state, society, and polity have demonstrated these features. In this chapter we examine these processes in detail and in chronological order. Our object is to introduce the key political forces and individuals, explore their roles in making and sustaining the Nepali state, explore their modes of interactions with the society, and probe the material and ideational bases of the socio-political structures.

THE MAKING OF A PATRIMONIAL STATE: FROM MONARCHY TO RANA REGIME (1769–1951)

The eighteenth century was a transitional period in the history of state formation in South Asia. It witnessed the eclipse of earlier imperial political

33

formations, and the rise of new principalities and empires. The most formidable new political power was obviously the English East India Company, which defeated the local ruler of Bengal in a minor fracas on the banks of Ganges on 23 June 1757 by bribing his disloyal general.[2] This rather unremarkable episode established the foundation of long-standing British Empire in South Asia. While the other parts of South Asia witnessed the formation of new princely polities, in the central Himalayan mountain valleys, on the north of the Indo-Gangetic plain, Prithvi Narayan (1723–1775), ruler of the tiny Gorkha principality, about fifty miles west of Kathmandu, embarked upon an assault of the Kathmandu valley. For twenty-six years, he organized blockades, sieges, and assaults that ultimately enabled him to conquer the valley comprising sixty local kingdoms. Prithvi Narayan and his successors did not stop with this formidable achievement and went on to further expand their kingdom, incorporating the Himalayan foothills as far as Sikkim in the east and the Kangra Valley in the west. They thus gave birth to another princely polity in South Asia.[3]

Yet there exists a fundamental difference between this principality and other princely states that emerged in different corners of South Asia in the late eighteenth century. Many of these princely polities collapsed under the sway of British imperial rule in the region and those that survived were frozen into a time warp by the British through indirect colonial control.[4] But while the formidable British colonial empire and other South Asian princely states floundered in the twentieth century under the twin impact of the rise of nationalism and republican democracy, Prithvi Narayan Shah's Gorkha kingdom did not disappear from the map of South Asia. Rather, the hill kingdom experienced a gradual transition to become the nation-state of Nepal. Not surprisingly, modern Nepali nationalists describe Prithvi Narayan as the unifier of their country. Moving a step ahead, Nepali royalists project the crown as the symbol of national unity. Nepal is thus a rare exception among eighteenth-century South Asian princely polities to have enjoyed such longevity and in the process to have successfully made a claim to be a nation-state in the twentieth century.

The longevity of this eighteenth-century Gorkha monarchical polity was not accidental. In many ways it can be attributed to the indirect colonization of Nepal that began with the compromise negotiated between the Nepali court and their formidable South Asian neighbor the British Empire in India. After a brief Anglo-Gorkha War (1814–1816), the Treaty of Sagauli signed by the Gorkha monarch with the East India Company in 1816 defined the outer parameters of the monarchical polity. This treaty stopped the process of expansion that the Gorkha kingdom undertook in the earlier period and transformed Nepal into a de facto dependent territory of the British Indian Empire.[5] A British resident was placed in the royal court of Kathmandu to supervise the process of governance. The resident played a crucial role in local politics. Indeed, the crown that ruled Nepal, to borrow a phrase from Nick Dirk's now famous work, was a hollow crown.[6]

In a situation of externally imposed restrictions on political dynamism for an expanding princely polity, the very power of the monarch as a military leader had been curbed; this substantially contributed to the weakening of the monarch's hold over the court. The monarchical crisis deepened as a series of minors succeeded to the throne. Many of these new rulers had little ability or desire to rule. Not being able to engage in wider military conquests, courtiers now concentrated in orchestrating intrigues, fractional fighting, and coups. Not surprisingly, after 1816 the monarchy as an institution was gradually weakened by internal squabbles. As elsewhere in South Asia, the British resident's presence and his occasional dabbling in court politics further contributed to growing fractional squabbles among courtly elites.

With the royal household mired in chronic fractional wrangles, Jang Bahadur Kunwar Rana, a powerful member of the court, usurped real power. In 1846 he massacred many members of the royal household and compelled the king to appoint him as the prime minister. Through the *Lal Panja* edict of 1856, the monarch transferred power to Jang Bahadur Kunwar and his direct male heirs. Thus, the Rana family became the hereditary prime ministers and de facto head of the state. Under the Ranas (we use the plural when we refer to the entire Rana clan which produced long lines of prime ministers), Nepal became a model patrimonial state where political rights and economic rights converged, in the sense that political power claimed ownership of all resources. Even the royal household depended on the Rana family for access to throne. Ranas, on the other hand, in order to gain further legitimacy, arranged marital alliances with the royal family, thereby transforming the royal Shah family into an extension of the Rana family. While the monarch remained titular head of state, the Rana family became the true power of the land.[7]

To further consolidate his rule, the founder of the Rana family, Jang Bahadur Kunwar Rana assumed the title of Maharaja of Lambjang and Kaski and also assumed control over the army as the commander in chief. Being the patriarch of the patrimonial state, Ranas distributed largesse among members of the family and established a precedent of honor call, which implied that the prime minister would recruit from his extended kin the highest-ranking members of bureaucracy in an institutional manner. The lower level of bureaucracy was selected on the basis of demonstration of loyalty to the regime, acceptance of gifts, and bribes. This obviously created a wider network of patron-client relationships and a culture of sycophancy pervaded all levels of the bureaucratic elites.[8] As in any patrimonial state the real source of power was the ruling elites' tight control over the army. Rana's position as hereditary commander in chief gave him substantial power to exercise this control.

Jang Bahadur Kunwar Rana also shrewdly recognized that the military oligarchy needed religious sanction in order to secure obedience of their subjects. He also understood that a religious structure could be utilized to create a hierarchical social order that would buttress his authority. Here the earlier process of state formation under the Shah dynasty, and myths and legends associated with the princely family and the evolution of the caste system, provided the impetus for the construction of new religious social order. The social system of the new Nepali state drew upon the caste structure of the *Parbatya* people of the middle hills or areas surrounding the Kathmandu valley. In the late eighteenth century the caste system in this region consisted of *Bahuns* (Brahmins) at the top followed by *Chetris* (*Khastriyas*) with a tiny minority of the royal caste among them, namely *Thakuri*. These high castes supervised the political system and extracted surplus both in kind and labor from low caste artisans.[9] With the expansion of territory, the Nepali monarchy in the pre-Rana days bolstered the economic and political positions of upper caste elites through official appointments and land grants.

In a carefully constructed myth that traced back the origin of the Shah dynasty to the fabled Rajput warriors of the Chitor dynasty of Udaipur in present day Western India, the royal rulers of Nepal established their credentials as authentic ruling elites of Rajput origin. According to a legend propagated by the royal household, in the sixteenth century, a warrior from this dynasty named Jagdeva Khan conquered the principality of Kaski and secured the title of Shah from the Mughal Emperor. The creation of this myth reflected a shrewd move to placate both the Mughal overlord of South Asia while also establishing the grounds within which to claim a role as protector of the Hindu religion. But there was more to this claim.

By tracing the royal household's lineage to Chitor Rajputs, royal mythmakers also claimed a direct line of descent from the Hindu god Vishnu and thus constructed an ideological patina of divine right to rule. Indeed, complex religious rituals had been used to legitimize the crown as the symbol of divine lineage. The founder of the Gorkha kingdom, Prithvi Narayan Shah, introduced the central sanctification process by drawing upon Tantric and Buddhist traditions of the land. The coronation ceremony of the king, given the title of *raja abhisheka* in accordance with Sanskritic tradition, bestowed upon the ruler divine status as an incarnation of Vishnu.

For religious sanction the Shah dynasty also appropriated *Indra Jatra*, a royal festival of the indigenous Newar population of the Kathmandu Valley, as a symbol of their conquest of the Malla kingdoms. Every year toward the end of the monsoon season monarchs erected a ceremonial pole at the medieval palace, *Hanuman Dhoka*, in order to affirm the crown's sanctified role as the unifier of heaven and earth. Another important feature is the blessing of the king by the "living goddess," Kumari. Prithivi Narayan Shah used the latter to gain instant legitimacy, when he sealed his conquest of Kathmandu during the *Indra Jatra* festival and placed himself before the Kumari to receive immediate sanctification as the ruler of Nepal.[10]

Clifford Greertz, in his well-known work has described such elaborate rituals concerning the Hindu monarchy in Bali as the Theatrical State.[11] Such complex rituals and claims provided wider ideological legitimacy for the ritualized expression of the crown's power. In Nepal, Hindu rituals thus acted as an ideological sanctifier for the regime but also constituted a source of legal structure. This became more pronounced as the Rana regime came to enjoy quasi-sovereignty as a British protectorate.

In 1854, Jang Bahadur commissioned Brahmin interpreters of religious texts and administrators to codify Hindu canonical laws. Through a fourteen-hundred-page document entitled *Muluki Ain* (law of the land), he sought to establish a legally sanctioned hierarchical social order based on Hindu caste ranking.[12] Caste, as Nick Dirk asserts, was embedded in a political context of the crown's authority in pre-colonial South Asia.[13] In Nepal the caste structure sustained the patrimonial despotism of the Rana family. It upheld royal honor, associated notions of power, dominance, and order. Although within the Gorkha kingdom, earlier Hindu practices had never been sharply delineated from diverse religious traditions emanating from Buddhist or animist heritage, *Muluki Ain* forcibly assimilated within the Hindu caste hierarchy a range of hill and plain ethnicities. Hill ethnicities, such as the Gurung and Magar (often described as tribals, currently styled as Janajatis), were placed into the middle ranks of the caste hierarchy under Bahuns and Chetris, compelling the former to acculturate and work within the system.[14] The stratification stipulated in this legal code influenced a wide range of policies. The *Muluki Ain* classified penalties for crimes according to caste, determined laws over land tenure and trading privileges and institutionalized economic dominance of upper caste elites over subaltern social groups ranging from Janajatis (tribals) to Dalits (untouchables located at the bottom of the social hierarchy below the organized caste system).[15] This social order that privileged caste hierarchy with Bahuns (Brahmins) at the top is described in modern Nepali political discourse as Hindu Brahminical order. It had been economically sustained by an agrarian political economy based on a complex tenurial structure.

A complex tenurial arrangement based on broadly four-fold classifications evolved under Rana rule: 1) the *Raikar* land from which the state directly received revenue but in which the state was divested of ownership rights in favor of an individual on conditional contracts; 2) the *Birta* tenure whereby tenure holders enjoyed direct control over land in return for part payment of revenue to the state; 3) *Gunthi* tenure whereby tenure holders enjoyed direct control over land in return for part payment of revenue to the state (the *Gunthi* lands were donated by the state or individuals for religious or philanthropic purposes, and exempted from tax); and iv) *Kipat*, a form of communal tenure prevalent in the Eastern Hills regions for Limbu minorities.[16] Despite variations these tenures actually supported the parasitic rent-receiving upper caste land-owning elites. *Birta* and *Gunthi* provided the basis of Rana control over the land tenure system. The Rana regime was not simply a predatory patrimonial regime. It also constructed a political economy of surplus extraction by a centralized political authority sanctified and legitimated through the Brahminical social order. The very formation of Nepali identity privileged high caste Hindu linguistic cultural traditions.

The Ranas not only privileged Sanskrit and Nepali as the language of the court but projected it as the language of the people as well. Again, Janajatis (sometimes referred to as tribals, but we prefer to use the Nepali term) had to accept high caste linguistic culture, and similarly untouchables had to operate and perform labor within this social order. Indeed, elite resistance to linguistic culture led to the accidental renaming of the national language as Nepali. In the 1920s, when the Newars, an ethnic group of the Nepal valley, claimed their language as Nepali, the Gorkha government gave the national language the same name, privileging it from a range of amorphous names such as Parbatya, Khas, or Gorkhali, at the same time styling the kingdom as Nepal.[17] They thus actually created common national nomenclature for a people, land, and government, and a critical category for the projection of national identity.[18] Soon the British provided external legal sanction in 1923 by recognizing the Nepali court as an independent sovereign state and thus placed the country on the world map distinguishing it from the maze of princely states that dotted South Asia under British tutelage.

Externally supported by the British and internally organized through Hindu Brahminical order, the crown claimed legitimacy as the protector of the *Sanatan Dharma* (literally meaning traditional religion, as Hinduism came to be called by its followers) while the Rana regime reinforced and preserved the social hierarchy associated with it. Ranas imposed a strict isolationist policy so that the "corrupting influence" of the outside world did not penetrate the princely polity.

This system, however, survived because of the active tolerance of the British of such affairs in Nepal. The topography of the new state actually made it more dependent on the British Indian territory. Many parts of Nepal were more accessible from India than from the Kathmandu valley. Although the border with India was porous, it was shielded by thick forests located in Terai—the extension of the Indo-Gangetic plain that the British allowed Nepal to retain. The British support for the regime may be explained in terms of their dependence on the Rana regime for the supply of military labor from the Himalayan kingdom. The British protected this state and projected it as a sovereign political entity. The Nepali state that came into existence under Ranas perfectly fitted the British imagination of Oriental Despotism. Colonial modernity thus sustained the only Hindu monarchy and its associated state-sponsored hierarchical structure.

RISE OF ROYAL DOMINANCE: DEMOCRACY, DEVELOPMENT, AND PRINCELY DICTATORSHIP (1951–1979)

As in all pre-capitalist states, in Nepal the process of state formation, its method of social restructuring, and surplus extraction from peasants were accompanied by various forms of resistance at different levels of society. These acts of resistance may be typified into two clusters: peasant insurgencies and elite dissatisfaction. Apart from undocumented everyday resistance, Nepal experienced peasant insurgencies under the Rana regime. The historic resistance to the Rana regime offered by Lakhan Thapa, a former captain in the Royal Nepalese Army, represented a form of peasant rebellion whereby a peasant leader emulated and sought to introduce a utopian just rule based on the Hindu notion of *Satya Yuga* (Era of Truth, when gods intermingled with humans).[19] Though these rebellions could not undermine the regime, they left behind a trail of legends that would be reinterpreted and claimed by various political groups in the post-Rana era.

In contrast to peasant insurgencies, elite resistance played a crucial role in undermining the Rana regime. Though elite resistance often could not be distinguished from fractional competition for access to wealth and patronage of the Rana regime, many upper caste Hindu elites who benefited from the *Muluki Ain* found it difficult to accept the patrimonial rule of Rana leaders and wanted to play a larger role in politics. Education and exposure to outside events indeed played a critical role in shaping elite resistance to the Ranas.

The Rana rulers were apprehensive that education would undermine their control over society. This fear was articulated by Prime Minister Chandra Samser Rana himself, who established Tri-Chandra College, the first institution of higher education in Nepal in 1918. At the inaugural ceremony of this institution, he reportedly lamented that the opening of this institution would be the death knell of the Rana regime. Yet education was necessary for ruling elites to run the administrative structure. Jang Bahadur Kunwar, the founder of the Rana regime, appointed an English tutor for his children in the Rana palace and thus established a dual system of education whereby upper elites moved to embrace Western education, leaving traditional Sanskrit and Nepali education for lesser elites.[20] Ranas regarded education as the exclusive privilege of the ruling elite and opposed any form of public instruction system for the people. Knowledge was regarded as the symbol of social status as well as a tool for dominance over the society.

To their great dismay, as time progressed the Ranas could not oppose the opening up of several new English middle and high schools, including a girls' high school in Kathmandu. Even the rural areas experienced changes as Gorkha soldiers, many of whom had learned to read and write while serving in the British army, sought to provide rudimentary education to children. It would be, however, wrong to overestimate these developments prior to the constitutional revolution of 1950–1951. Before 1950, Nepal had only 310 primary and middle schools, eleven high schools, two colleges, one normal school, and one special technical school. Even in the early 1950s, the average literacy rate was 5 percent. Literacy among males was 10 percent and among females less than 1 percent. Only one child in one hundred attended school.[21] But though numerically insignificant, many young members of these educated groups from high caste families went to Patna University, Banaras Hindu University, or other universities in India for higher academic or technical training. In India their exposure to wider nationalist and socialist movements had contributed significantly to the political revolution that ultimately led to the overthrow of Rana rule in 1951.

Socialism, with its emphasis on state control of the economy in a situation of near complete absence of capitalistic growth, promised to many educated elites a short cut to rapid modernization particularly because educated elites would then be able to play the role of technocratic managers of the state. Impressed by Indian socialists such as Ram Monohar Lohia, Acharaya Narendra Dev, and others, exiled Nepali intellectuals organized the Nepali Congress Party in Calcutta in 1947. This organization later flourished as a premier political party in Nepal. Within two years of the establishment of the Nepali Congress, in a clandestine meeting of Marxist radicals in Calcutta, there came into existence a nucleus of Communist organization.[22]

With the British departure from India (15 August 1947), the Rana regime lost its most powerful foreign sponsor. The Nepali Congress decided to use this as an opportunity to step up their action against the Rana regime. It is not surprising that from the late 1940s with the coming of Indian independence, the Nepali Congress launched an armed struggle to depose the Rana regime. The Congress further stepped up their political activities against the Rana regime through violent insurgency. In November 1950, this culminated into an open rebellion. Communists extended lukewarm support to the movement as they suspected that the intention of the struggle was to restrict Communist influence in Nepal. They thought that the government of India would not allow Communists to have a say in Nepali affairs and would emerge as a distant overlord. The struggle took a dramatic turn when reigning Nepali monarch Tribhuvan Shah, a mere figurehead, escaped from Rana control and took shelter in Delhi. Ranas attempted to dethrone the monarch. They appointed Gyanendra, a three-year-old grandson of Tribhuvan, as the king. This was met with dissension in the army.

The king's departure led to far more violent insurgency. Rebels from India launched attacks on the army in Terai plains on the Indian borders. Though rebels captured towns in Terai they had to retreat in the face of counterattacks by the army. However, military confrontations sparked off political uprising in hills. Towns of the hills witnessed massive demonstrations. Demonstrators demanded the return of the king. Meanwhile, following classic guerilla tactics insurgents infiltrated into the remote hill areas of the west and east. In these hilly terrains conventional army operation proved to be difficult. Soon political turmoil took its toll on the army. Local commanders now opposed the government moves. A series of regions slipped out of government control. By the end of January 1951, towns such as Palpa, Pokhara, and even parts of Gorkha district fell into rebel hands. By this time, low-level military officials resigned their commissions in protest, and troops were beginning to surrender to the rebels.

In the meantime, New Delhi insisted on a solution of power sharing between monarchy and party political apparatus. This came after a negotiation with the Rana government that began on 24 December 1950 in Delhi. On 8 January 1951, Prime Minister Mohan Shamsher Rana promised the restoration of the king, amnesty for all political prisoners, and elections based on adult suffrage no later than 1952. In February 1951 the king returned from India and a new settlement was effected between the Ranas, the royal court, and the Nepali Congress, which represented an emerging party political apparatus.[23] Thus the 1950 uprising was an elite rebellion with the potential for establishing a popular accountable government. It was a product of anti-colonial nationalism and emerged victorious due to the collapse of colonial rule in India. Yet in reality this victory was a compromise between the monarchy and an emerging party political apparatus. King Tribhuvan's reluctance to intervene and the Indian government's attempt to retain a weak and divided authority in Nepal allowed this power sharing to continue. For India, political stability in Nepal appeared more important than the pursuance of the lofty cause of democracy. Ironically, such a weak and fragmented political system could hardly provide political stability.

As there was no clear systematic structure of political representation in Nepal, this complex duality of the political system with New Delhi acting as "distant sovereign" created ground for intense factional squabbling for access to political power within the Congress, between the Congress and representatives of the former Rana regime, and within ambitious members of the royal circle. Members of a nascent intermediate class mostly composed of upper caste elites accessed political power through an emerging party political apparatus. Remnants of the Rana regime organized their own political organization—the Gorkha Parishad. Communists also established their presence through various organizations working within groups like students, peasants, and so on, and a wider coalition of like-minded political parties, namely, the United Democratic Front. Soon at least thirty-two political parties emerged. Within months of the slackening of the Rana rule in 1951, intense politicization of elite social groups drawn from intermediate classes ensued.

While the United Democratic Front (UDF) organized street agitations for a fully functioning democracy, Prime Minister Mohan Shumsher Jang Bahadur Rana was reluctant to resign. He was ultimately compelled to do so on 13 November 1951 and with his resignation Rana rule came to an end.[24] Throughout 1951, Nepal experienced the outbursts of street demonstrations, political uncertainty, and the spectacle of the Ranas and court playing a hide-and-seek game over the political process of government formation. Interestingly, similar political drama would be played out almost four decades later in 1990, during another democratic movement. The resemblance of the situation was further highlighted by the attempts by radicals, suspected of affiliation with the Communist Party, to capture political power in 1952. The *Kishan Sangh* (peasant association) led by K. I. Singh started a peasant rebellion in the country and demanded implementation of forced land redistribution. Though Singh was placed under arrest, earlier in January 1952 members of the *Raksha Dal* (defense guards), allegedly backed by Communists, occupied the airfield, radio station, the post and telegraph office, and even a part of the *Singh Durbar* where many government offices were located. They liberated radical leader K. I. Singh. K I. Singh demanded an all-party government including Communists but excluding *Gorkha Dal* (popularly referred to as *Khukri Dal*, or knife-wielding gang)—a quasi-terrorist organization comprising supporters of former Rana ruling elites. The rebellion, however, was defeated and Singh fled the country. But uncertainty continued, owing to institutional brittleness, accompanied by intense factional squabbles within the ruling Congress.[25]

The monarchy and Nepali Congress continued to share political power. On 4 July 1952, King Tribhuvan inaugurated an advisory assembly (Nepal Salahkar Samity). He promised that this assembly would guide the country to democracy. The king also promised the election of a national constituent assembly as demanded by democratic parties and especially by revolutionary Communists—this is also similar to the demands made by Maoists in Nepal today. Interestingly, as King Tribhuvan appointed the Nepali Congress leader M. P. Koirala as the prime minister of the country (allegedly on the advice of the Indian ambassador to Nepal), an unseemly quarrel broke out between M. P. Koirala, the prime minister, and his brother B. P. Koirala, the leader of the Nepali Congress Party. The squabble could not be resolved despite the mediation of Jai Prakash Narayan, a well-known socialist leader from India.

Finally when both factions failed to compromise, the king appointed old Rana elements as cabinet ministers. On 4 September 1953, the assembly was dissolved and the king gained an upper hand. The king enjoyed the support of the royal army, which enabled him to declare emergency. Meanwhile, a United Democratic Front of Communists continued to organize both in urban and rural areas demanding an all-party government.[26] Mutual suspicions between leftists and conservative political elements grew; the left feared a right-wing conspiracy and the conservatives feared a full-fledged revolution. The Nepali Congress, a centrist political party representing the nascent intermediate class, remained trapped by the rivalry between two brothers leading two factions of the party, namely the Nepali Congress and Nepali National Congress. These intense tragicomic factional rivalries almost prefigured what would happen fifty years later. Such rivalries, ideological confrontations, and fragmentation of political forces enabled the monarchy to consolidate its hold over the political system of the country. Between November 1951 and 1955, the monarch appointed a number of short-lived cabinets. Many of these cabinet members had no wider political base in the country. The monarch scrupulously avoided inviting the Nepali Congress Party headed by B. P. Koirala, who had the largest political following. In the end, King Tribhuvan accumulated a substantial degree of power for the royal house as he declared unambiguously in January 1954 that "the supreme power in every sphere vests solely in us."[27] This obviously included the most important of all power—control over the army. Indeed, it was King Tribhuvan, despite his pro-democracy demeanor, who systematically undermined democratic political setup.[28]

This process received a further boost in 1955 when King Mahendra succeeded his reclusive father King Tribhuvan. King Mahendra was not too keen to continue with democratic experiments. Mahendra toured the country, met local elites, and sanctioned government funds to build up a direct patron-client relationship between the palace and local notables. He constantly humored smaller political parties whose political clout depended on royal patronage. He even promoted delegates from politically active groups to represent the government. However, political circumstances were not very favorable to Mahendra. Internationally, on the south of the border, Indian government was putting pressure for an open representative system. On the north, Chinese Communists were now in Tibet. Within Nepal, the growing strength of Chinese Communists had obviously encouraged factions of revolutionary Communist movements. The Nepali Congress was also gaining new popularity and was threatening to launch a civil disobedience movement for more democratic reforms. All these factors compelled the king to hold elections on 18 February 1959.

Nonetheless, King Mahendra cautiously prepared his way for elections. He did not accept the Nepali Congress's demand for the election of the constituent assembly. According to the earlier negotiations with King Trib-huvan, a constituent assembly would actually draft the new constitution. This implied that the king would have very little control over the process of the drafting of the constitution. Indeed, Mahendra not only departed from this promise, but also planned his own political game. As political parties of all persuasions were busily preparing for the elections, the king appointed a commission to draw up a new constitution. As a suave politi-cian, the king presented it as a gift to the nation on 12 February 1959, with the elections only one week away. Under the new constitution, the king would control the national assembly as the head of the state. From a con-stitutional perspective, such control would provide the monarch with the power to dismiss the national assembly at will. More importantly, the monarch as the head of the state would continue to exercise control over the army, which was undergoing a thorough retraining under Indian mili-tary advisors.

Despite such restrictions placed on the emerging democratic political sys-tem, the election constituted a step forward toward a constitutional regime. Predictably, the Nepali Congress emerged victorious in the election. The scale of victory was, however, unexpected: they secured 74 seats in the 109-member parliament. Did the victory of the Nepali Congress represent the breakdown of the patrimonial state and the constructed Brahminical Hindu order that provided legitimacy to it? The answer is no. First, the Nepali Con-gress leadership was composed of Bahuns, Chetris, and Newars, who consti-tute a substantial minority of the hill population but were primary benefici-aries of the constructed ethno-religious social order enforced by the Rana patrimonial state. The election in 1959 followed formal democratic princi-ples in practice. In 1959 eligible voters numbered approximately 4.25 mil-lion, of which 42 percent exercised their franchise. Following the "first past the post system," one candidate was elected for each of the 109 seats on the basis of a majority of votes polled. Nearly five hundred candidates repre-senting nine political parties contested the poll.[29] However, the predomi-nance of upper caste candidates actually indicated the continuation of the legacy of a *Muluki Ain*–based ethno-religious order in a different form whereby economic, cultural, and social resources of upper caste Hindus were transformed into political capital. A cursory glance at the ethno-religious composition of those elected reveals the near absence of untouchables and only a sprinkling of Janajati (tribal) candidates. (See Table 1.)

The new government, despite continued uncertainty, adopted a program of democratization of the polity and egalitarian reforms of the economy with far-reaching consequences. B. P. Koirala emerged as a crucial player in the economy, pursuing land reforms, the ending of the autonomy of princi-palities (*rajjya*) in western Nepal hills and thus undermining the hold of the former aristocracy over the economy and favoring his own base among an

Table 1.   Ethnic-Caste Division of Candidates
in the Election of 1959

Caste/ Ethnic Group	Candidates Percentage
Hill Bahun	23.91
Chetri	29.83
Newar	11.11
Hill Tribal	11.83
Occupational Caste	0.24
Total	76.92
Plain Group	
Terai Bahun	5.55
Landed Caste	7.48
Trader Caste	5.43
Terai Tribal	3.11
Muslim	1.08
Total	22.68
Unidentified	0.40

Source: Harka Gurung, *The Sociology of Elections in Nepal,*
1959 to 1981 Asian Survey, vol. 22, no. 3 (March 1982): 309.

emerging intermediate class encompassing rich peasants, urban traders, and service elites. He also strengthened party control over the newly constructed bureaucracy, appointed Congress sympathizers in top positions, and even restricted direct contact between the palace and officials.[30] This period witnessed a critical development in the organization of state bureaucracy.

During the 1950s and 1960s a new bureaucratic apparatus of the state came into existence that became the core of the government of Nepal. In the 1950s, two major administrative systems were formed. These two entities were formally constituted as a civil service and palace secretariat.[31] In 1959 the elected Congress ministry tried to curb the power of the palace over bureaucracy by organizing a special development bureaucracy. These new bureaucrats would manage the foreign aid that poured into Nepal following its constitution as a nation-state and would report back to the cabinet. The control over bureaucracy thus remained central to the operation of the state and the linkage between political elites and the people. The king soon realized that if the elected government were able to control the bureaucracy, then he would lose an important access to political power. More importantly, the Congress ministry proved to be successful in dealing with a substantial number of issues. In 1960 the government revised a crucial Trade and Transit Treaty with India. It was also successful in negotiating the Gandak River Project that established free provision of water to Nepal. In the sphere of foreign policy Koirala was able to steer a middle course between India and China. He successfully established diplomatic ties with the United States, the Soviet

Union, China, France, and Pakistan. To revitalize Nepali economy after the poor execution of the first five-year plan (1956–1961), the government took steps to introduce the second plan (1962–1965). Indeed, against all obstacles, it was a moderately successful democratic government that embarked upon reforming the patrimonial legacy of the state formation of the Rana regime.[32]

As the Nepali Congress increasingly consolidated its grip over the system, the monarch waited for an opportune moment to strike back. In the 1960s, as border tensions between India and China increased, the monarch also became alarmed over the pro-India tilt of the Nepal government under the Nepali Congress. He also realized if he struck against the democracy movement, India would find it difficult to support a full-fledged insurgency in Nepal for fear of instability in the sensitive buffer state. The monarch had four advantages over the democratic forces. First, he controlled the army, which was indeed the most crucial source of political power in Nepal. Second, he was the head of the constitution. The new democratic regime operated under a constitutional system that was created by the monarch himself and thus he could dismiss the government at will. Third, he shrewdly realized that once the Congress regime was toppled from power many ambitious politicians would work with him if he could devise a political system that could accommodate their ambitions. Finally, the monarch realized that he could still take advantage of his role as a custodian of the Hindu ethno-religious order. Thus, when this democratic experiment was merely eighteen months old, the king in a swift move in December 1960 dissolved the government, incarcerated major leaders and workers of all political parties, and banned their activities. Nepal reverted to absolutist monarchy. As the king estimated there was little concerted opposition to this takeover and any possibility of revolutionary attack from India was scuttled by the Indo-Chinese border dispute in 1962. The Indian government had no wish to destabilize Nepal further.

King Mahendra appointed an ad hoc committee to inquire into a possible form of governance that would suit Nepal's cultural tradition. The committee surveyed political institutions in Yugoslavia, Egypt, Pakistan, and Indonesia in order to determine whether recent constitutional experiments in these countries could be instructive in the establishment of a Nepali political system. This survey of an eclectic mix of various sorts of authoritarian regimes enabled the monarch and his advisors to appoint an appropriately quasi-democratic political system. A *panchayat* system was set up in order to synchronize with the Hindu ethno-religious order constructed by the regime. According to tradition, five village elders well versed in the *Vedas* (sacred texts of Hinduism) and Hindu religious texts used to advise and govern villages in "traditional" Nepal. The king now claimed a rare synthesis of tradition and modernity and invented a new tradition to bolster his authority.[33] In 1962 he declared Nepal a Hindu state, which reinforced his role as the custodian of tradition and could effectively assist him in cashing in on the myth of the monarch as an incarnation of Vishnu (Hindu god who sustains the world).

In the new constitutional arrangements of the *panchayat* regime, it became apparent that the monarch would continue as the sovereign ruler of Nepal, and all powers—executive, legislative, and judicial—would be vested in him. He would exercise his authority with the assistance of a specifically selected development bureaucracy and royal rule would ultimately depend upon the axis of military and bureaucracy. However, the monarch carefully maintained a semblance of democratic political representation.

In 1962 King Mahendra introduced a new constitution to institutionalize the royal hold on the political structure of the country. The new constitution, amended in 1967, envisaged a three-tier political structure. At the lowest level were the village *panchayats* and at the other end of the spectrum there would be an apex body called the national *panchayat*. While the primary units were to be directly elected by the local population, the secondary units were to be constituted by members of village and town *panchayats*. The national *panchayat* was to be formed through a complex voting system whereby diverse professional organizations, class-based unions, and members of zonal *panchayats* were to send representatives.

Class here signified not real social formations, but arbitrarily defined social categories by the Nepali monarchical order. These categories were then utilized to constitute a constituency for the national *panchayat*. The new constitutional arrangement banned political parties. Elections to *panchayats* were designed on a non-party basis. By replacing the mere formal democracy of 1950s, the Nepali monarchy attempted to preserve and freeze the socio-political system of the country within a carefully stipulated hierarchical political order.

This new order proved to be a hotbed of factional squabbles among disgruntled political leaders who entered the system in order to access power and prestige. Popular representatives were blocked through official manipulation of the small number of electors. The patrimonial state thrived under the *Panchayati Raj*. Indeed, the system operated as a vast patron-client network machine whereby people knew that only bureaucrats enjoyed true political power and, in a resource-scarce economy, government appointments would provide steady income. As a consequence, people searched for powerful men who could provide them access to government jobs. These powerful men had their own networks of local powerful men. A culture of sycophancy pervaded the society. This personalized political culture based on networks of political powerbrokers pervaded even the party political apparatus, and hence every political institution remained fragile and witnessed constant factional competition for resources. The monarch, royal household, and centralized bureaucracy under royal command would emerge as the most powerful network of influence.

The *panchayat* system projected the image of a Brahminical Hindu social order through a carefully constructed notion of Nepali citizenship based on a particularistic cultural concern. Burghat provides the most perceptive analysis of the new political culture. Calling the public life under *panchayat* system a counterfeit reality, Burghart reminds us that under the new constitution, public order in Nepal was represented by the king, who, through the government, monopolized claims to all aspects of public service. Thus Nepali government required a particular type of citizen who had internalized Nepali cultural traits—namely, the Hindu devotion to the monarch. Yet the system appeared to be a counterfeit reality because although the official discourse maintained that there existed a harmonious relationship between the Nepali ruling dynasty and people, the Nepali state did not have the power to suppress opposition within Kathmandu itself and thus the party political system operated within public life in a semi-clandestine manner. The ruling dynasty continued to claim to provide public service in the form of a "gift to the people" of self-governance through the partyless democracy of *Panchayati Raj*, which represented all social classes and perfectly suited the harmonious Hindu cultural tradition of Nepal devoid of social conflicts.[34]

DECAYING ROYAL AUTOCRACY AND THE RESURGENCE OF THE DEMOCRACY MOVEMENT (1972–1990)

On 31 January 1972, after ruling the country for seventeen years, King Mahendra passed away. His son Birendra was supposedly a man of liberal inclination. It was expected that his education at Eton College and Harvard would incline him more toward democracy. When Birendra ascended the throne, it became apparent that the *panchayat* system was showing signs of cracks. Government candidates were losing elections. More importantly, Mahendra's policy of courting Chinese support now proved to be a failure. Entangled in domestic power conflicts during the days of the Cultural Revolution, China experienced a temporary eclipse in international politics. On the other hand, buoyed by the victory in the India-Pakistan War of 1971, India exerted more pressure on Nepal, so that the Nepali monarch had to revise the trade agreement with India. Stringent conditions further tightened India's economic control over Nepal. India pressured the government to show more tolerance to the democratic movement. However, Birendra was reluctant to compromise. His strategies of dealing with the opposition soon paved the way for a new pattern in Nepali politics that would anticipate a more constitutional form of government in the country.

King Birendra's ironfisted strategies soon became evident in his treatment of Nepali Congress leader B. P. Koirala. B. P. Koirala and his associates sought a compromise with Nepali monarchy. But when on 30 December 1976, Koirala and his close associate, Ganeshman Singh, arrived from India in Kathmandu, the government promptly arrested them and appointed a tribunal to try them for sedition. This action provoked mass protests on the streets of the capital and the government released Koirala in June 1977, ostensibly on the grounds of ill health. Koirala went to United States for treatment, but on his return to Nepal in November 1977 the government again arrested him at the airport. Though urban areas witnessed considerable agitation for his release, Koirala had to undergo five treason trials in early 1978. This led to a change in the strategy of the opposition forces. They expressed their loyalty to the crown but opposed the king's government. This obviously indicated a move toward the acceptance of constitutional monarchy by the Congress party and a search for compromise.

The movement for democracy, however, did not collapse despite the new strategy and compromising tone of the Nepali Congress. As elsewhere in South Asia, students and diverse urban social groups continued to protest against *Panchayati Raj*. In a largely non-urban society like that of Nepal, streets in the capital often acted as a political theater where the government and opposition tested their strength politically. These street movements are generally led by students who enjoyed access to information and trust of the people because of their cultural capital. In many instances, students were thus looked upon as the most critical political players who could ignite the urban political society through mass demonstrations. Thus, on 6 April 1979,[35] massive students' demonstrations ignited urban centers. This movement ended with King Birendra's announcement of a national referendum on the *panchayat* system, which would be held on the basis of universal adult franchise and a secret ballot.

On 2 May 1980 the referendum was held and nearly 54.7 percent voted to retain the *panchayat* system with 45.3 percent voting for a multiparty system. The referendum made it clear that it would be difficult to defeat the *panchayat* system through ballot. Various vested interest groups involved with the *panchayat* system had wider resources due to government patronage. The patron-client network, along with the backing of state-sponsored intimidation, was able to maintain a stable degree of support in rural areas.[36] The referendum thus created further disenchantment with the system. Though B. P. Koirala accepted the verdict, many other Congress and Communist leaders were reluctant to do so. The royal establishment realized that they had to concede further ground in order to avoid a revolution from below.

On 16 December 1979, the king announced three fundamental reforms: all elections would be held on the principle of adult franchise, the prime minister would be selected on the recommendation of the legislative council, and the council of ministers would be responsible to the national legislature. This obviously indicated a move toward parliamentary democracy.[37] But in reality the constitution did not undergo radical changes. The *panchayat* system remained supreme where various influential but not always popular powerbrokers predominated and influenced the decision-making process. Thus the referendum furthered the nature of national polarization along ideological lines between supporters of the partyless *panchayat* and those who favored party politics. The *panchayat* system continued to be characterized by individualized intrigues and corruption tainted members of the government and bureaucracy and further eroded the legitimacy of the system. Signs were evident that despite factional struggles within the system and within the Communist and Congress opposition, any serious international crisis could plunge Nepal into mass upsurge, particularly in the urban areas. As the system witnessed decay and institutional brittleness became evident, its legitimacy waned among the people. The state increasingly had little capacity to absorb external shocks to the polity and economy.

THE DEMOCRACY MOVEMENT AND THE COMING OF PARLIAMENTARY DEMOCRACY IN 1990

The historic referendum of 1980 relaxed the political system. Party activists openly voiced their opposition to the *panchayat* system. They were also keeping the political temperature high and waited for an opportunity to strike back. Their opportunity arrived with an externally induced shock. When King Birendra brokered an arms deal with China in 1989, India severely restricted entrée routes to commerce for landlocked Nepal. This act paralyzed the economy. Mounting economic tensions created conditions for widespread popular movement against the government.

This pro-democracy political movement gained momentum at a time when Asian countries were experiencing a slow transition to democracy. In the Philippines in 1986, Marcos was toppled from power through a massive popular upsurge, and in Pakistan the violent and mysterious death of Zia Ul Haq paved the way for the restoration of civilian rule. In Bangladesh, the popular struggle against General Ershad intensified. In India the Congress party was removed from power for only the second time in the post-independence history of the subcontinent. More importantly, Eastern Europe was passing through a phase of political upheaval. The visuals on television of popular movements against various ruling Communist parties impressed upon Nepali political activists and urban intermediate social classes that the time was ripe for action.

By 1990, popular discontent acquired a more concrete shape. Even the fractious left parties came together and gave birth to a United Left Front. An internally divided Nepali Congress extended the hand of cooperation to the Left Front in order to end the *panchayat* system. Political parties began their agitations on 18 February 1990. This was of immense symbolic value as it was celebrated as Democracy Day in Nepal commemorating the 1951 revolution. The new democratic revolution now proved to be a consequential event.

For the next fifty days, public meetings, strikes, demonstrations, and confrontations with police paralyzed Kathmandu and other urban centers. The police sought to suppress the movement by arresting thousands of people and resorting to violent strategies. But repression only contributed to the spreading of the movement. A cross-section of the urban population comprising traders, artisans, and professionals confronted the police in large numbers. On 6 April, when protestors marched toward the palace, perhaps led by the Maoist Mashal group, police fired indiscriminately into the unarmed crowd. Police brutality transformed the capital into a battle zone with barricades being erected to prevent widespread deployment of troops. Birendra took no more risks. He removed the ban on political parties. Soon protracted negotiations between the king and leaders of the Nepali Congress and United Communist Party of Nepal (Marxist-Leninist) were underway.[38] Again, what was gained through battle on the street was slowly surrendered through palace negotiations as leaders proved to be unwilling to risk an uncontrolled social revolution in the country. A constitutional settlement was reached but not through an elected constituent assembly. The political agenda of the revolution of 1950 remained unfinished. This hindered progress toward a stable constitutional base for a democratic political system.

Although the new constitution clearly stipulated people as the ultimate source of sovereignty in contrast to the *panchayat* system, the king managed to preserve his control over the army as the supreme commander in chief. The new constitution also provided him with extensive emergency powers and control over palace-related issues, including succession. Nepal became a parliamentary system with a bicameral legislature comprising 205 seats in the House of Representatives (*Pratinidhi Sabha*), elected by universal suffrage, and a sixty-member National Assembly (*Rastriya Sabha*) in which the king could nominate ten members while the other fifty seats were to be indirectly elected by the House of Representatives and an Electoral College.[39] This historic compromise contained seeds of future confrontation.

Democratic pluralism opened up new avenues of political mobilization. As in neighboring India,[40] political openness had led to new assertiveness of lower castes against the constructed Hindu ethno-religious order, which underpinned the monarchical system of governance. The Nepali monarchy legitimized its claim as the symbol of unity by evoking supposedly Hinduized cultural traditions of Nepal. Since the advent of the new royalist government in 1950, the monarchy promoted the distinctiveness of Nepali identity through a cultivated image of harmonious Hindu traditions that integrated the nation. This tradition acted as a bulwark against revolution as the monarch still encouraged the belief that the crown was not only the custodian of *Sanatan Dharma*, but also the incarnation of Lord Vishnu. Yet in Nepal the democratic movement had to challenge this fundamental premise of the state in order to make room for those who were assigned the lowest position in Nepali Hindu social hierarchy. More importantly, as Nepal experienced state-sponsored reforms in caste structure from 1960s onward, upper caste elites sought to tighten social control mechanisms in order to safeguard their positions.[41]

Thus, not surprisingly the coming of democracy in the 1990s led to an intensification of ethnic activism. For the first time in the history of Nepal, Janajati (tribal) movements evolved into a mass movement and opened up new debates concerning their status in Nepali society. Religion in this context had been integrally related to cultural linguistic identity since Nepali and Sanskrit were both languages identified with elite Hindu culture. These languages were promoted at the expense of the distinct cultural heritage of ethnic groups. The Nepal Janajati Mahasangh, formed in 1990 as a coalition of indigenous groups, agitated against the continuation of Sanskrit as a compulsory subject in schools. In the 1991 census, many people refused to identify Nepali as their mother tongue. Indeed, in Nepal the census of 1991 reported that only 50.3 percent claim Nepali as their first language and the distant second was Maithili—a dialect of Hindi. While 11.9 percent of the population claimed Maithili as their second language, the census reported nearly thirty-two languages spoken in Nepal.[42] Although some Janajatis have distinct languages, like the Rai and Tharus, others have more diffused dialects. Many other caste and ethnic groups also have their own languages, which are not recorded in the census. These diversities have thus made it difficult for the articulation of any homogenous Nepali identity based on a national language. However, at the same time, it would be wrong to identify minority coalitions premised on ethnic allegiance as homogenous and harmonious. As in any society such identities are plural and open to contestations. Complicated arraignment of linguistic and ethnic identities made such alliance more fragile. A sense of belonging to higher ranks also permeated the social attitudes of Janajatis in relation to the Dalit population.

Complex interactions with diverse social groups, extensive geographic spread, and diverse aspects of identities based on region, gender, and class obviously acted as hindrances to the articulation and organization of a wider social movement and also to the framing of a common identity. Nonetheless, the assertion of this identity had so profoundly shaken Nepali polity that all established political parties and particularly parliamentary Marxists and Maoists had to articulate the grievances of ethnic minorities. The language of class had to recognize and incorporate a language of distinctive ethnic cultural heritage. There was much wider accommodation of such ethnic demands under democratic government in the 1990s. This was more clearly discernable in the broadcasting of Radio Nepal in Newari and Maithili, and later on eight other languages. Resources were also allocated toward language and textbook development for primary school education in various mother tongues.[43] Democratic Nepal experimented with an ethnic pluralism that sought to address the historical wrongs committed by the Hindu patrimonial state.

The new political establishment in Nepal was, however, clearly aware of the possibility of ethnic fragmentation of Nepali society that the eighteenth-century founder of the Gorkha state Prithvi Naryan Shah had fondly described as a harmonious conglomeration of four *jatis* (castes) and thirty-two *jats* (subcastes). Caste hierarchy comprised three categories: *Tagadharis* (twice born); *Janajatis*, who were often derogatorily referred to as *Matwali* (liquor drinking); and *Pani Nachalne* (from whom water could not be accepted). The *Tagadharis* (or people who wear sacred thread) include Nepal's highest castes: Bahuns, Thakuris, and Chetris. At the middle were *Matwalis*, or liquor drinkers, who include most of Nepal's Tibeto-Burman and Indo-European non-caste ethnicities who were often described as "tribal" for their distinctive social organization. The *Pani Nachalne* were those from whom high castes would not accept drinking water, or, in other words, they were excluded from normal social interactions. These groups mainly comprised untouchables or Dalits associated with specific traditional occupations. Upper caste Hindus, such as Bahuns (Brahmins), Chetris (Khastriyas), Thakuris (members of the royal clan), and Newars (traders who practiced a combination of Buddhist and Hindu rituals), continued to dominate public life. Subcastes constituted smaller socially endogamous unit of wider caste ranks, such as Bahuns or Chetris. As discussed earlier, the caste system constituted a critical component of the strategy of governance by the patrimonial Rana state. Though caste discrimination was officially banned by the state in 1962, it hardly lost its significance in the social and political life of Nepal. The relationship between caste and class constituted a critical source of debates about Nepali society. Indeed, many scholars have argued that class had surpassed caste as a marker of social and economic cleavages in Nepal.[44] Indeed, these views were more appropriate for 1980 when caste mobilization remained subdued. Rather it would be more natural to suggest that caste structure acted as a social signifier, which actually legitimated and justified class division.[45] (See chapter 2 for details.)

From the perspective of differences in wealth, access to political power, and cultural capital, Nepali society could be divided into rather amorphous

social classes, which had its resemblance to Marxist notions of class super-
ficially. Indeed, small ruling elites drawn from the highest class, who also
belonged to Thakuri caste, had substantial presence in the trade and commerce. However, the most politically articulate social groups belonged to a
growing, intermediate class consisting of government officials, large landholders, merchants, and a segment of affluent peasants.[46] A sizeable section
of the population consisted of marginal farmers and landless agricultural
workers.

Despite the emergence of new forms of social stratification along class
lines, in many instances cultural capital, economic assets, and political
power were concentrated in the hands of upper caste elements. The advent
of democracy signaled new forms of social and political movements by hitherto marginalized social groups such as Dalits and Janajatis for recognition
of socio-cultural rights, which were denied to them by Hindu monarchy.

To prevent such disintegration, the constitution explicitly prohibited political parties that campaigned exclusively on regional or ethnic affiliations
from participating in general elections. This potential divisiveness along
ethno-religious lines was evident in the activities of the Mongol National
Organization, which championed a federation of Tibeto-Burmese states
and the end of monarchy that preserved Hindu dominance. Indeed, in the
first general election only two such parties were allowed to participate: the
Rastriya Janamukti Party and the Sadbhavana Party. The latter represented
Maithili-speaking settlers of Terai from the north Indian state of Bihar.

In the new Nepal the projection of Hinduism as the state religion was
perceived as a critical imposition of a monolithic ethno-religious structure
on heterogeneous religious traditions at societal level. Newar Buddhists,
many of whom were sympathetic to the parliamentary Marxist movement,
demanded from the inception of the democracy movement the creation of
a secular state in Nepal. Secularists argued that religion constituted a personal affair of Nepali citizens. It had been brought to public affairs in order to bolster monarchical regime. More importantly, Dalits, or former untouchables who were historically marginalized by *Muluki Ain* and the
institutional structure of Hinduism, were critical of the retention of Hinduism as a national religion. Many observers of Nepali politics described
these movements as communal.[47] The term "communal" in Indian English
refers to sectarian mentalities. The very use of the term communal invokes
a stale statist language that refused to recognize the democratic aspirations
of suppressed minorities. Despite these historic developments the new
Nepali polity was a historic compromise. This was probably more aptly reflected in the constitution that describes Nepal as "a multiethnic, multilingual, democratic, independent, indivisible, sovereign, Hindu, Constitutional monarchical kingdom." In other words, the monarch insisted on

retaining Hindu kingdom in the nomenclature as that particular description reflected the special status of the monarch as head of a distinctively Hindu Nepali society.

FRAGMENTED DEMOCRACY AND POPULAR DISENCHANTMENT (1991–2005)

On 12 May 1991, under the new constitution the first general election took place in Nepal. The election generated wider political debates in Nepali society and revealed a clear trend toward two-party polarization centered on Nepali Congress and Communist Party of Nepal [United Marxist-Leninist—hereafter CPN (UM-L)].[48] Besides these parties, there existed a number of smaller parties. Prominent among them were National Democratic Party (NDP) and Nepal Sadbhavana (Goodwill) Party. The NDP was comprised of former supporters and activists of the pre-1990 *panchayat* regime and Nepal Sadbhavana Party, a small regionalist party of Terai, primarily associated with the people of "Indian descent." Rastriya Prajatantra Party emerged as a distinctive minor force, a part of wider spectrum of center right political parties in Nepal.[49]

Among all these parties, Nepali Congress emerged as the premier political party of Nepal. The Nepali Congress had a distinct ideological and organizational advantage over its opponents. In popular perceptions the Nepali Congress became synonymous with multiparty democracy. Not surprisingly, the Nepali Congress Party won 110 seats in the 205-member House of Representatives. Though theoretically the Nepali Congress Party claimed to have a socialist agenda, in reality its message of socialism was much diluted. Its proclivity toward socialism was reflected in its advocacy of a mixed economy, equitable distribution of the national product, participation of labor in production management, equal dignity and rights to all people, government help for oppressed peoples, and social security for the old and disabled.[50] These programs obviously reflected a critical choice for radical social restructuring. However, in terms of executing them in practice the party followed a policy of moderate conciliation and retained close connections with the palace.

The Nepali Congress Party operated patron-client mobilization and various political power brokers sought refuge in the party in order to access resources of the center. The party sought to monopolize government offices and retained control over important mass media. Despite pressure for privatization of television, radio, and print media, such as *Rising Nepal* and *Gorkha Patra*, Congress retained control over these organs. As the party veered to the right, it failed to implement any serious structural reforms. On the contrary, it sought to accommodate more landed elements in order to consolidate anti-Communist forces.

Soon the party gained access to new resources and followed the model of patron-client relationship in building mass bases. Internal squabbles within the party increased manifold. There was a growing tendency toward the centralization of party political apparatus and denial of power to grassroots-level cadres. The government and party activities centered on individual leaders who sought to establish their exclusive arena of political control. In many ways they represented their Indian namesake without the charisma of a political dynasty. The result was debilitating factional squabble that paralyzed the party. The party became identified with Hindu upper-caste elites of intermediate social background. The severity of inner party wrangling was reflected in the fact that within three years of his election, Prime Minister Koirala had to resign. He lost a parliamentary vote due to the abstention of thirty-six members of his own party. This phenomenon continued to haunt the party. The party returned to power in 1995 when the minority government of CPN (UM-L) lost in a parliamentary vote of confidence. A coalition government of Nepali Congress, RPP, and Sadbhavana was formed. However, constant inner bickering and absence of stable political focus led to the collapse of the alliance, which resulted in a CPN-UML-RPP coalition. This government itself lost power six months later to another NC-RPP coalition. In 1999 the third general election after the restoration of democracy resulted in the Nepali Congress coming back to power with an absolute majority in the House. Krishna P. Bhattarai became prime minister for the second time.

In a way the Nepali Congress became the party of establishment. They continued to operate through patron-client networks relying on power brokers. The result was a glaring contradiction between rhetoric and reality; egalitarian rhetoric that leaders employed during the 1990 pro-democracy movement was not practiced by leaders themselves. The remoteness of the leader, expropriation of resources allocated for development, and unavailability of leaders during crisis undermined the confidence of the people. The party could win popular votes because of the Nepali inclination to move in with the winner in the hope of a trickle-down effect of development activities of the state.

In many ways the right to information, separation between judiciary and executive, and right to association provided people with critical abilities to judge and deliver a verdict. Ordinary people were deeply dismayed by the performance of the Nepali Congress. It became amply clear that despite the support of the urban intermediate classes, Congress could not continue to hold on to the most politically conscious segment of the people. Urban artisans, unskilled workers, and areas with a tradition of organized peasant movement tended to vote against the Congress. It had to rely increasingly on powerbrokers to deliver votes in remote areas of western Nepal and Terai. These areas, indeed, later became the most powerful locations of Maoist rebellion. The political process enabled people to develop critical abilities but did not provide them with alternatives to deselect insensitive elected representatives. This resulted in wider disillusionment.

More importantly, bureaucratic functionaries who operated distributional networks in rural areas that provided the rural poor with access to resources often acted in a high-handed manner. The bureaucracy continued to perceive such operations as an attempt to augment the production and consumption base of society, but they conducted their operation as if they were giving these as gifts to the people, the way the monarchy earlier conceptualized services to the poor. Thus while popular political culture became more critical and effectively scrutinized every aspect of state functioning, patterns of operations of the ruling political party continued to mimic older monarchical patrimonial tradition. This caused an enormous gap between rhetoric and quotidian reality of governance. It is legitimate to ask, if the Nepali Congress had failed to perform, why could not the opposition provide a way out?

As expected a coalition of various Communist parties emerged as a major political force in Nepali politics with the Communist Party of Nepal (United Marxist-Leninist), a constituent of the United Left Front, securing sixty-nine seats in 1991 in the first general election. The thirteen seats went to three other Communist parties of the United Left Front. Indeed, new elections in November 1994 resulted in a hung parliament; the CPN (UM-L), which emerged as the single largest party, formed a minority government. Nepal was possibly the first constitutional monarchy in the world that experienced an elected Communist Party government in an era when Communist movements were retreating elsewhere in the world. CPN (UM-L) was itself a coalition of different trends within the Communist movement and was thus faction-prone in terms of ideological orientations of diverse trends within the movement. Personal rivalries, long-standing misunderstandings, and problems in effecting the transformation from an underground political movement to a mainstream parliamentary party had plagued the movement. However, a serious gap between theoretical pronouncements of the party and its growing role as the mainstream alternative within the Nepali political system took hold over time.

The CPN (UM-L) characterized the Nepali state as "semi-feudal" and "semi-colonial."[51] This characterization was based on the original thesis adopted by the CPI in 1950 in India and later on gained currency among Communist revolutionaries of Naxalite tradition.[52] The establishment of a self-sufficient economy and political republic was the stated aim of the party. However, as the party became more integrated within the political system associated with constitutional monarchy, it moderated its republican rhetoric.

In the sphere of foreign policy CPN (UM-L) stood for a far more favorable trade treaty from the Nepali perspective with India. But it had to modify its stand in this regard. Another important legacy of the party was its struggle for land reforms and close links with peasant movements in the eastern part of Nepal. Indeed, this is an area where the party could be clearly distinguished from the Congress. The party was also perceived to have played a significant role in the liberation of bonded agricultural workers in the Tharu areas of Terai. However, the party could not develop a sweeping land reform program during its brief stay in power. The party remained steadfastly committed to its demand for a secular state in Nepal and the abolition of the caste hierarchy including the practice of untouchability. Yet ironically, in hill areas the party developed an image of the party of Bahun because of the predominance of Bahun leadership.[53] Indeed, the party aimed at broad-based social coalition in both class and ethnic terms. It wanted to unite ethnic minorities, urban workers, the rural poor, and middle classes within the broad aim of establishing a people's democratic state.

However, its multiple images and ideological flexibility made it difficult to identify a clear, coherent, and effective political image. Unfortunately, the party remained deeply mired in intra-party heuristic ideological disputes and experienced splits before the third election causing serious damage to its electoral fortunes. The constant permutation and combination among different factions over the interpretation of party lines, and the existence of diverse types of Marxist parties outside its fold has obviously hampered its ability to win elections.

The party had an organizational network in rural areas and soon after the democracy movement it won over several segments of the ethnic minority community even in the remotest villages. Its reliance on cadres obviously freed the party from the need of developing a patron-client network of strongmen. But during its brief stay in power the party hierarchy promoted its disciplined cadres to important positions with the aim of influencing government policies and consolidating its hold of the state.[54] Increasingly the party came to be viewed as the party of the establishment. With the rise of the Maoist insurgency many CPN (UM-L) supporters at grassroots level switched loyalties to the Maoist forces as the rhetoric of the two movements seemed to be confusingly similar, though their political practices differed widely.

Apart from the Nepali Congress Party and the Communist Party of Nepal (United Marxist-Leninist) alliance, four other parties qualified for national party status, which meant they polled more than 3 percent of the total votes cast. Of these the Nepal Sadbhavana Party had been traditionally identified with people of recent Indian descent in the Terai region located on the border of India. There were parties representing the former *panchayat* establishment. Splinter groups of the Nepali Congress floated their own political parties. But the two trends comprising Nepali Congress and CPN (UM-L) remained the most crucial political establishments in Nepal.

Democratic politics transformed Nepal in many ways. The right to information, the right to organize associations, and the separation of the judiciary, executive, and legislature constituted remarkable improvement in terms of political rights of the people. Growing activism through party political activities and NGO organizations changed the profile of the country. People participated in elections enthusiastically. The voter turnouts in various elections bear testimony to the fact. In the first election, of a total of more than eleven million voters, about seven million, or 65 percent, cast ballots, of which slightly more than 4 percent were declared invalid on technical grounds. However, in subsequent elections, voter turnout did not decline.[55] Indeed, even in the midst of recent political turmoil according to a random survey of 3,249 people in 163 polling stations, including 31 in urban and 132 in rural areas, conducted by the International Institute of Democracy and Electoral Assistance (IDEA), two-thirds of respondents in July 2004 preferred democracy as a form of government and criticized monarchical intervention in the democratic process from October 2002.[56]

Yet it would be wrong to suggest that democracy provided political stability in Nepal. Factional wrangles within all types of political parties that Nepal experienced produced a rapid turnover of governments throughout the period. The following (Table 2) drawn from Gellner's work indicates the depth

Table 2.   Governments in Nepal 1990–2002

Prime Minister	Parties	Length	Dates
K. P. Bhattarai	Congress +ULF Interim	13 months	4/19/90–5/25/91
G. P. Koirala	Congress Majority	43 months	5/26/91–11/28/94
M. M. Adhikari	UML Minority	9 months	11/29/94–10/09/95
S. B. Deuba	Congress-NDP-NSP Coalition	18 months	9/11/95–3/11/97
L. B. Chand	NDP-UML-NSP Coalition	6 months	10/06/97–3/25/98
G. P. Koirala	Congress minority	5 months	3/26/98–8/25/98
G. P. Koirala	Congress-ML Coalition	4 months	8/26/98–12/22/98
G. P. Koirala	Congress-UML-NSP Coalition	5 months	12/23/98–5/26/99
K. P. Bhattarai	Congress	10 months	5/27/99–3/9/00
G. P. Koirala	Congress	28 months	3/10/00–7/22/01
S. B. Deuba	Congress	14 months	7/23/01–10/4/02

Source: David N. Gellner, "Introduction: Transformations of the Nepalese State," in D. N. Gellner, ed., *Resistance and the State: Nepalese Experience* (New Delhi: Social Science Press, 2003): 14.
Congress—Nepal Congress Party founded by socialist leader B. P. Koirala; United Left Front—formed to fight the *panchayat* system in 1989 and dissolved when the three ULF ministers left the interim government; UML Communist Party of Nepal (United Marxist-Leninist)—originally professed revolution but now operate within parliamentary system; NDP (National Democratic Party)—party of former supporters and activists of pre-1990 *panchayat* regime; NSP (Nepal Sadbhavana [Goodwill] Party)—small regionalist party of Terai, primarily associated with people of "Indian descent"; ML (Communist Party of Nepal [Marxist-Leninist])—splinter group from UML in March 1998, rejoined in 2002.

of instability. The popular mood was reflected in the widespread saying as Gellner represented it in his well-known essay: "Under the Ranas only the aristocracy fleeced the country, under the guided democracy elites fleeced the country, under [the] democracy the common person has the right to fleece the country."[57] The ethno-religious order of the patrimonial state remained operative and class-based inequality corresponded in complex ways to ethno-religious inequality. A constructed Hindu ethno-religious identity continued to inform and influence political culture. The dominance of upper caste males in the political structure continued to be a feature of Nepal. The inability to perform and the constant quest for resources allegedly for personal gains marked by factional squabbles—a characteristic feature of patrimonial state—had obviously contributed to popular disenchantment and cynicism. This paved the way for a royal coup on the one hand and Maoist peasant rebellion on the other.

As Nepal's democratic political system experienced chronic political instability, a section of Maoist political factions decided to organize a people's war in Nepal to initiate revolutionary transformation from below. In coalition with a few other left-wing political groups, representatives of the Maoist faction of the Nepal Communist Party founded the United People's Front (SJM) in early 1991. The SJM was active in parliamentary politics and became the third-largest party in the House of Representatives in 1991. By 1993, the SJM began to splinter. In 1995, Pushpa Kamal Dahal, known as Comrade Prachanda, left the SJM to form the Communist Party of Nepal (Maoist), which would remain outside of politics and begin guerilla fighting. The two organizations remained close, however, and the SJM was often identified as the political wing of the CPN (Maoist).

ROYAL COUP: MONARCHY AND DEMOCRACY

The democracy movement of Nepal placed King Birendra in a dilemma. He astutely submitted to the democracy movement in April 1990. But from the beginning the palace bureaucracy bargained hard to retain emergency powers for the monarch. The king cautiously studied the situation. Ostensibly he never transgressed the limit of his responsibility as constitutional monarch. By 1997, when democracy had reached its nadir, with three coalition governments being formed and dismantled in a single year due to factionalism within the party political apparatus, the monarch consulted several politicians behind the scenes. The Maoist insurgency actually strengthened the hands of the monarch. Birendra's refusal to deploy troops to suppress the Maoists further exhausted elected leaders. It has been rumored that the king maintained a channel of communication with the rebels.[58] This clandestine connection was an adroit move that enabled the monarch to obtain political benefit from the growing strength of Maoists at the expense of political parties.

Within the royal circle, there were hints of impatience over such a carefully stipulated policy of neutrality and studied patience. It became clear that his brother Gyanendra favored a more confrontational strategy. However, the studied neutrality of King Birendra gained him popularity, exposed the inability of quarreling democratic leaders to contain insurgency, and the monarch increasingly looked like a symbol of unity and stability. In the final days of his life, Birendra was possibly preparing for a return of the monarchy to the center stage of politics. His control over the army and paramilitary forces, and his wide-ranging emergency powers would have enabled him to assume more responsibility slowly but steadily. Yet he was robbed of this opportunity on 1 June 2001 when he died supposedly at the hands of his highly intoxicated, lovesick son.

The regicide in Nepal was a mystery. The assassination took place on 1 June 2001 when the entire family attended a customary monthly ceremony at Nararyanhithi Palace in Kathmandu. It has been alleged that Crown Prince Dipendra, infuriated by his mother Queen Aishwarya's refusal to allow him to marry the girl he loved, killed his entire family with a machine gun and then attempted suicide. The *Raj Parishad Sthayi Samiti* (Privy Council) was immediately consulted. It was a statutory, high-powered body comprising the prime minister, the leader of the opposition, and representatives from all recognized political parties. This institution came into existence in 1990 after the advent of democracy in Nepal. The Privy Council declared the comatose Dipendra the new monarch. Predictably, on 3 June, King Dipendra passed away and his uncle Gyanendra took over as monarch. These events took place with a bewildering speed. Turnover of three kings in four days proved to be a highly disturbing and historically unprecedented event that deeply destabilized the institution of monarchy.

The stunned palace bureaucracy sought to censure news from people. As a consequence, in popular perception the monarchy as an institution further lost credibility. Gyanendra was an unfortunate victim of historic circumstances when he was crowned as king in 1950 by the Ranas in the wake of the flight of his father to India. His son Paras had always been portrayed in the Nepali media as irresponsible and high-handed. His involvement in a hit-and-run accident in an intoxicated state so infuriated people that nearly half a million people signed a petition demanding his arrest.

Given the high level of unpopularity of Gyanendra and his family, it was not unusual that many viewed them with suspicion. All incongruities concerning the violent death of King Birendra further contributed to the public distrust of Gyanendra. The cremation of dead bodies of royalties without autopsy, Gyanendra's absence during the family ceremony, and the survival of Gyanendra's son Paras from the incident encouraged conspiracy theorists to circulate rumors that went against Gyanendra and his family. The informed and concerned public was also surprised by the inability of five thousand palace security guards to intervene and prevent the massacre.[59] Political tension also increased when the inquiry commission, headed by Chief Justice Keshav Prasad Upadhyay, formed to inquire into the royal deaths, published several contradictory evidences. Empowered by the parliament and cabinet, the commission actually interrogated royal witnesses, including the present Queen Komal Rajya Laxmi Devi Shah. It appeared that there were serious inconsistencies in the statements issued by palace officials and new royal family members. More importantly, the credibility of the commission appointed by the new monarch suffered a jolt at the outset, as one of the members nominated to the commission, Madhav Nepal, opposition leader and general secretary of the Communist Party of Nepal (United Marxist-Leninist), declined to join. According to him the commission was unconstitutional, as it was formed without consulting the cabinet. Meanwhile, Maoist leader Baburam Bhattarai, in an article in the Kantipur Daily, alleged that the palace massacre was a replay of the Khot massacre that led to the birth of the Rana regime. In typical revolutionary nationalist hyperbole, he alleged that the Research Analysis Wing of the Indian secret services was behind the massacre. He also hinted at the involvement of "Western imperialists" in the gory event. These criticisms from both parliamentary party political apparatus and Maoists hardly pleased Gyanendra, the new monarch.

Gyanendra took a more proactive position in the politics. Within six weeks of Gyanendra's coronation, Prime Minister Koirala resigned from his office on 19 July 2001, admitting his failure to suppress the insurgency. New Prime Minister Sher Bahadur Deuba announced a ceasefire and engaged in protracted negotiations with Maoists. The Maoists revived the old demand of the 1950 revolution that a constituent assembly should be elected to draft a new constitution for the country. As talks floundered, Gyanendra intervened in the political process directly by declaring a state of emergency on 26 November 2001. The monarch then extended the emergency, introduced draconian laws like TADO (Terrorist and Disruptive Activities [Control and Punishment] Ordinance),[60] and dissolved the lower house of the national parliament to remove potential parliamentary opposition to the emergency regime. In his next move on 4 October 2002, by invoking Article 127 of the Nepali constitution, which allows the king to "issue necessary orders" to remove "any difficulty" "in connection with the implementation of the Constitution," he dismissed Deuba's government and appointed his own cabinet and a prime minister to run the administration. Constitutional experts doubted the legality of the measure as under Article 36(1) of the 1990 constitution, the monarch could only appoint the leader of the majority party in parliament as prime minister. In the case of the absence of a majority the king could dissolve the parliament and order fresh elections. However, on this occasion the monarch dissolved the parliament and assumed the role of executive head of the administration. Thus a three-way split occurred in Nepali politics with the monarch and palace establishment placing themselves at the helm of the administration, the party political apparatus now raised a demand to return to democratic procedures, and the Maoists continued their insurgency with the rallying cry of the election of a constituent assembly.

As the death toll mounted, international pressure from donor countries increased for negotiation and popular opinion demanded a respite from violent conflict. Bowing before such overwhelming pressure, the monarch entered into a ceasefire agreement with the Maoists in January 2003. Negotiations continued for nearly seven months. The talks gradually entered into a deadlock as it became clear that the Maoists would not surrender their central demand for the election of a constituent assembly to redraft the constitution. The crown would not accept such demands on the grounds that this could transform Nepal into a republic. The negotiation, however, broke down when on 17 August 2003 the Royal Nepalese Army at Doramba carried out an operation in which nearly nineteen Maoists lost their lives. Maoists cited this as a violation of the spirit of the negotiation and retreated from talks.

As the negotiation collapsed, the political parties organized a mass movement for the restoration of civilian government. Finally on 2 June 2004 the monarch once again appointed Surya Bahadur Thapa as the prime minister of a multiparty government, which promised peace talks with the Maoists and early elections. It became clear that without the consent of Maoists it would be impossible to hold elections in the country. Political parties also could not provide an alternative solution to the problem. In the meantime, government troops and the insurgents continued to clash, with the death toll reaching nearly eight thousand people. Violations of human rights became routine matter on both sides. Nepal slowly plunged into anarchy and chaos. The monarch finally engaged in a desperate gamble. On 1 February 2005, King Gyanendra usurped all executive powers of state through a proclamation of emergency in the country. The palace coup thus again ended democratic political possibilities. The crown obviously blamed political parties for not taking a unified approach against terrorism and their inability to hold elections in time or initiate social, political, and economic justice. Yet a careful scrutiny of events reveals that monarchical manipulation also played a significant role in dismantling the democratic political apparatus. The palace never accepted constitutional monarchy and the crown slowly but steadily gained ground through intrigues, manipulation, and overt use of force while party political forces squandered their moral capital in factious squabbles.

CONCLUSION

The royal coup on 1 February 2005 was able to take place because of the brittleness of democratic political institutions in Nepal. In the absence of well-defined organizational structures, political parties found it more convenient to operate through the patron-client network that had served the patrimonial state so well. These networks promoted intense inner party factional squabbling over access to resources and thus resulted in a high level of political volatility and instability. In this situation the monarchy emerged as a seeming source of strength and stability in 2001. However, the massacre of the royal family undermined that perception. Many ordinary Nepalis refused to accept the simplistic palace interpretation of the story of the royal massacre. This prompted the monarchy to move toward a military solution to its political problems. The historic compromises of 1990 enabled the monarchy to retain control over the army and to declare emergencies, and thus circumscribed the ability of elected officials to exercise full control over the palace. The monarchy used this opportunity and suppressed parliamentary democratic institutions. The royal coup of 2005, however, further delegitimized monarchy as an institution of governance and intensified Maoist revolutionary activities and party opposition to the institution. This eventually produced a grand acceptance of the opposition and the alienated monarchy by a very large segment of the populace.

NOTES

1. Ali Riaz, *Unfolding State: The Transformation of Bangladesh* (Ontario: de Sitter Publications, 2005): 263.

2. See: Ramkrishna Mukherjee, *The Rise and Fall of the East India Company: A Sociological Appraisal* (New York: Monthly Review Press, 1974); see also: P. J. Marshall. *East Indian Fortunes: the British in Bengal in the Eighteenth Century* (Oxford: Clarendon Press, 1976).

3. See for details: K. Pradhan, *The Gorkha Conquests: The Process and Consequences of the Unification of Nepal with Particular References to Eastern Nepal* (Calcutta: Oxford University Press, 1991).

4. For a detailed social history of the British Empire in South Asia, see: C. A. Bayly, *Indian Society and the Making of the British Empire* (Cambridge: Cambridge University Press, 1988).

5. N. R. L. Rana, *The Anglo Gorkha War 1814–1816* (Kathmandu: NRL Rana, 1970). See also: L. E. Rose, *Nepal: A Strategy for Survival* (Berkeley: University of California Press, 1971).

6. N. B. Dirks, *The Hollow Crown: Ethnohistory of an Indian Kingdom* (Cambridge: Cambridge University Press, 1987). For a brilliant revision of Dirk's ideas about the

same kingdom, see: Daud Ali, *Courtly Culture and Political Life in Early Medieval India* (Cambridge: Cambridge University Press, 2004).

7. R. Shaha, *Modern Nepal: A Political History 1769–1955, Volume I (1769–1885)* (New Delhi: Manohar, 1990).

8. See for a sociological explanation of this political culture: D. B. Bista, *Fatalism and Development: Nepal's Struggle for Modernization* (Calcutta: Orient Longman, 1991).

9. For details, see: David N. Gellner, "Introduction," in *Nationalism and Ethnicity in a Hindu Kingdom: The Politics of Culture in Contemporary Nepal*, ed. David N. Gellner, Joanna Pfaff-Czarnecka, and John Whelpton (Amsterdam: Hardwood Academic Publishers, 1997), 8.

10. See: Holly Gayley, "Gyanendra's Test—Nepal's Monarchy in the Era of Democracy," *Harvard Asia Quarterly*, 13 April 2005, http://www.fas.harvard.edu/~asiactr/haq/200201/0201a009.htm.

11. Clifford Geertz, *Negara: Theatre State in Nineteenth Century Bali* (Princeton: Princeton University Press, 1982).

12. András Höfer, *The Caste Hierarchy and the State in Nepal—A Study of the Muluki Ain of 1854* (Innsbruck: Universitatsverlag Wagner, 1979).

13. Dirks, *The Hollow Crown*.

14. See Nancy Levine, "Caste, State, and Ethnic Boundaries in Nepal," *Journal of Asian Studies* 46, no. 1 (1987): 71–78, quoted in Holly Gayley, "Gyanendra's Test: Nepal's Monarchy in the Era of Democracy," *Harvard Asia Quarterly* (13 April 2005).

15. Levine, "Caste, State," 71–78.

16. L. Rose and E. Fisher, *The Politics of Nepal: Persistence and Change in an Asian Monarchy* (Ithaca: Cornell University Press, 1970): 29–33. For details of the operation of Nepalese economy, please see: D. Seddon, *Nepal: A State of Poverty* (New Delhi: Vikas, 1987), and D. Seddon, P. Blaikie, and J. Cameron, *Nepal in Crisis: Growth and Stagnation at the Periphery* (New Delhi: Oxford University Press, 1980).

17. Richard Burghart, "Political Culture of Panchayat Democracy," in *Nepal in the Nineties: Version of the Past, Visions of the Future*, ed. Michael Hutt (New Delhi: Oxford University Press), 3.

18. Burghart, "Political Culture of Panchayat," 3.

19. Marie Lecomte-Tilouine, "The History of the Messianic and Rebel King Lakhan Thapa: Utopia and Ideology among Magars," in *Resistance and the State: Nepalese Experience*, ed. D. Gellner (New Delhi: Social Science Press), 244–78.

20. See for details: *Nepal*, Library of Congress, Nepal Country study, http://countrystudies.us/nepal/ (10 June 2005).

21. See for details: *Nepal*, Library of Congress.

22. Nepali Humanist Jai Prithvi Bahadur Singh, a member of the Rana family, went into self-exile for his Marxist beliefs even earlier. Deepak Thapa, "Radicalism and the Emergence of Maoists," in *Himalayan People's War: Nepal's Maoist Rebellion*, ed. Michael Hutt (Bloomington: Indiana University Press, 2004), 22.

23. For details, see: T. Louise Brown, *The Challenge to Democracy in Nepal: A Political History* (London and New York: Routledge, 1996).

24. Levi Werner, "Government and Politics In Nepal: II," *Far Eastern Survey* 22, no. 1 (14 January 1953), 5–10.

25. Werner, "Government and Politics," 5–10.
26. Werner, "Government and Politics," 5–10.
27. R. Shaha, *Modern Nepal: A Political History 1769-1955, Volume II, 1885–1955* (New Delhi: Manohar, 1990): 303–5. Also quoted in Brown, *The Challenge to Democracy in Nepal*, 29.
28. See for analysis: Brown, *The Challenge to Democracy in Nepal*, 29–30.
29. Harka Gurung, "The Sociology of Elections in Nepal, 1959 to 1981," *Asian Survey* 22, no. 3 (March 1982), 304–14.
30. See for details: B. Joshi, L. Rose, and L. E. Rose, *Democratic Innovations in Nepal: A Case Study of Political Acculturation* (Berkeley: University of California Press, 1996).
31. Merill R. Goodall, "Bureaucracy and Bureaucrats: Some Themes Drawn from the Nepal Experience," *Asian Survey* 15, no.10 (October 1975): 892–95.
32. Brown, *The Challenge*, 33–41.
33. Naryan Khadka, "Crisis in Nepal's Partyless Panchayat System: The Case for More Democracy," *Pacific Affairs* 59, no. 3 (Autumn 1986), 429–54.
34. Burghart, "The Political Culture," 1–13.
35. Students ostensibly brought out the procession to protest the execution of Prime Minister Bhutto of Pakistan by the authoritarian military dictators on the same day.
36. See for details: L. R. Baral, *Nepal's Politics of Referendum: A Study of Groups, Personalities and Trends* (New Delhi: Vikas, 1983). See also: T. B. Smith, "Nepal's Political System in Transition," in *Political Participation and Change in South Asia: The Context of Nepal*, ed. M. Dharamdasani (Varanasi: Shalimar, 1984), 29–30.
37. Khadka, "Partyless Panchayat System," 429–54.
38. For details of this revolution, see: Martin Hoftun, William Raeper, and John Whelpton, *People, Politics and Ideology: Democracy and Social Change in Nepal* (Kathmandu: Mandala Book Point, 1999).
39. See for details: Ram Kumar Dahal, *Constitutional and Political Development in Nepal* (Kathmandu: Ratna Pushtak Bhandar, 2001).
40. For Indian case, see: Kanchan Chandra, *Why Ethnic Parties Succeed: Patronage and Ethnic Headcounts in India* (Cambridge: Cambridge University Press, 2004).
41. See the analysis of Brown, "The Challenge," 52–53.
42. Quoted in Thomas A. Marks, *Insurgency in Nepal* (Carlisle, PA: U.S. Army College Strategic Studies Institute, December 2003), 4.
43. For details of ethnic politics, see: Harka Gurung, *Nepal: Social Demography and Expressions* (Kathmandu: New Era, 1998).
44. D. Seddon, P. Blaikie, and J. Cameron, *Nepal in Crisis: Growth and Stagnation at the Periphery* (New Delhi: Oxford University Press, 1980), 53.
45. C. Meillassoux, "Are There Castes in India?" *Economy and Society* 2, no. 1 (1973): 89–111.
46. For a detailed discussion of the concept of class formation and the role of intermediate classes in societies located on the periphery of global capitalist economy, see: Riaz, *Unfolding State*, 2–31.
47. See for the use of the term: Martin Hoftun, "The Dynamics and Chronology of the 1990 Revolution," in *Nepal in the Nineties: Version of the Past, Visions of the Future*, ed. Michael Hutt (New Delhi: Oxford University Press), 14–27. Also see: Dha-

nendra Purush Dhakal, *Jana Andolan 2046 (Mass Movement 1990)* (Kathmandu: Bhupendra Purush Dhakal, 1992).

48. Krishna Hachhethu, *Party Building in Nepal: Organization, Leadership and People, a Comparative Study of the Nepali Congress and the Communist Party of Nepal (Unified Marxist-Leninist)* (Kathmandu: Mandala Book Point, 2002).

49. Lok Raj Baral, ed., *Nepal: Parties and Parliament* (New Delhi: Adroit, 2003).

50. See for details: Krishna Hacchethu, "Political Parties and the State," in *Resistance and the State: Nepalese Experience*, ed. D. Gellner (New Delhi: Social Science Press), 133–77.

51. See for details: CPN (UM-L), "PMPD," http://www.cpnuml.org/cpnuml.html (2 October 2005).

52. Naxalite refers to a revolutionary Maoist movement in India between 1967 and 1971. A radical section of Communist Party of India (Marxist) in 1967 started a movement of forceful land-grabbing for landless agricultural workers and peasants in Naxalbari region of Darjeeling district of West Bengal, India. Soon this movement moved out of the fold of the parliamentary socialist movement sponsored by Communist Party of India (Marxist). The movement adopted the path of radical political insurrection based on Maoist doctrine. A new political party emerged under the name of Communist Party of India (Marxist-Leninist) as opposed to its parliamentary counterpart CPI (M). The original movement was suppressed by the Indian state in 1972, but many splinter groups continued to function in different corners of India. See for details: Sumanta Banerjee, *India's Simmering Revolution: the Naxalite Uprising* (London: Zed, 1984).

53. See for details: Hacchethu, "Political Parties," 133–77.

54. Hacchethu, "Political Parties," 133–77.

55. See for details: *Election of the Kingdom of Nepal*, http://www.election-commission.org.np/ (2 August 2005).

56. See: *IDEA Report Dialogues on Constitutional Processes in Nepal*, http://www.idea.int/asia_pacific/nepal/upload/NEPAL_longVersion_final%20_2_.pdf (3 August 2005).

57. D. Gellner, "Introduction: Transformations of the Nepalese State," in *Resistance and the State: Nepalese Experience*, ed. D. Gellner (New Delhi: Social Science Press, 2003): 15.

58. M. Hutt, "Introduction," in *Himalayan People's War: Nepal's Maoist Rebellion*, ed. Michael Hutt, p. 8.

59. See for details of these events: Sudhanshu Ranjan, "Bad time for regicide," *Al-Ahram Weekly Online* (21–27 June 2001), 539.

60. Clause 9 of the TADO revised on 12 October 2004 is of particular concern to human rights organizations. It specifically states that "If a security official feels the need to prevent a person from carrying out any terrorist and disruptive activity, such a person can be kept under house arrest for a maximum period of one year, six months at his [Security Official's] discretion and another six months after obtaining permission from the home ministry, in any place after fulfilling common humanitarian conditions." In 2005 there were nearly two hundred reported cases of forced disappearances. See for details: *Statement of Asian Human Rights Commission*, http://www.ahrchk.net/statements/mainfile.php/2004statement/211/ (25 July 2005).

2

Ethnicity and Politics in Nepal

Ethnicity had always been a critical but subdued component of the Nepali polity but it has now become an open and hotly contested terrain of politics. Ethnicity is viewed here not as a given static identity based on existing cultural symbols or social traditions; rather, it is conceptualized in terms of contestation for national identity by different socio-demographic entities. As the monarchical state claimed Nepal to be a monolithic Hindu nation, different social entities marginalized within the constructed Hindu hierarchy transformed their diverse ascribed identities into characteristics of indigenous nationalities in order to claim Nepal as a multinational state. This chapter seeks to outline the dialectics of this contestation over national identity. In the course of this contestation, it is argued that the monarchical state lost its legitimacy as a governing entity and thus experienced deeper crises of existence.

STATE FORMATION, THE PROCESS OF CENTRALIZATION, AND ETHNIC CATEGORIZATION OF THE POPULATION

Prithvi Narayan Shah, the ruler of Gorkha principality, whose conquest provided Nepal with its current geo-political shape, famously described his newly conquered kingdom as the land where four estates and thirty-six castes existed in perfect equilibrium. The conquest of Nepal by the Shah dynasty not only provided the country with an increasingly unified political system, but also laid the foundation of a unifying social organization based on a Hindu Brahminical notion of caste hierarchy. Indeed, the territorial

unification of an ecologically diverse, ethnically heterogeneous land re-
quired a unifying social mechanism of control that would buttress the hold
of a centralizing polity: hence, the Shah rulers privileged the Hindu caste hierarchy of ruling Parbatya elites. The term *Parbatya* refers to high caste
Hindu groups of the middle hill region in Nepal comprising Bahuns,
Thakuris, Chetris, and their occupational caste retainers now described as
Dalits, or former untouchables. Broadly speaking, Nepal, at the time of
Prithvi Narayan Shah's conquest, had three distinctive caste systems: Parbatya, Newar, and Terai. More importantly, there also existed major cultural
differences between Indo-Aryan-language-speaking Hinduized Parbatya
groups, Tibeto-Burman-language-speaking diverse hill ethnicities with their
belief system occasionally influenced by Buddhism and Shamanism, and
Mundari and Dravidian-language-speaking residents of the Terai region
practicing their own autochthonous religious rituals.

In the midst of this complex mosaic of languages and cultures, Shah
rulers imposed a framework of accommodation and ranking through internal colonization of these various ethnicities by privileging high caste
Nepali-speaking Parbatya Hindu social groups, both culturally and materially. The new pattern of taxation, the promotion of certain Brahminical
rituals, and the Khas/Gorkhali/Nepali language in the functioning of the
state and the extension of central government's support to emerging Hindu
land-holding elites led to the consolidation of a Hindu kingdom. Indeed,
according to Harka Gurung, in the nineteenth century Hinduized elites migrated continuously from dry western regions to the humid eastern regions
of the kingdom, bringing with them new agricultural technologies and untouchable artisan castes, and developing more sedentary and productive
agricultural practices such as terracing and irrigation that further marginalized non-Hindu inhabitants who relied on cultivation and pastoral activities for their livelihoods.[1] Similarly, the advanced economic conditions
of Hindus convinced the local population of the ritual powers of Hindu
gods and goddesses who increasingly became part of local quotidian religious rituals.

The incipient Nepali state under the Shah rulers between 1768 and 1844
thus created a framework of domination through the construction of a
Hindu social order that simultaneously incorporated as well as marginalized various other ethnicities within this broad, unifying, but also ethnically discriminating social order. Thus, the Nepali state had from the beginning a particular ethnic outlook based on Parbatya Hindu values. The
state as a ruling entity as well as a resource extracting and distributing mechanism remained in the hands of high caste Parbatya Hindus who excluded
others. The sole exception to this process happened to be high caste Newars,
who had evolved a separate caste system prior to the Gorkha conquest of
Kathmandu valley. Being urban residents for a long time period, these high

caste Newars had accounting, trading, financial, and administrative skills that proved to be indispensable in running the affairs of the state. Thus the new social configuration appeared to be a Hindu high-caste-dominated state with a sprinkling of high caste Newar administrators and traders.

Rana rulers further consolidated the social stratification along caste lines through a formal countrywide legal code. The infamous *Muluki Ain*, introduced on 5 January 1854, served to divide the society clearly in terms of a Hindu caste hierarchy. The term *Muluki Ain*, derived from two Perso-Arabic words *Mulk* (country), and *Ain* (law), actually sought to promote the new legal system as the comprehensive code of law for the entire land. This code of law stipulated a five-fold classification of Nepali society along the following lines:

- *tagadhari* caste groups, or wearers of holy thread castes;
- caste group of non-enslavable alcohol drinkers (*namasinya matwali*);
- caste group of enslavable alcohol drinkers (*masinya matwali*);
- impure but touchable caste; and
- untouchable caste.

This five-fold classification, though never a fully enforceable system, provided the broad framework through which the Rana rulers made claims on the resources of their subjects, both in terms of the extraction of material and human labor. This classification fundamentally established the pattern of social negotiation among diverse social groups within the land. Many within non-Hindu ethnic communities now acquired wealth and displayed nominal loyalty to Hindu symbols and thus acquired positions of privilege, hence there took place stratification within these communities.[2] Indeed, in the nineteenth century the Hindu state that the Rana rulers established gained a certain degree of acceptance among elites of middle castes, who otherwise in many instances were conscious of their solidarity due to a common ancestry and of sharing specific linguistic and cultural phenomena vis-à-vis high caste Hindus. According to Andras Hofer, this identity is relational in the sense that it "is an outcome of an interplay between self-assessment and outside assessment."[3] Thus, under the Rana rulers, Nepali society on the one hand adopted a universal unifying symbolism of rank and order, but on the other hand it created permanent visible marks of consolidated social hierarchy whereby elites of particular ethnic groups presented their cultural organizations as naturally superior to others because of their control over centralizing state machinery. The Hindu state thus enabled certain ethnic groups, namely high caste Hindus, to establish control over the mechanism of the state. In the later era, when Nepal embarked upon a scheme of modernization with the demise of the Rana state, such identities were presented as the naturalized national identity of the Nepali population.

As Nepal self-consciously embarked upon a project of nation formation under monarchical leadership from 1951, "one language, one people, one dress" became the rallying cry of the new regime. The idea of nation now overlapped with the traditional notion of royal realm. In 1960, soon after the royal coup that displaced the democratically elected government from power, King Mahendra promoted a new ideology of harmonious Nepali identity. In the constitution promulgated by the monarch in 1962, the king announced Hinduism to be the state religion of Nepal. This very announcement obviously distinguished Nepal from its officially secular but predominantly Hindu neighbor India and at the same time buttressed his own authority as the custodian of this unique "Hindu Nepali" culture. He also sought to cash in on the popular belief based on certain verses in the *Geeta*, the sacred Hindu text, that the king represents the incarnation of Lord Vishnu. These declarations not only affirmed the Hindu character of the state and polity, but also accentuated the marginalization of population groups who were not included in the Parbatya caste. Though a new constitution replaced the *Muluki Ain* promulgated in the Rana era, it actually rationalized the domination of high caste urban elites. This rationalization was done through the prism of the then globally fashionable ideology of modernization theory. Indeed, Joanna Pfaff-Czarnecka sums up the situation brilliantly when she states:

> The modernization rhetoric, especially the dualism thesis, was built upon the idea that peripheral societies were divided into two sectors: a dynamic one, "modern," seeking and able to integrate with the global (economic) system; and a second sector, devoid of links with the developed poles, traditional, and stagnating. In striving to establish development ideals, the elites promoted the image of villagers as backward . . . claming that the traditional forms of life among non-Hindus were opposed to progress.[4]

This very contention had actually played a crucial role in continuing the structure of internal colonization of primarily non-Hindus who were assigned a low status in the astrictive caste structure created during the Rana regime.

The monarchical state thus continued to follow the policies of the Rana regime in Nepal. The domination of high caste elites now became institutionalized and naturalized through the ideology of modernization and national identity. The very pattern of elite formation during the modern era reflected this deeply entrenched ethnicized high caste Hindu domination. Nepal's census data continue to reveal a very complex social mosaic whereby diverse linguistic groups and castes coexist together. The Nepali census did not use caste as a category of social enumeration between 1951 and 1991. It was from 1991 that the census produces more reliable data for caste in Nepal. According to the 2001 census, for example, Bahun and Chetri—two of the most dominant castes—constitute only 12.7 percent and 15.7 percent of the population respectively.[5] More importantly from a linguistic perspective, only 48.6 percent of the population listed/registered Nepali as their first language.

Thus, Nepali-speaking, high caste Hindus constitute only a small minority of the population. Yet these communities constituting 29 percent of the population dominate the bureaucracy and political parties, and boast a much higher literacy rate than the remainder of the population. For example, according to the 1991 census only 3.1 percent of workers were employed in the organized labor market. They were categorized as professional, technical administrative, and clerical employees. In these salaried professions nearly 34 percent were Bahuns, 17.4 percent were Chetris, and 14.1 percent were Newars. Interestingly, only these three communities constituted nearly 70.2 percent of all graduates in Nepal.[6] The senior level permanent bureaucracy had far higher representatives of these three communities. In 1990, according to Harka Gurung, Bahuns, Chetris, and Newars constituted 87 percent of permanent secretaries of the Nepali government, nearly 92 percent of additional secretaries, 88 percent of deputy secretaries, 94 percent of joint secretaries, 96 percent of assistant secretaries, and 92 percent of section officers.[7] Given this domination of high caste Hindus over government jobs, it is not surprising that the average per capita income of the officially recognized fifty-nine indigenous groups, or nationalities, in 2004 was 15,630 rupees (U.S. $211) while the per capita income of Nepal was 20,689 rupees, according to the Nepal Living Standard Survey.[8]

These communities also came to dominate the Nepali political scene. In three different general elections held during a relatively peaceful climate in 1959, 1991, and 1994, the combined strength of Bahuns, Chetris, and Newars in the House of Representatives far exceeded other communities. In 1959 nearly 79 percent of legislators belonged to these categories, in 1991 the number declined to 73.6 percent of the legislators but it further increased to 79.5 percent in 1994. Indeed, the number of Bahun members in the House of Representatives increased from 27.5 percent in 1959 to 42 percent in 1994.[9] This was indeed a remarkable performance for a community constituting less than 13 percent of the population. Details of cabinet reshuffles involving 104 ministers between 1991 and 1997 reveal that nearly forty-two were Bahuns, eighteen Chetris, and ten Newars.[10] More importantly, the contrasts become stark when one finds that the Dalit community (declared untouchable by the Rana-dominated state) despite constituting nearly 13 percent of the population elected only four representatives in the legislative assembly during the quasi-democratic era.[11] These data obviously indicate that since inception, even during the quasi-democratic era, the Nepali state remained under the domination of a minority elite group. A critical reason for such continued domination by privileged minority ethnic elites even under democracy may be located in the institutional structure of the state in

Nepal during the quasi-democracy era. The introduction of the institution of a "first past the post system" in Nepal and the lack of affirmative action policies continued to buttress the domination of particular ethnic groups, i.e., high caste Hindus who have exercised control over the state since the inception of a unified Nepali polity.

This obviously contributed to the crises of the state. The participation of Dalit youths in the Maoist movement bears testimony to the level of alienation of Dalits from the political processes. Similarly, because of the urban bias of development, the rural population has been isolated from the functioning of the state. There is no doubt that the 1990 constitution made Nepal more sensitive to pluralism as the constitution declared Nepal to be a multiethnic, multilingual, democratic, independent, indivisible, sovereign Hindu, and constitutional monarchical kingdom under clause 4; nevertheless, it was still a far cry from providing equal opportunities to the non-Hindu population. It thus occasioned no surprise and even little resistance when after the restoration of the House of Representatives on 25 April 2006, Nepal was declared a secular state (see chapter 7 for details). The growing consciousness among the marginalized population of the discriminatory practice of the Nepali state had obviously made them aware of changes required in terms of state religion. Secularism was then a much-needed rectification of the inherent bias in the monarchical structure of governance in Nepal and is thus popularly regarded as a move toward the dismantling of the institutionalized structure of discrimination against marginalized social entities.

FROM ETHNICITY TO NATIONALITY: THE RISE OF THE JANAJATI MOVEMENT IN NEPAL

Nepal is a land of diversity. Not only does the country possess three ecological zones (comprising the northern Himalayan tundra region, the middle hills of central Nepal, and the Indo-Gangetic plains in Terai), but the social mosaic of the country includes nearly 101 caste and ethnic groups. There are nearly 123 living languages in Nepal.[12] Table 3, based on the 1991 census, demonstrates the complexity of Nepal.

According to the 2001 census there are at least seven major language groups in the country apart from numerous languages spoken by tiny minorities. More importantly, despite the predominance of ascribed caste status as a framework of social differentiation and stratification, none of these social groups live in hermetically sealed communities practicing autonomous cultural traditions. Rather, most communities live in a situation of interdependence whose inter-communal cultural practices are often governed in reference to caste codes. However, such codes are neither static nor

Table 3.   Major Ethnic and Caste Divisions

(1) **Parbatyas** (Nepali-speaking) (40.3%)

Bahuns	12.9%
Thakuris	1.6%
Chetris (formerly **Khasas**)	16.1%
Others	9.7%

(2) **Newars** (Newar- or Nepali-speaking) (5.6%)

Bahuns	0.1%
Uray (Tuladhars etc.)	0.4%
Maharjans (Jyapus)	2.3%
Others	2.1%

(3) Other hill or mountain ethnic groups ("tribes") (Speaking other Tibeto-Burman languages or Nepali) (20.9%)

Magars	7.2%
Tamangs	5.5%
Rais	2.8%
Limbus	0.6%
Sherpas	0.6%
Gurungs	2.4%
Others	2.9%

(4) Madhesis (Speaking north Indian dialects, including Awadhi, Bhojpuri, and Maithili) (32.0%)

(a) Castes	16.1%
(a) Ethnic groups	9.0%
(c) **Muslims**	3.3%
(d) **Marwaris**	0.2%
(e) Sikhs	0.1%

Source: Based on 1991 census data (Nepal, Central Bureau of Statistics 1993: II, Part VII, Table 25).

uniform. Caste structures are often intersected by emerging class fissures in rural communities. This diversity is as much real as is the institutionalized forms of discrimination against particular communities in Nepal because of their location at the bottom of the caste structure. More importantly particular ethnic groups had a consciousness of their identity within the local context. As historian John Whelpton asserts, Tamangs located north of the Kathmandu valley were aware of the distinctions between them and other ethnicities, particularly Hindu caste groups but were not aware of any national Tamang identity.[13] The growing movement toward cultural awareness among these various non-Hindu ethnicities who were placed in the "wine drinking" middle and lower middle caste orders by the *Muluki Ain* of 1854 did spread throughout Nepal from the 1980s onward with the rise of literate educated elites among these communities. By the 1990s, with the arrival

of a quasi-democratic political structure, Nepal had witnessed far more as-
sertive movements toward the realization of "ethnic" rights. In many instances, ethnic identities emerged as a dynamic relational concept whereby
people deliberately engage in constructing ethnic identities to combat social marginalization arising out of ascribed ethnic identities by the state and
dominant high caste Hindu elites.

The most important example of the development and construction of
such ethnic identities may be located among the Tharus. Indeed, the term
Tharu refers to dispersed groups of people located in the inner Terai region
despite the widespread presence of malarial fever and dense forests in the
nineteenth century. Arjun Guneratne, a scholar of the formation of Tharu
identity, argued that various communities among the Tharu people did not
have any common linguistic or cultural ties. Indeed, they were dispersed
over a very large tract/stretch of land extending over the vast Terai region of
Nepal with diverse social practices and marital customs. However, the Rana
state's categorization of Tharus as "enslavable wine-drinking caste" provided a unifying framework for social interaction among Tharus for a common identity to combat such a derogatory categorization. This quest for
identity had been further bolstered under the monarchical state when a
large number of high caste hill men settled down in the Tharu areas in Terai
and in many areas took over their land.

In an increasingly multicultural rural milieu, the Tharu people sought to
develop a more positive identity. With the spread of literacy and education
there came into existence a well-educated Tharu elite from among the
Tharu land-holding classes. These educated land-owning elites pioneered
Tharu cultural and political activities and many of them became political
elites at the national level. They formed a Tharu welfare society in the later
years of Rana rule and became critically involved in the political and social
mobilization of the Tharu community. Though these national level elites
constituted a miniscule minority among the Tharu people, land-holding
local elites who were constantly threatened with degradation of their status because of the slippery slope of economic and social mobility in Nepal
had become a link between national level Tharu elites and the overwhelming majority. The very term "backward" now became a unifying factor among the Tharu people. Tharu activists even exhorted ordinary Tharus
to register Tharu as their language in the census in order to impress the authorities with their numbers. The very notion that they belonged to a dis-
possessed and deprived *adivasi* (indigenous) community became a source
of pride among the Tharu people.[14] Thus the process of modernization
and social contradictions generated by internal colonization and related
developmental activities led to a situation whereby people embraced their
ascribed identity and transformed it into site of resistance. The presence of
poor Bahun settlers in the Terai region in this context became to many

Tharus the visible marker of the other—a symbol of *Bahunbad*, or Brahminical Hinduism.

The Tharu experience is not an isolated case of identity formation. The formation of cultural associations for the purpose of revival and reconstruction of "indigenous" cultural identities became a common feature in Nepal. Indeed, among the Tamang, a dominant ethnic group in the northern fringe of the Kathmandu valley, a Tamang cultural association known as the Nepal Tamang Ghedung was set up in 1956 headed by Santabir Lama. In the 1960s clashes occurred between Tamangs and Jartis, as they called high caste villagers in Dhadin and Nuwakot districts. In a similar way, among the Limbus the domination of local Bahun elites and the abolition of a communal tenure holding pattern known as Kipat generated animosity toward Brahminical domination and the *panchayat* system of governance. Even Newars, who were part of the elites under Gorkha rule, had actually asserted their differences from high caste Hindus and when in 1969 the monarchical government banned Newar radio broadcasting, Newar activists protested, and formed a new organization called *Manka Khala* (cooperative group). These activists organized meetings for the introduction of Newar as a medium of instruction in schools as well as for the restoration of radio broadcasts.

In the 1980s new attempts at organizing a wider platform among non–high caste social groups including the Newars were made. Indeed, Newar community organizations played a critical role in organizing a movement for the introduction of the Newar almanac as opposed to the "Indian" Bikram Sambat calendar. In 1980 prior to the referendum on the *panchayat* system, there came into existence a platform called Magrauli—an organization that sought to represent four major Janajatis: Magar, Gurung, Rai, and Limbu. In 1982 the Nepal Sarbajatiya Manch (Forum for All Nationalities in Nepal), an umbrella organization of various local organizations, was created. This was followed by the Nepal Matribhasa Parishad in 1985 whereby all non-Nepali-speaking people sought to question the reason for a national language in Nepal. By the late 1980s Nepal thus witnessed a political ferment among leaders of Janajati groups in Nepal. By the end of 1989 a new forum was set up, known as the Janajāti Māhā Sangha. Defining the meaning of the word Janajati as "nationalities," the new organization styled itself in English the "National Federation of Nationalities," implicitly rejecting labels such as ethnicity, caste, and tribe.

From the late 1980s urban intellectuals were also challenging the notion associated with modernization theory that Janajatis constituted the backward segment of the population who needed to be "modernized" in order to accommodate the process of economic development. In a landmark research work entitled *Fatalism and Development: Nepal's Struggle for Modernization* published in 1991, Nepali anthropologist Dor Bahadur Bista argued that Nepal could develop rapidly if it could shed the imported Indian Brahminical ideology steeped in the culture of clientelism (*Chakari*) and nepotism (*affne manche*). He blamed Nepal's current developmental failures on the fatalistic Brahminical religious ethos imported from India and argued that Nepal's future lay in the "indigenous ethnicities," who were less influenced by such principles and whose simple work ethic would provide a way forward. Alan Macfarlane, an anthropologist, compared this work to de Tocqueville's *Ancien Regime* or Weber's famous protestant ethic thesis and Taine's *Notes Upon England*. Notwithstanding the high merits of the work, such scholarly assaults on Brahminical Hinduism prepared the ideological ground for new types of ethnicity-based politics. Indeed, as Nepal entered the 1990s, the word "ethnicity" had been discarded by Janajati politicians in favor of the term "indigenous nationalities." The new cultural elites and Janajati intellectuals now invested in reconstructing traditions and histories and argued that Nepal had been inhabited by various Tibeto-Burman and Mundari and Dravidian-speaking groups long before the migration of Indo-Aryan communities. Thus, the term Janajati now gained a new prestige as an alternative for indigenous nationalities. Following the United Nations and ILO declaration of the decade from 1995 as that for the rights of indigenous people, the idea of indigenous nationality gained new acceptance among ethnic leaders. More importantly, with the influx of INGOs in Nepal and their emphasis on working among local communities and fostering community identities, this process was further bolstered. The political language of the new Janajati movement now drew upon current global discourses about the rights of indigenous people to resist the Hindu state's encroachment on their rights as much as in the past ruling high caste Hindu elites borrowed from modernization theory to justify and rationalize the ongoing internal colonization of marginal populations.

The nationality question now became a common expression for Janajati resistance against the monarchical state's attempt to use nationalism to privilege a high caste Hindu cultural ethos. This again demonstrates the dialectical process of nation formation. The high caste Hindu elites' attempt to construct a monolithic Nepali identity had been challenged on the same premise by Janajati leaders who claimed that Nepal was a multinational state. For Janajati leaders the projection of a monolithic national identity represented a form of internal colonization of the indigenous population by immigrant high caste Hindus. However, the movement for Janajatis now primarily assumed the form of a social movement. The charismatic Cornell-educated anthropologist and social activist Dr. O. M. Gurung, who is currently heading the Nepal Janajati Mahasangh, has steadfastly refused to transform it into a political party. Rather, he identified the movement as a social movement and his organization a part of wider civil society organizations in Nepal.

In the 1990s, however, many Janajati leaders made efforts to develop exclusive racial labeling for their movement. They claimed themselves as "Mongol," a derivative of Mongoloid races, in order to popularize the notion that they were racially oppressed by Caucasoid Hindus in Nepal. Gopal Gurung, a journalist and the editor of Kathmandu-based journal *New Light and Thunderbolt*, promoted an organization entitled the "Mongol National Organization." Claiming that the people of Nepal were to be divided into two different groups, Aryans and Mongols, Gopal Gurung and his followers argued that Mongols constituted an indigenous oppressed "Mongol race." The idea was to present the plight of Janajatis, in the words of Susan Hangen, a scholar studying this particular political entity, as racial oppression in Nepal. The activists felt the term "racial oppression" would attract international attention.[15] However, this group had a limited base in eastern Nepal and had never been allowed to contest the election under the 1990 constitution for its exclusive ethnic political appeal. In the 1990s the Janmukti Party was set up to gain recognition as the party of Janajatis but they remained a non-starter. In other words, the movement of Janajatis in Nepal had traveled through many routes that sought to present their marginalization even in terms of racial repression by the state based on physical features of the population. Yet the complex social mosaic of Janajati groups did not enable such ethnic political entrepreneurs to translate their ideology into a reliable support base.

During the quasi-democratic era, in different regions of Nepal, Janajati groups tended to vote for two major political forces in the country—the centrist Nepali Congress and the center/left CPN (UM-L). Yet as the Janajati movement gained momentum, the Maoists sought to accommodate their anger into their movement by organizing the Akhil Nepal Janajati Sangha. While Maoists in the early stages of their movement promised the right to self-determination to the Janajati movement, increasingly they moved toward the idea of federalism. In the words of the Janajati movement's foremost intellectual, Krishna Bhattachan, the Maoist movement actually preempted the possibility of a Janajati-based revolution.[16] In the words of Dr. O. M. Gurung, the leader of NEFIN, the right to self-determination would fragment Nepal. He preferred autonomous regions organized along federal lines.[17]

Indeed, given Nepal's complex social mosaic of castes, ethnicities, and nationalities, it would be difficult for any particular group to emerge as a powerful ethnic block in any region of the country to exercise the right to self-determination based on notions of nationality carved out of a putative ethnic origin. Rather, multilingual, multinational (ethnic) alliances would seek to work toward a secular democratic Nepali state. They might try to address the issue through the prism of compensatory affirmative action policies. This way they hope to prevent occasional flash points between Bahuns and marginalized but more populous locally predominant ethnic groups. Federalism is currently favored as a solution to the unitary exclusionary patrimonial monarchical state. However, it is important to recognize that there were very few areas dominated exclusively by one nationality/ethnic group. Thus, any major reorganization would involve complex representation of various ethnicities at local, regional, and national governments in the case of a reorganization of the Nepali polity along federal lines. Scholars even suggested the creation of a house of nationalities based on equitable representation and a combination of affirmative action along with educational instruction in the first language of a community.[18] The experiment is now on for an inclusive stake-holding state as opposed to a patrimonial state in Nepal. Yet one unavoidable conclusion that can be reached about the current process is that the crises and the loss of legitimacy of the state are clearly evident through the rise of the Janajati movement. Not only has the patrimonial monarchical state failed to address the needs of the population, but it has also functioned as an ethnicity-based exploitative state. Once this character of the state had become decipherable, the state became further disembedded as a political entity from the rest of society.

DALIT RESISTANCE: THE MOVEMENT TOWARD AN INCLUSIVE STATE

The term *Dalit* is a product of an ongoing political struggle of occupational groups, who were declared untouchables in Nepal by the state in the past, to claim humane treatment. During the Malla period, for example, Jayasthiti Malla (1382–1395) famously ordered a ranking of sixty-four different strata among the Newars of Kathmandu valley. He was also infamous for his edicts that identified certain occupational groups as untouchables. Many Gorkha rulers, even prior to the conquest of Kathmandu valley, also reinforced strict caste divisions. Ramshah Gorkha, for example, notoriously prescribed the wearing of distinctive apparel for different caste groups and compelled low caste groups to live in mud-constructed houses as opposed to brick-built houses reserved for high castes. Certain occupational groups were also segregated in unhealthy unsanitary quarters of towns. This tradition of segregation and marginalization of Dalits was further upheld by the Rana state. The *Muluki Ain* of 1854 placed certain groups in the ranks of *Pani na Chalne choi chito Halnuparne,* or an impure group of people from whom water could not be accepted. This assignment of low ritual status for Dalits had much wider implications. Not only were occupational working groups segregated but they were denied access to resources necessary for a decent life. Materially, they were assigned to hereditary occupations and were in many instances enslaved through debt bondage.

The hold of the caste system became so pervasive that not only had Hindu high castes relegated them to the margins of society, but even non-Hindu middle castes also in their quotidian life treated these occupational castes as untouchable. Even within the ranks of the so-called untouchable communities there developed a sense of hierarchy. Thus the ascription of untouchable identity to a community led to the internalization of the notion of untouchability among victims and created fatalistic dispositions. It also transformed certain occupational groups, such as ironsmiths and potters, into an army of readily available workers in a labor scarce economy whereby their labor could be demanded, controlled, and deployed at the will of the high caste Hindu landed elites. Hindu apartheid thus had a profound economic as well as socio-religious logic.

After the collapse of Rana rule the government enacted the Civil Rights Act of 1955 and the Defamation Act of 1963, which aimed at eliminating untouchability. In 1963 under the new *Muluki Ain* untouchability as a social practice was declared illegal. In 1971 Nepal endorsed the provision in Article 6 of the International Convention of Elimination of Racial Discrimination and Untouchability. Yet all these laws had been based on a liberal premise that recognized untouchability as an individual prejudice. It failed to recognize the wider socioeconomic premise of untouchability whereby a vast number of people had been rendered a socially invisible, politically disenfranchised, and economically deprived subject population. More importantly, as the law continued to regard religious freedom as a fundamental aspect of human rights, it permitted a certain form of untouchability to be practiced as tradition. The most cited example of the latter was the New Nepali Civil Code (amended in 1992), which recognized the right of high caste Hindus to practice traditional religious rituals that continued to separate and segregate untouchables from Hindu religious sanctuaries. The discrimination against Dalits thus continued unabated.

In everyday life, it had been observed that even when Dalits were allowed to work as domestic labor they were not allowed to enter the kitchen, and in many instances when Dalits performed household chores, the high caste Hindus purified their house by sprinkling holy water from the Ganges and cow's urine after the work was completed. However, certain crucial household works were reserved for Dalits, such as the work of the *dai*, or midwife, whereby *Chamar* (traditionally a leather workers' caste) women were specially appointed to assist mothers with childbirth. High caste communities still did not allow marriages between ritually impure Dalit caste groups and higher castes. Even when a high caste or intermediate caste man married a Dalit girl, he had to leave his community and accept the status of untouchable. Dalits were prohibited from entering temples and places of public worship.

Dalits had much more restricted access to community resources. They were often prevented from fetching water from village wells. Their attempts to open restaurants or shops dealing with groceries were not encouraged, as high or intermediate caste Hindus would not visit their shops. Dalit boys were discriminated against in public schools and in many instances had to observe strict caste segregation in classes. Dalits were often not appointed as teachers because this would imply that high caste students would have to heed to their words and pay respect to them. This discrimination in terms of accessing educational institutions was reflected in the fact that according to the 2001 census, literacy rates among Dalits (33.8 percent) were much lower than the national average (53.7 percent). Nearly 80 percent of Dalits were illiterate in the Terai regions though in the hill regions the literacy rate was much higher among them (31.51 percent). It had been observed that direct financial support provided to Dalit students led to their increasing participation in schools while the withdrawal of such support contributed to the decline in their attendance. In many instances, Dalits were so poor that they could not even provide proper apparel for their children to cover their bodies in order to enable them to attend schools.[19]

This economic deprivation had a direct bearing on the economic position of Dalits. Indeed, many Dalits were forced to work as bonded workers categorized as *Haliya, Khali,* and *Charuwa*.[20] *Haliya Pratha* stands for bonded work and *Khala Pratha* means forced labor. Workers employed under these systems were paid in food grains and were not provided with wages.[21] Despite the official act of rescinding bonded labor systems, few attempts were made to address the plight of Dalit bonded workers. Indeed, the land-poor Dalit communities in many instances resorted to various strategies to survive such economic marginalization. For example, one landless group of Badi women survived by engaging in sex work. The government denied citizenship to Badi children, as it was compulsory for children to produce their father's name on the certificates. In most cases this meant that the children of sex workers would not be provided with a citizenship certificate.

Women among Dalit households, according to Durga Sob, President of the Feminist Dalit Organization Kathmandu Nepal, bear a triple burden. They were socially ostracized and economically deprived for being Dalits and had to earn their livelihoods through hard work while they had to face sexual exploitation from high caste males. The burden of inter-caste marriage fell upon them, as they were not accepted into the families of the men. More importantly, in many instances they were forced to become sex workers and were victims of trafficking. At home, the distribution of food, resources, and access to better life opportunities were often clearly skewed in favor of men. This situation was reflected in two important ways: first, the literacy rate among Dalit women was much lower than that among Dalit men and the national average for women and men; second, Dalit women had a much shorter lifespan in comparison to men and to the national average for women and men. For example, according to Sob, Dalit women of the Mushahar community in Terai had an average life expectancy of forty-two years as opposed to fifty-five years, which was the national average according to the 1991 census.[22]

The Dalit resistance movement had now taken the shape of a social movement primarily organized through several NGOs. There also existed a Federation of Dalit NGOs. Dalit NGOs provide conditions for the deciphering of the plight of Dalit communities in Nepal and lobby international organizations as well as the Nepali government to act in a proactive manner to end racial and cultural discrimination of Dalits. Dalit NGOs also organized various local consciousness-raising movements among the Dalits and sought to provide an outlet for Dalit anger at their deprivation. There were numerous attempts made to initiate programs that would address directly the plight of Dalit communities. However, despite such efforts, Dalit representations at the political level remained muted and rather restricted. Throughout the democracy era, Dalits could elect only four representatives to the Nepali parliament despite having 13 percent of the population, while at village and town levels their representation in decision-making bodies remained low. Indeed, political parties were hardly active in promoting Dalit causes despite having Dalit leaders and special branches of their organizations dedicated to them. Dalits were represented by others and were often not allowed to vote by the landed elements in villages. The combination of class, caste, gender oppression, and socially institutionalized prejudices had made it difficult to organize Dalits. More importantly, the very marginalization of Dalits in all aspects of life had drawn them more toward the CPN (Maoist) and its seemingly revolutionary solutions. Reports indicate that Dalit women and men constitute as many as one-third of ordinary combatants in the CPN (Maoist)'s forces though at the highest level the party's leadership remained in the hands of two Bahun leaders. Indeed, in a personal interview, Janajati leader of the CPN (Maoist) Suresh Ale Magar, argued that the Maoists view the issue from the perspective of dialectical materialism, and rather than the caste background of the leadership they would like to analyze the role of the party in "smashing semi-feudal remnants" of social oppression in Nepal.[23]

As in the case of the Janajati movement, the state lost its neutrality in the perception of Dalits. An emerging Dalit intellectual and political community had recognized the failure of the state to protect and promote their interests. Indeed, they had recognized the ethnic as well as the class character of the state. By documenting and articulating their grievances they created the condition for the social alienation of an exclusionary Hindu state from the rest of the population.

HILLS AND PLAINS:
REGIONAL CONFLICTS AND THE QUEST FOR THE
MEANING OF CITIZENSHIP

The Terai is a vast region located just south of the foothills of the Himalayas that stretches from Arunachal Pradesh in India in the east to Himachal Pradesh in the west, covering more than one thousand kilometers of land. A part of the Terai fell within the boundary of the kingdom of Nepal under the provisions of the Treaty of Sagauli signed in 1816 between the ruling elites of the Gorkha kingdom and the English East India Company in India. The Terai region in Nepal is a 26 km by 32 km wide belt of fertile plain in the southern part of the country. Stretching from east to west this region covers about 17 percent of the total land area. However, within Nepal, between the Chure hills, rising abruptly to the north of the southern plains, and the Mahabharat range in central Nepal, there are several valleys which resemble Terai in terms of geographic and climatic features and are hence called the Inner Terai. Though Terai had been sparsely populated and the least-developed region in Nepal, today it has become the center of economic activities, with large industrial and trading centers sprouting up in different parts of Terai and absorbing large number of immigrants from hills. As Terai began to attract economic attention, it also witnessed the development of regional ethnicity based social and political movements and had the potentiality to become a flash point between Nepal and India. We have already described the formation of the Tharu movement in the Inner Terai region. However, the most critical sources of discontent often stemmed from the Madhesi community in Terai who constituted a substantial segment of the population in Terai.

The term *Madhes* refers to Madhyadesh, which originally meant central realm in terms of the Hindu political canons of Nepal but generally came to refer to the plain land, i.e., India. Thus, Madhes had a connotation of being different from Pahad Desh (or hill country) in the everyday language of the people.[24] This etymological root of the word has a direct bearing over the political contestation concerning the identity of the people inhabiting the region and the claim of regional discrimination made by the political activists who belong to the region. The word *Madhesi*, or inhabitant of Madhes, had been used to signify people of Indian descent. This reference is actually a historically anachronistic construct as many of these people inhabited the region for nearly two centuries and thus predated the formation of the boundaries of nation-states in South Asia. Maithili, Bhojpuri, and Avadhi are widely spoken languages in the region. Indeed, Mithila had been the center of cultural activities in this region for many centuries and in the past the Maithili language had been widely used in the literature of the Kathmandu court as it had been elsewhere in South Asia. Maithili also happens to be the second most important language of Nepal. According to the census of 2001 nearly 12.8 percent of the people speak Maithili in Nepal. This is followed by 7.4 percent speaking Bhojpuri and 2.4 percent who speak Avadhi. In other words, these languages primarily spoken in the Terai region actually demonstrate the links between the Nepali people inhabiting this region and their neighboring regions in India. However, regional leaders from Terai often claim that Hindi is the lingua franca of the region and should be recognized by the state as the second language. During the early 1950s after the restoration of monarchy Hindi came to enjoy equal status with Nepali. Gajendra Narain Singh, then a congressman who later worked within the *panchayat* system and became a founder of the Nepal Sadbhavana Party, insisted in parliament (1959) on speaking in Hindi. Though he was supposedly allowed to speak in Hindi, his speech, Madhesi activists allege, was not recorded in the parliament.[25]

Indeed, regional identities became the major force behind the mobilization of a segment of Terai's population against the supposed discrimination organized by the state. The long list of discriminatory policies prepared by Madhesi activists included lack of investment in Terai by the government, the failure to distribute land along the East-West Highway to the Terai population, the low per capita income of the Terai people, particularly Dalits, who constitute nearly 37 percent of the local population, and, above all, the denial of citizenship certificates to the people for their alleged dual nationality.[26] The citizenship issue actually brought into existence the Terai-based Sadbhavana through a cultural movement that aimed at making the claims of the Terai population heard in Kathmandu. The most crucial issue was the strict criterion followed by the government on the issue of the citizenship certificate. Indeed, the cross-border linkages among the Terai population with Indian people across the border, the constant to and fro movement of the people between Terai and north India as well as the fear of mass migration compelled the Kathmandu-based regime to adopt a stringent attitude in relation to the issuing of citizenship certificates to people who inhabit Terai particularly to those who married across the border or had relatives in north India. In 1984, Dr. Harka Gurung, a hill-based intellectual, headed a commission on immigration that recommended far more stringent control over migration from India. The result was the formation of the Sadbhavana Council in Terai. Initially started as the Nepali Sadbhavana Parishad, the organization was formed as a cultural advocacy forum to raise the concerns of the Madhes on a national level. The founding members were active in the Purbanchal Congress, which later became integrated into the Nepali Congress. The five founding members of the Sadbhavana Council were Rajeswor Nepali, Balaram Nayak, Ramjanak Tiwari, and Sankar Keriya, along with Gajendra Naryan Singh. They selected the name *Sadbhavana* (good will) to demonstrate that Pahadi and Madhesi could act in unison.

The Sadbhavana Council under the leadership of Gajendra Narayan Singh became the Sadbhavana Party in the wake of the introduction of a quasi-democratic system in 1990. The party, however, secured only a limited number of seats in Terai. Indeed, many members of the Sadbhavana Council actually opposed the formation of the party and joined the Congress instead. They believed that it would be better to lobby for the demands of the Madhesi rather than float a new political organization.[27] The Koirala family, who traditionally led the Nepali Congress, with their base in Birat Nagar had maintained connections with the Maithili community and thus had a substantial following in the region. Similarly, the fragmentation of the Terai community in terms of allegiance to different caste and ethnic identities and the domination of Maithil Bahuns and Kayasths over the Sadbhavana Party actually prevented the emergence of a Pan-Terai movement. The party itself underwent a split in 1998 soon after the death of Ganjendra Narayan Singh, its founder. Singh's widow Anandi Devi led the larger fraction of the party and joined the pro-democracy movement, while Badri Prasad Mandal, the leader of the opposite camp, declared loyalty to the king. Indeed, throughout the 1990s, a vast majority of the Terai electorate voted for major national parties. The Sadbhavana Party gained new access to power after the democracy movement, and hoped to play a critical role in the creation of a federal polity. Indeed, in the words of Anil Kumar Jha, a rising young leader of the party, the only solution to the issue of regional discrimination could be the reorganization of Nepal along federal lines.[28] This indicates the depth of alienation of the relatively moderate political forces in Terai from the male high-caste-dominated hill population.

Yet the Terai problem could not be easily resolved through the federal reorganization of Terai. Indeed, the complex ethnic mosaic of Terai would make it a contentious issue. For example, the Maoists' proposal to reorganize Terai into five different regions—Kochila Pradesh, Mithila Pradesh, Bhojpur Pradhesh, Awadh Pradesh, and Tharuwan Pradesh—provoked the ire of various segments of Madhes communities. This had been interpreted as a critical blow to the demands of a unified and autonomous Madhes. In the last two years the Madhes issue has taken a strange twist. A Maoist leader from Terai, Matrika Prasad Yadav, resigned from all positions within his party citing discrimination against the Terai population. Meanwhile, Yadav fell out with his colleague Jaya Krishna Goit. Goit is a lifelong Communist who began his career in Bishnu Bahadur Manandhar's Communist Party. In 1990 he joined the UM-L but he was recruited to the CPN (Maoist) by Matrika Prasad Yadav. Appointed the first chairman of the Maoists' Terai Mukti Morcha, Goit left the Morcha in 2004 and formed the Terai Janatantrik Mukti Morcha (TJMM) after Yadav replaced him as chairman. This organization soon engaged in vigilante action against Maoists alongside the Nepali Army who were embroiled in counterinsurgency measures.

But the issue could not be put onto the back burner. Recently, as the peace negotiation picked up in the hills, Goit has turned his attention to settlers in Terai from hill regions. Active in Sapatari district, he was able to kidnap a few hill settlers, and threatened Terai landlords from the hills with confiscation of land and possible closure of factories owned by traders from the hills. He also had allies in another group called Terai Tiger. He is arguing for secession of Terai from Nepal and the formation of an independent state of Madhes. Though he currently enjoys little support among Madhesi politicians, it is clear that if the reorganization of a unitary monarchical polity does not satisfy Madhesi activists, they may change their methods of agitation. The issue evokes such a strong response from Terai that a July 2006 UN report, from the Office of the Coordinator of Humanitarian Affairs, stated: "The situation was rather volatile in Tarai [sic] districts."[29] Thus the failure of a hill high caste monarchical Hindu state in weaving a clear and effective all-embracing Nepali identity had now caused such deep fissures in Nepali polity that it would require very adept consultation concerning the reorganization of the polity.

CONCLUSION

The contestation over ethnicity is not simply symptomatic of emerging ethnic conflicts in Nepal. Ethnicity had not been a ready-made identity for the majority of the people in Nepal. Rather, it had been constructed and had been used for the purpose of the interests of the state and of a particular ethnic group. The declaration of Hinduism as the state religion represented a process of social categorization of people for the purpose of governance. Hinduism represented a constructed unifying caste-based ethnic symbolism that ranked the population in order to gain access to land resources and labor of diverse segments of the population. As the twentieth century progressed, this Hindu identity had been reinvented as the symbol of national identity thus permanently placing a large segment of the population under a disadvantage. With the spread of education and the emergence of new elite groups among marginalized segments of the population there developed a new trend to challenge and expose the limited ethnic prism of the state. This prompted resistance to the idea of Nepal as a monolithic Hindu nation-state governed by a unique monarchy representing the cultural ethos of the land.

Nepal's journey to the secular modern form of polity, however, cannot be put into a straitjacket of ethnic conflict. The people resisted a demeaning ethno-religious or regional characterization of the state through diverse means. On the one hand, they sought to record and reinvent various sorts of identities to reclaim Nepal as a multinational state, and, on the other hand, drew various international discourses of rights to challenge the state's claims. This obviously meant that rather than the evolution of one singular interpretation of identity, Nepal experienced multiple forms and expressions of diverse identities ranging from nationality to regional identity. Thus Nepal underwent a radical transformation in terms of political processes of identity formation. While this opened up new possibilities for the reorganization of the polity along federal lines, it also deepened the crises of the monarchical state.

NOTES

1. Harka Gurung, *Nepal Social Demography and Expressions* (Kathmandu: New Era, 2001): 170.

2. Joanna Pfaff-Czarnecka, "Debating the State of the Nation: Ethnicization of Politics in Nepal—A Position Paper," in *Ethnic Futures: The State and Identity Politics in Asia,* ed. Joanna Pfaff-Czarnecka, Darini Rajasigham-Senanayeke, Ashis Nandy, and Edmund Terrace Gomez (New Delhi: Sage Publications, 1999): 54.

3. Andras Hofer, *The Caste Hierarchy and the State in Nepal: A Study of Muluki Ain of 1854* (Lalitpur: Himal Books [reprint], 2005): 11.

4. Joanna Pfaff-Czarnecka, "Debating the State," 57.

5. Harka Gurung, *Social Demography Nepal Census 2001* (Lalitpur: Himal Books [Second Edition], 2005): 5.

6. Gurung, *Nepal Social,* 99.

7. Gurung, *Nepal Social,* 100.

8. Marty Logan, "NEPAL: A Nod to Indigenous People," *Interpress Service News Agency,* 31 August 2006, http://www.ipsnews.net/news.asp?idnews=34495 (31 August 2006).

9. Gurung, *Nepal Social,* 102.

10. Gurung, *Nepal Social,* 102.

11. Tulsi Ram Pandey, Surendra Mishra, Damber Chemjong, Sanjeev Pokhrel, and Nabain Rawal, "Forms and Patterns of Social Discrimination in Nepal," *UNESCO Kathmandu Series of Monographs and Working Paper,* 8 (Kathmandu: UNESCO, 2006): 28.

12. "Languages of Nepal," http://www.ethnologue.com/show_country.asp?name =NP (1 September 2006).

13. John Whelpton, *A History of Nepal* (Cambridge: Cambridge University Press, 2005): 178–79.

14. Arjun Guneratne, "Modernization, the State, and the Construction of a Tharu Identity in Nepal," *The Journal of Asian Studies* 57, no. 3 (August 1998): 749–73.

15. Susan Hangen, "The Emergence of a Mongol Race in Nepal," *Anthropology News* 47, no. 2 (February 2006): 12, http://www.aaanet.org/press/an/hangen.html (31 August 2006).

16. Krishna B. Bhattachan, "Possible Ethnic Revolution or Insurgency in a Predatory Hindu State," in *Domestic Conflict and Crisis of Governability in Nepal,* ed. Dhruba Kumar (Kathmandu: Center for Nepal and Asian Studies, 2000): 135–63.

17. Interview with Professor O. M. Gurung, Kathmandu, 7 July 2006.

18. Mahendra Lowoti, "Inclusive democratic institutions in Nepal" *Himal Assocation*, Kathmandu, http://www.himalassociation.org/baha/baha_conf_mahendralawoti.htm (1 September 2006).

19. Pandey, Mishra, Chemjong, Pokhrel, and Rawal, "Forms and Patterns," 19–29.

20. Statement of Tek Tamrakar, representative of the Human Rights Consultant Feminist Dalit Organization (FEDO), Nepal; deposition before Sub-commission for Promotion and Protection of Human Rights, Working Group on Minorities Twelfth Session, Geneva, Switzerland.

21. Anit Srestha, "Dalits in Nepal: Story of Discrimination," *Asia Pacific News* 30, 2002, http://www.hurights.or.jp/asia-pacific/no_30/04.htm (31 August 2006).

22. Durga Sob, "Dalit Women: The Triple Oppression of Dalit Women," Asian Human Rights Commission, Human Rights Solidarity, http://www.ahrchk.net/hrsolid/mainfile.php/2001vol11no08/1169/ (2 September 2006).

23. Interview with Suresh Ale Magar, Kathmandu, 8 July 2006.

24. Richard Burghart, "The Formation of the Concept of Nation-State in Nepal," *The Journal of Asian Studies* 44, no. 1 (November 1984): 101–25.

25. Rajendra Mahto, "Nepal's Terai People Neglected," *Madhesi*, 4 August 2006, https://madhesi.wordpress.com/2006/08/04/nepals-terai-people-neglected/ (3 September 2006).

26. Rajendra Mahato, "Nepal's Terai," (3 September 2006).

27. Sushma Joshi, "Goodwill Hunting," *Madhesi*, 31 July 2006, https://madhesi.wordpress.com/2006/07/31/goodwill-hunting/ (2 Sept 2006).

28. Anil Kumar Jha, personal interview, Kathmandu, 28 June 2006.

29. Suman Pradhan, "Terai on a Slow Burn," *Madhesi*, 21 August 2006, https://madhesi.wordpress.com/2006/08/21/tarai-on-a-slow-burn/ (2 September 2006).

3

Economic Crisis and the Lack of Performance Legitimacy

Despite adopting ambitious plans, efforts made to create a developmental infrastructure, receipt of substantial external assistance, and dutiful implementation of structural adjustment programs prescribed by the Breton Wood institutions during the last five decades, Nepal remains among the poorest nations in Asia, with the highest level of poverty in South Asia.[1] Persistent underdevelopment characterized by massive social and economic inequities has become the defining characteristic of the country. The absolute numbers, such as per capita GDP of U.S. $271 and 32 percent living below the poverty line, and comparative standing of the nation, reflected in the Human Development Index—ranked 136 among 142 countries in 2003—demonstrate the dismal state of the economy and its impact on the lives of the people in Nepal. They are the all too obvious signs of the failures of the Nepali state and its ruling elites to deliver social goods. In the words of Devkota, "the persistent poverty is a single but a significant indicator of failure of the socioeconomic development goal mentioned in different planning documents. All stakeholders of development such as politicians, planners, bureaucrats, entrepreneurs, and donors were ineffective to arrest the feedback loops of poverty."[2] We argue in this chapter that economic failure contributed to the weakening of the legitimacy of the state and thus contributed to the crisis that Nepal faces today. A combination of a lack of ideological hegemony (discussed in chapter 1) and what we call a "lack of performance legitimacy" of the state and the ruling group accentuated state failure in Nepal.

What we mean by the performance legitimacy is that in a non-democratic (and/or quasi-democratic) political environment, incumbents may continue to survive despite having little popular political support if they can produce economic growth or deliver the basic economic necessities to a broad section of population. Popular acquiescence to the incumbent regime, under this circumstance, is directly linked to the economic performance of the regime, rather than its ideological underpinning or political organization. Within this framework, economic performance comprises service delivery and the ability to transform the productive sectors to generate surpluses for the maintenance of the economic and political structures and profit for the beneficiaries of these systems.

In the context of Nepal, weak performance legitimacy is a result of both the structure of the state, which required unremitting extraction of resources, and a host of other factors. Some of these other factors stemmed from the policies pursued by the Nepali elites, including the monarchy and the political establishments, but some are intrinsically related to the geopolitical location of Nepal, its peripheral position within the global economic system, and the geographical formation of the country. We shed light on some of these factors to illustrate the argument that economic distress has been corrosive to the authority of the Nepali state.

The discussion deals with exogenous factors, endogenous factors, and ecological factors, respectively. The exogenous factors include the external dependency of the Nepali economy owing to its geo-political location and the global power-play during the Cold War era; the endogenous factors include the issue of the absence of redistributive reforms, and the adoption of lopsided urban-centric development strategies; and the ecological factors probe the distinctive geography of Nepal.

EXOGENOUS FACTORS

1950 is a watershed in the history of Nepal and a defining moment for the nation, not only because it heralds the beginning of dramatic domestic political changes (chapter 1), but also because it shaped Nepal's interaction with the external world, both politically and economically. In some ways, India and the global powers rediscovered Nepal in that year and the country entered into a perpetual dependent relationship with these external actors, which have since then restricted the economic sovereignty of the country.

Geo-Strategic Limitations and the Economic Sovereignty of Nepal

While geography, common ethnic and linguistic identities, and shared history produced a close relationship between Nepal and India, two treaties signed in 1950 shaped the relationship between these two states. They are the Treaty of Peace and Friendship, ratified in July 1950, and the Treaty of Trade and Commerce, ratified in October 1950. It is well to bear in mind that both these treaties were signed with the Rana regime, which was at that time losing its grip over the Nepali polity. The Treaty of Peace and Friendship, in addition to the formal recognition of each other's sovereignty, territorial integrity, and independence granted rights equal to those of its own citizens to the nationals of the co-signatory residing in its territory. Under the Treaty of Trade and Commerce, which has greater importance for our discussion in this chapter in regard to the economy of Nepal, India recognized Nepal's right to import and export commodities through Indian territories and ports. Customs could not be levied on commodities in transit through India.

These treaties have been treated with suspicion by the Nepalis, and both politicians and the common people have described them as unequal and an unfair imposition on Nepal. From the Indian point of view, the security treaty, signed after the Communist revolution in China in 1949 and China's annexation of Tibet in 1950, was a pre-emptive bid to secure its Himalayan frontier. Simply stated, "If British India regarded Nepal as a buffer between the Indian and Russian empires, independent India considered it as a 'principal barrier to India' defending the northern frontiers."[3] Various steps followed the treaty demonstrating India's anxiety in regard to the security aspects of their relationship. These include establishment of a military mission in 1952, the signing of a memorandum for the joint coordination of foreign policy, and the establishment of Indian security posts on Nepal's northern frontier.

Chinese control over Tibet halted the trans-Himalayan trade and a relationship dating back millennia between Tibet and the Kathmandu valley. This made Nepal more economically dependent on its southern neighbor while politically the presence of China provided a certain amount of diplomatic leverage to ruling elites in Kathmandu. Notwithstanding such a diplomatic advantage, Nepal's problems may be explained as those of a mini-state that entered into the international political arena in the era of the Cold War, when not only the Soviet Union and the United States competed for global hegemony, but India and China were also locked in a contest for leadership of the emerging Afro-Asian nations. Both these giant neighbors assiduously courted Nepal while at the same time they restricted Nepal's economic and political ambitions. For Nepal, India posed a greater threat than the erstwhile colonial rulers, because independent India's influence on Nepal in cultural and religious terms was all-pervasive.[4] Precisely because of such similarities, Nepali political elites struggled to assert their distinctiveness and independence in order to prevent their country from being absorbed into the "mother culture."[5] The economic relationship between Nepal and India had to be located against the background of this hypersensitive attitude on the part of the Kathmandu elites and the patronizing platitudes of New Delhi's ruling elites.

While the transit facilities provided to Nepali commodities under the trade treaty of 1950 was helpful to the Nepali economy, clauses stipulating a similar tariff structure for both countries, detrimental to the Nepali industry, were also part of the deal.[6] The Nepali government insisted that Indian insistence on a common tariff for goods imported from a third country implicitly put pressure on Nepal to agree to a customs union. However, since India had a much wider resource base and a larger economy, any such union would have naturally placed the Nepali economy at a disadvantage particularly because it would have reduced Nepal to the position of a supplier of raw materials to the Indian manufacturing industry.

The specific clause related to a common tariff was removed by the Treaty of Trade and Transit, concluded in 1960 when Nepal was under the rule of the popularly elected Nepali Congress government headed by B. P. Koirala. The 1960 treaty even enabled Nepal to impose a protective tariff in order to shield its infant manufacturing sector from Indian competition. However, the 1960 treaty was replaced by the treaty of 1971. This treaty included a clause that stipulated that Nepal's exports to India should comprise 90 percent of Nepali or Indian, or Nepali and Indian materials. This too had been interpreted as a move detrimental to Nepali industry. The issue of transit remained contentious throughout the 1970s. The Nepali government argued that the issue of access to seaports by a landlocked country should be based on international law while trade between Nepal and India could be considered a bilateral issue. India under the Janata Party's government accepted this demand and signed a new treaty with Nepal in 1978.

Regardless of such agreements, the India-Nepal trade relationship seemed to be fraught with difficulties. This situation was obviously worsened by the Nepali monarchical regime's inability to deal dexterously with the Indian relationship. The Nepali monarchy, often irked by India's persistent support to democratic forces as well as demands for special privileges, sought to diversify diplomatic links and declare Nepal a zone of peace. The monarchy often invoked anti-India feelings with the aim of deflecting attention from the dismal internal political and economic situation. In order to counter Indian influence they also courted China's support causing much anxiety in New Delhi. This strategy of balancing Indian influence with Chinese support also contributed to a further hardening of Indian suspicions of the Nepali monarchy. In 1989, this strategy of counterbalancing India by making deals with China led to a serious diplomatic imbroglio between India and Nepal over the trade and transit treaty.

In 1988 King Birendra negotiated with China a special deal for arms purchase. In retaliation India decided to flex its economic muscles. The opportunity for India arose in 1989 when India and Nepal had to renegotiate the Trade and Transit Treaty.[7] Since the treaty had expired in March 1988, a temporary extension until 23 March 1989 was in place. Although a rudimentary draft for the new treaty had been prepared in 1988, India insisted that two separate treaties concerning trade and transit should be coalesced into one. As Kathmandu disagreed, on 1 March 1989 the Indian embassy delivered a letter warning that the transit treaty between India and Kathmandu would expire on 29 March 1989. Kathamandu retaliated by easing custom duties on Chinese goods. With the expiration of the treaty on 23 March 1989, India, not being a signatory to the international conference on the transit trade of landlocked countries, felt free to close all but two of the fifteen transit points between India and Nepal. The two transit points that remained open carried only essential items. Indians also subjected all goods entering Nepal through these two points to rigorous inspections. More importantly, with the lapse of another treaty on 31 March 1989, India squeezed the supply of petroleum-related products to Nepal. On 23 June 1989, with the expiration of a further agreement, India refused to renew Nepal's warehouse facilities in Calcutta Port. India also denied railway wagon facilities to move Nepali goods from Bangladesh to Nepal.[8] The consequences of these Indian measures were enormous for Nepal. It has been argued that the planned growth in Nepal's national economy dwindled from 5 percent to 1.5 percent in 1989–1990 as a result of the blockade.[9] India sent a stern signal that if Nepal desired to transform her special relationship with India into a "normal" one, India would tailor her policies accordingly.

As these instances of disaccord show, Nepal can ill afford to ignore the Indian influence over her economy. Apart from treaties and access to ports, Nepal's economic dependence on India is also reflected in the fact that India is her largest trade partner, investor, donor, and supplier of arms. Despite significant efforts made by the Nepali government to reduce dependence on India, it is clear that it cannot be lessened without a massive restructuring of the Nepali economy. Nepal's manufacturing base is weak and its growth is contingent upon India's control over trade routes. Nepal's most vital economic region—Terai—is not only located close to the Indian border but is also closely integrated into the Indian economy. For example, important market towns in Terai have evolved in response to the business conducted in Indian railway. These towns in the Terai constitute the most important trading points between the two countries. All transit points of trade and commerce between India and Nepal are located in these towns.

This economic relationship between Nepal and India has obviously imposed structural constraints on Nepal's ambition to develop her resources and to become economically self-reliant. However, this goal, or at least a move in this direction, could have been achieved through external assistance received from the donors. But neither the donors nor the Nepali regimes seem to have this on their minds. Instead, the donors have had a different agenda to pursue.

The Donor Agenda and the Nepali Economy

While Nepal has received aid from foreign sources since the Second World War, it was the establishment of a diplomatic relationship with the United States in 1947 that brought the country into the fold of global politics and opened the door for external actors beyond India to play a role in its economy. Moreover, the Communist revolution in neighboring China in 1949 increased global interest in Nepal. Much to the annoyance of India, the United States signed a major four-point technical assistance program with Nepal in 1951. Akin to the Monroe Doctrine of the United States vis-à-vis South America,[10] India has always viewed Nepal as its backyard and considers any other country's interest to be intrusive behavior. This agreement was seen in similar vein. The apparently innocuous technical program was an acknowledgement of the United States' concern with the enormous influence of India on Nepal and the perceived necessity to have a foothold to counter any plausible future influence of China. Further economic relationships with other countries were established when Nepal became a member of the Colombo Plan.[11] But these new relationships did not lessen the formidable presence and enormous influence of India. King Mahendra, who came to power in 1955, made a move to reduce Indian influence. This was due to his dislike of India for its perceived role as the primary patron of the democratic movement in Nepal. Mahendra sought to curb Indian influence, not only by gaining wider international recognition for Nepal, but also by searching for new donors for Nepal's developmental projects.

By then Nepal had been rediscovered by the global powers, thanks to the Chinese annexation of Tibet. When King Mahendra embraced a new slogan of diversification of Nepal's foreign relations based on equal friendship, he was able to open diplomatic channels beyond great powers such as the United States, the United Kingdom, the Soviet Union, China, and India. His success was evident from the fact that by 1959 Nepal had been able to obtain recognition from twenty-four countries as opposed to a mere five in 1951. In the 1960s, the king was able to assert more independence in foreign policy as the border war between India and China brought Nepal's geo-strategic importance to the fore. During this period King Mahendra established trading relationships with China, Pakistan, and East European Communist countries, and at the same time through India obtained new donors in Japan and from among the Western European powers.[12]

A combination of Mahendra's skill as a deft negotiator and the superpowers' own strategic interests increased the flow of foreign assistance from the United States, the Soviet Union, and China throughout the 1960s. However, once Nepal's strategic utility declined due to the changing global political situation, Nepal fell behind in drawing assistance from the major powers. For example, as the United States followed a policy of rapprochement with China in 1971, U.S. aid to Nepal started dwindling. While between 1962 and 1965 Washington had contributed nearly 40 percent of Nepal's total aid, it declined to 23 percent between 1970 and 1975, and to 12 percent between 1976 and 1985.[13] This demonstrates that, as elsewhere, U.S. assistance to Nepal was driven by U.S. strategic interests. Interestingly, the decline in U.S. aid also reduced the help from countries such as the Soviet Union and China. The limited involvement of China in developmental activities such as establishing a trolley bus line in Kathmandu, leather and shoe, brick, and tile factories in different parts of the country and to a lesser extent that of the Soviet Union such as building cigarette and sugar factories, a hydroelectric plant, and a part of the East-West Highway in the 1950s were directly related to their perception of Indian and U.S. activities. As the Indo-Soviet relationship improved and the United States retreated from providing bilateral assistance, the Soviet presence in Nepal decreased to an insignificant level.

With the gradual cooling down of the Himalayan cold war of the 1950s and the 1960s, the nature of aid also changed in Nepal in the 1970s. Rather than direct exercise of geo-strategic interests through bilateral aid, advanced industrial nations now exercised control over Nepal's economic future through multilateral agencies. The 1970s saw the beginning of a massive involvement of multilateral agencies in Nepal's developmental projects. Apart from the World Bank and the IMF, eleven aid agencies associated with the United Nations and eight private foundations such as the Ford Foundation were involved in providing assistance to Nepal. Increasingly the World Bank and the Asian Development Bank came to play a crucial role in delivering aid and developing projects as well as directing developmental activities. They were assisted by the British government's development agency (the Department for International Development, DfID) and the United States Agency for International Development (U.S.AID) in running these programs. In 1976 the World Bank established the Nepal Aid Group. By 1987 this group included sixteen countries and six international agencies. From the late 1980s onward, this group provided the largest share of aid to Nepal. The loan share of foreign aid also increased from 4 percent in the period in 1960s and 1970s to 25 percent in the 1980s.[14] By the 1990s, INGOs such as Oxfam, Christian Aid, and the American Himalayan Foundation came to dominate development activities.

Foreign aid has played a crucial role in Nepal's economy over recent decades, but instead of enhancing productivity it has become an economic burden. Nearly 78 percent of the total actual outlay of Nepal's second plan (1962–1965) and nearly 56 percent of the third plan (1965–1970) were financed by foreign aid. A World Bank report in 1990 claimed that between 1976–1977 and 1987–1988, the proportion of foreign financing in development expenditure was higher than 49 percent. Narayan Khadka notes that foreign aid contributed to nearly 70 percent of the public investment in Nepal's seventh plan (1985–1990).[15] In terms of contribution to the Gross National Product of the country, in the late 1980s the share of foreign aid increased from 8 percent to almost 13 percent.[16]

Despite the flow of aid Nepal's economic performance remained mediocre during the absolute monarchical period. Between 1965 and 1989 Nepal's GDP growth rate was a dismal 0.6 percent. The agricultural sector, primary employer in Nepal, witnessed a growth rate of 1.1 percent while Nepal's population grew by 4.5 percent. Between 1970 and 1989, Nepal's debt burden increased from $3 million to $1.3 billion. As of 2005, out of the total GDP of U.S. $5.5 billion, about U.S. $1.7 billion is the value of debt.[17] According to one estimate Nepal's debt service as a percentage of exports of goods and services increased from 3.2 percent in 1980 to 16 percent in 1989.[18]

By the mid-1990s the aid flow to Nepal started to decline rapidly, yet the country has not become less reliant on external sources for its development. In 1994/1995, aid contributed 56.50 billion rupees of the development expenditure; it had reached 68.50 billion rupees in 2004/2005.[19] Despite the alarming level of external dependency, the Nepali government continues to rely on external assistance resulting in a growing debt service for Nepal. The amount of per capita debt had reached U.S. $14.70 in 2001 according to World Bank estimates.[20] As such aid is not only causing damage to its present state of economy but also mortgaging its future to the donors, it has also created a mindset of dependence that has often led planners to plan not in terms of available resources but in terms of possible availability of aid from abroad. One can easily realize the principal reason behind this mindset when one notes that the auditor general of Nepal commented in 2001: "There are no records of how much aid and loans are brought into the country. We have repeatedly demanded with the government to come up with a mechanism to keep track of these amounts to avoid irregularities and misuse of funds but that has not happened."[21]

ENDOGENOUS FACTORS

Over the last five decades, central to the development discourses and economic strategies in Nepal has been the idea of *vikash*—the literal meaning of which is "development." But in the context of Nepal, *vikash* signified not the economic transformation of society alone but also the process of centralization of state power. The ascendant monarchical regime used the word *vikash* as a metaphor for a "harmonious way of nation building" by drawing upon the theme of "modernization of [the] economy."

This economic strategy has been biased toward externally funded, urban-centric, bureaucracy-driven economic growth. While the earlier tribute-extracting patrimonial state of the Rana regime siphoned resources from the countryside into the urban metropolis of Kathmandu in alliance with rural landed elements, the new monarchical regime appropriated foreign aid provided by external donors within the limits of the capital's urban environs. The infrastructural development projects of the state actually pushed agriculture onto the back burner and undermined rural development. Thus the historic core-periphery relationship between Kathmandu and the interior, earlier fostered through internal colonization under the Rana regime, continued to characterize the process of economic development in Nepal under the new monarchical regime after the demise of Rana rule. At the same time, by refusing to implement land reforms the state allowed absentee landlords to remain the dominant economic player in the countryside. The rural property regime remained extremely unequal although a vast majority of the people resided in the countryside. The overwhelming majority of Nepali peasants earned their sustenance from subsistence farming based on small plots.

The urban male bias of development strategies also contributed to a rapid increase in population. The low literacy rate among rural women, their lack of access to an organized labor market, and their lack of influence over decision-making processes within the family all contributed to population growth. The population explosion caused enormous environmental degradation that in turn contributed to economic problems. Finally as the literacy rate increased and a quasi-monarchical democracy opened new avenues of political mobilization, politically conscious women, Dalits, agricultural workers, and bonded laborers challenged old forms of social domination. All of these reinforced extreme inequality at multifarious levels and made poverty in Nepal a "deep and complex" problem.[22]

Developmentalism and Centralized Economic Governance

In a sharp departure from tradition, King Tribhuvan on 17 February 1951 addressed the nation as "beloved people" as opposed to "nobles of the land."[23] This signaled a new era in political discourse in Nepal as "people" took precedence over the "nobles." This shift was consequently reflected in the policy documents including those relating to the economy. But even more importantly, this marked the beginning of the era when the Nepali state started projecting itself as the edifice of national unity. The state also sought to provide substance to this claim by trying to create a national economy and at same time establish its total control over the economy.

To exercise state control over the economy the government of Nepal opted for state-guided planning to pursue its political economic agenda of development. This endeavor was consistent with the global trend of state-led economic planning, both ideologically and pragmatically. Examples were available at both ends of the ideological spectrum: while the Marshall Plan to steer the economic recovery of Europe stood at one end, the presumed success of the Soviet Union was evident on the other. Additionally, the "Soviet success" had wide popularity among ruling elites and development mandarins in neighboring India, which had influenced the Nepali elites.

While planning was no doubt necessary for social and economic transformation in the incipient stage of the formation of the national economy, the state-led model proved to be an inadequate top-heavy structure in Nepal where the knowledge of the state of the economy and statistics were unknown to planners themselves. For example, when the first five-year plan was announced in 1956, there was no planning commission. The first planning agency was established in the country on 1 March 1957. It comprised thirty-one members, including the heads of the Indian Aid Mission, the U.S. operations mission, the UN Technical Association, and representatives of the Ford Foundation. This indicated that the planning commission was a controlling body where heavyweight foreign donors sought to assert their presence.

Control became a key factor in running the affairs of the planning commission. As the Nepali political system remained unstable in the 1950s, the political players sought to impose their control over the system. This is reflected in rapid changes in the planning commission over succeeding decades. The first planning body, appointed by the Praja Parishad government headed by Tanka Prasad Achayarya, was dismissed by the next government formed under the leadership of K. I. Singh in August 1957. Within less than six months King Mahendra had appointed a new planning board with his brother Prince Himalaya as its head. Later in 1958 the new democratically elected government under the Nepali Congress Party replaced this commission. The planning board that worked to formulate the second plan was dismissed by the king when he assumed direct political control of the country. The battle to control the planning commission demonstrates that planning was perceived as an instrument of control over the emerging national economy and thus heavyweight political players felt the necessity of establishing their sway over the newly emerging institution rather than simply ensuring institutional continuity and effectiveness.

The primary reason for such a predilection on the part of the state could be located in the monarchical regime's anxiety to establish a political-economic presence in every aspect of life. The claim to initiate *vikash* or development remained the most critical ideological apparatus available to the regime to legitimize itself in the public eye. The monarchy as an institution of governance was engaged in constant competition with party politicians to establish their credentials as legitimate and appropriate custodians of Nepali citizen-subjects' interests.

Historically the Nepali state following unification in 1769 had to accommodate various powerful forces within the tribute-extracting modes of political governance of the Gorkha state. Under the Gorkha and Rana regimes, quasi-independent principalities enjoyed a greater degree of internal autonomy in return for their nominal acceptance of the suzerainty of the Kathmandu-based regime. The new Nepali royalist political regime at Kathmandu was not content with the loose confederation of diverse kinds of polities and isolated economies that Nepal had under the Rana rulers. The new Kathmandu regime opted for establishing centralized control over the polity and economy. This was aptly reflected in their rallying slogan "one leader (monarch), one language (Nepali), one religion (Brahminical Hinduism), and one nation." The state controlled by an ascendant monarchical establishment thus sought to impose a centralized bureaucratic structure on their rickety inheritance from the Rana regime with the hope of homogenizing the nation and its fragmented economy. The state thus became a central actor in the process of political economic transformation and engaged in building its own capacity to rule. Planning was viewed as the scientific way to deliver this capacity to govern.

With their ideological emphasis on creating an integrated centralized national polity, Nepali rulers looked toward economic integration of a national market and therefore sought to overcome critical ecological hurdles in the way of diversity. Indeed, divided into three ecological zones, a northern Himalayan high altitude region, a middle hill region, and a thin strip of fertile plains in the south, Nepal comprises one of the most diverse geographic regions in the world. Secluded by mountain ranges and valleys, Nepal had isolated pocket economies linked with each other through mountain trails that often required long journeys.[24] Road networks remained poor[25] and previous regimes deliberately avoided constructing wider networks of paved roads, supposedly in fear of British incursions.[26] As the custodian of the emerging centralizing state, Nepali rulers felt that an extensive road network was imperative to create a unified market structure. Consequently, the government accorded primary importance to the development of infrastructure. Transportation and communications received over 36 percent of the budget allocations under the first five-year plan, resulting in nearly 565 kilometers of new roadways. However, this modest achievement came with a cost. During the first five-year plan, agriculture, including village development and irrigation, took second priority with about 20 percent of budget expenditure. Similar trends are discernable in the second plan, which covered three years (1962–1965), and the third (1965–1970) and fourth five-year (1970–1975) plans; in all circumstances the agricultural sector was that which lost most.[27]

Thus, in an economy characterized by isolated primarily subsistence-level terraced farming, the Nepali regime invested resources not in increasing the

productive capacity of agriculture but in improving infrastructure that
would establish a unified national economy, which in turn would buttress
the unitary structure of the state. More importantly, the infrastructural development took place in such a manner that Kathmandu was placed at the
center of newly emerging road networks.

In many ways this Kathmandu-centric approach also suited foreign
donor interests. For example, between 1952 and 1956 the Indian army
constructed a road linking Kathmandu with the Indian border. While Indians sought to establish direct contract with Kathmandu, this road induced substantial economic growth in Kathmandu valley. Nonetheless,
even when foreign donors were not keen to support the projects formu-
lated by the ruling regime in Kathmandu, the monarch used his influence
to obtain foreign assistance for projects that would enhance the control of
the monarchy. For example, to further boost Kathmandu's central authority, King Mahendra made personal efforts from 1959 onward in constructing an east-west road network in Terai that would connect Nepal's remote
western parts with eastern regions, and reduce Kathmandu regime's dependence on India. Major donors, such as India, the United States, and the
United Kingdom objected to the plan on the grounds of economic
efficacy. But a cross-country network, as Schloss rightly points out, would
enable the Kathmandu regime to penetrate the interior.[28] Despite the ob-
jections of major donors, King Mahendra through deft diplomatic maneu-
vering involving China, India, the United States, and the Soviet Union succeeded in constructing the road. This was done through political initiative
at the highest level. The king formed an East-West Highway Committee under his chairmanship comprising all cabinet ranking ministers in order to
secure local cooperation. Thanks to his relentless insistence, the East-West
Highway was completed in 1972. This roadway further consolidated Kathmandu's grip on the country, although the economic benefits of road con-
structions have often been greeted with skepticism by many scholars.[29] Yet
the East-West Highway became a symbol of development in Nepal and an
attempt was made to engrave it on the minds of future generations as such
by eulogizing it in school textbooks.[30] In a way, these roadways became the
most important visual symbol of the ruling regime's penetration into remote areas of Nepal. Thus the Kathmandu-based monarchical regime used
the all-embracing term "development" to project and consolidate its own
grip on the polity. Indeed, such roadways established Kathmandu's control
over strategic administrative centers but failed to provide wide and elaborate backward-forward linkage between all segments of the economy
boosting growth. But the government did not engage in the modernization
of existing networks of mountain passes and trails that had been used
by Nepali peasants for hundreds of years. The monarchy preferred more
visible but costly all-weather roadways. These roadways would buttress

monarchical control over the polity, make the geography of transportation Kathmandu-centric, and therefore draw resources there while such costly public works projects would impress the people with the government's ability to initiate "development."

The state also extended its sway over other institutions that would act as the backbone of the economy. The role of the government in the financial system in general and in the banking sector in particular is a case in point. The crucial role in the new financial system was played by the state and centralized bureaucratic elites. Nepal lacked a powerful commercial class to play a lead role in establishing banking sectors and thus providing a privatized foundation for the economy. The state hardly sought to assign private capital an independent role in developing the banking sector. More importantly, yet again Kathmandu emerged as the seat of control of the financial system of the country. Indeed, the first move toward the establishment of a state-controlled banking system originated in the Rana period. For example, the government owned 51 percent of the shares of Nepal's first commercial bank—Nepal Bank Limited—established in 1937. The government also controlled its operations to a large extent. With its headquarters in Kathmandu, Nepal Bank Limited and its branches in the interior enabled Kathmandu-based bureaucratic elites to exert their power over the newly emerging financial system. Similarly, the Rastriya Banijya Bank (National Commercial Bank) established in 1966 was also controlled by the state. Specialized financial institutions such as the Nepal Industrial Development Bank, established in 1959 with U.S. assistance, also remained under government control. Correspondingly, in 1966 the government established a Land Reforms Saving Corporation to finance land reform measures. The Agricultural Development Bank founded in 1967 which supplied credits to agro businesses and cooperatives was primarily controlled by the state which supplied 85 percent of the capital; nearly 21 percent came from the Nepal Rastra Bank, and 5 percent from cooperatives and private individuals. This bank also received assistance from the Asian Development Bank (ADB) and the United Nations Development Program (UNDP). All these banks had their headquarters in Kathmandu. No attempts were made to decentralize the financial system to cater to the needs of different regions. These extensions in credit networks enabled small business and entrepreneurial farmers to gain access to organized credit services. However, the monarchical state was unwilling to allow private capital to play a direct role in sustaining developmental institutions for fear of loss of control. An argument that social equity was the guiding concern of the state-led development process cannot be made in the case of Nepal because these efforts didn't benefit the poorer segments of the society. The Agricultural Bank, for example, after 1965 had granted loans to only 9 percent of the total number of farming families. The financial system that the state established was designed to help it retain unbridled control instead of being sensitive to the needs of the poor.

Bureaucracy: Exclusive and Powerful

One of the most significant outcomes of the centralized state-governed economy of earlier eras was the creation of a class of bureaucratic administrators with control over economic leverage of the society. This new class emerged out of the phenomenal expansion of the public bureaucracy in the 1950s and 1960s. The Nepali government passed the Nepal Civil Service Act in 1956, which grouped all civil employees of the government into two categories—gazetted services and non-gazetted services. Gazetted services included all those advertised by the government by notification in the *Nepal Raj Patra*, the government gazette. At the apex of the political system, fourteen ministries were created. These were served by permanent secretaries.

Yet, given the skill shortage and limited literacy levels, the government had to rely on the old elites. According to one estimate in 1951 there were only 321 primary schools with less than 1 percent of the children attending schools[31] while only around 2 percent of the adult population was literate.[32] The miniscule literate social group was confined to high caste Hindus primarily based in the Kathmandu valley. The Rana regime operated through an informal bureaucracy that actually provided important political positions to their family members and appointments were restricted to a few hundred families in the Kathmandu valley. The offices were located in officers' residences. The officers ingratiated themselves with their superiors by providing gifts and personal services. This relationship was widely known as the *Chakri* system, operated through patron-client networks. As a consequence, during the Rana era, Kathmandu-based Bahun and Newar families monopolized the bureaucracy, marginalizing a diverse mosaic of caste and ethnic groups in Nepal.

This situation scarcely changed after the 1950s despite (overall) emphasis on a supposedly open "meritocratic modern" bureaucracy. The highest echelon of the bureaucratic machinery was restricted to the same high caste elites. For example, in a rather revealing survey in 1975, Merill R. Goodwill, an advisor to the Nepal government on an intermittent basis from 1952 onward, reported that at the top there existed two groups of administrative officials who influenced the civil service, namely, the formally constituted civil administration and palace secretariat. According to Goodwill, most top civil servants were from two high castes—Chetris and Bahuns—and were born in Kathmandu.[33] The predominance of Kathmandu-born upper caste Hindu hill men continued to be a persistent feature of the Nepali civil service. Nearly a decade after Goodwill's experience, a newspaper report in 1991 presented a dismal picture of high caste domination. The report maintained that Bahuns and Chetris held 80 percent of the posts in the civil service, the army, and the police despite the fact that they constituted not more than one-third of the population. Even the eleven-member Council of Ministers in 1991 had six Bahuns, and hill Bahuns constituted six of the nine-member Constitution Recommendation Commission, which drafted the constitution in 1990 in the wake of the people's movement against monarchical absolutism. The importance of bureaucratic exclusivity assumes greater significance if we take into account the fact that the political system was highly exclusionary to the non-upper caste population. The representation of Dalits remained nearly nonexistent in the national parliament despite the fact that they constituted nearly 13 percent of the population.

Education: For Fewer

This high caste urban bias in highly placed jobs was also a function of the way educational institutions were concentrated in the country. As noted before, the Rana rulers were explicitly hostile towards mass education for fear of popular discontent. The only higher education institution was Trichandra College at Kathmandu. But the situation improved under the royal regime. In 1954 the government established the National Education Planning Commission. The government also appointed in 1961 the All Round National Education Committee and in 1968 the National Education Advisory Board. Finally, in 1971 the New Education System came into operation as an integral part of the fourth five-year plan (1970–1975). In 1975 the government instituted a policy of free and compulsory primary education. In 1990 Nepal initiated a twelve-year literacy program targeting eight million people between the ages of six and forty-five.

In the realm of higher education, in 1959 the government chartered the establishment of Tribhuvan University in Nepal. As of 2006 nearly 463 colleges are affiliated with the Tribhuvan University. Despite this achievement, it is apparent from even rudimentary statistics that there exists a clear urban bias in the education system. For example, according to the 1981 census 24 percent of the population was functionally literate. While in urban areas nearly 62 percent of the male population and 33 percent of the female population were literate, in rural areas the literacy rates for males and females were 33 percent and 9 percent, respectively. The gap between male and female literacy remains substantial. Approximately 35 percent of the male population was literate in 1981 but among the female population the rate was only 11.5 percent.[34] While in 2004 the adult literacy rate was estimated 45.2 percent, the discrepancy between males and females was stark: male literacy stood at 62.7 percent and female literacy at 27.6 percent. A rural and urban divide is also apparent in the fact that almost all major schools and educational centers are located in Kathmandu and the newly developed towns in Terai. It was apparent in simple issues such as the distribution of textbooks. While 30 percent of the thirty-four hundred thousand primary school-going students in 2002 received free government sponsored textbooks on time, in the far-flung rural districts the equivalent figure is only 15 percent.[35] Non-availability of textbooks on time is a clear indication of the quality of education in rural areas. The economic consequence of this situation was clear: the rural poor are excluded from an organized labor market that requires formal educational training and skills. This is truer for women who are excluded from the organized labor market in various ways, of which lack of access to formal education institutions is a significant one. As most Dalits are located at the bottom of the economic ladder, they are also excluded from formal education. Thus gender, caste, and rural and urban divide continue to inform skills formation and labor market operation in Nepal.

The Agrarian Sector and the Lack of Redistributive Reform

As with all pre-capitalist economies, agriculture remains the most significant source of employment and income-generating productive activities in Nepal. A cursory glance at Nepal's economy from 1951 to 2001 indicates that agriculture constitutes the most important employment provider in the economy despite its gradual decline as the most important contributor to gross national income. As agriculture provided sources of livelihood for the majority of the people, agrarian relations constitute the most crucial arena of the economy in Nepal and the fundamental source of underdevelopment in the country.

In many ways, Nepal's ecological diversity constitutes a significant hindrance to the expansion of the agricultural base of the economy. This is evident in the fact that the uncultivable snow-covered majestic mountains known as the Himalayan region occupy 35.2 percent of the land surface and barren hills stretch over 41.7 percent of the land. Only 23.1 percent of landmass is in the Terai hills. Overall, only 21 percent of the total land surface area is cultivated and uncultivated agricultural land constitutes roughly 7 percent of the region. In addition to adverse natural conditions the structure of agrarian relations has also contributed to the vulnerability of the vast majority of the rural population. Restricted economic opportunities are closely related to the skewed landholding pattern in rural areas. In 1990, 6 percent of the landowners controlled over 50 percent of the land.[36]

In the 1950s developmental measures in Nepal required sweeping land reforms that would provide the vast majority of tenure holders with a stake in landholding. At the time of the introduction of the first five-year plan in Nepal in 1956, nearly 95 percent of the country's population depended on agriculture for their livelihood. Nearly 80 percent of them were tenants without any security of landholding.[37] M. C. Regmi, the doyen of agrarian historians of Nepal, notes that three aspects of land relationship contributed to the economic insecurity of tenant cultivators in Nepal: 1) uncertainty of tenancy rights, 2) excessive rents, and 3) privileged form of land ownership and use. Insecurity of tenancy rights was caused by the absence of legal regulations concerning rent collection. Rents were determined more by density of population dependent on agriculture than in accordance to the productivity of soil. As a consequence, in highly populated regions such as Terai rents absorbed nearly two-thirds of the gross produce. In addition, landlords made additional impositions on the tenant, reducing the latter to a condition of serfdom.

Although the cultivators' record compilation act of 1956, and Land Reform Acts in 1957 and 1959 sought to improve the condition of tenants, many clauses could not be enforced due to the absence of effective implementation machinery. For example, the Land Reform Act of 1957 sought to restrict the collection of rent from tenants to one-half of the gross produce. It also provided tenancy rights to tenants who cultivated the land for a year and prohibited the landlord from evicting the tenant as long as the tenant continued to pay rent. The tenancy rights were made inheritable and saleable by the tenant without the consent of the landlord by the 1959 act. In order to protect the rights of the tenant, the government also made it compulsory to provide them with documents of tenancy holding. Regmi correctly pointed out that these acts did not improve the conditions of the peasantry because the actual costs of production were mainly borne by tenants themselves.

The Land Reform Acts did not lead toward the abolition of intermediary tenure holding as had partially happened in neighboring India and the then East Pakistan. This is understandable given the close relationship between absentee landlords and the ruling monarchical regime or even Nepali Congress leaders. In the initial stages the palace establishment, in order to consolidate their power, sought to cripple the influence of the Rana aristocracy but only up to a point. Institutional hindrances as well as lack of intention to implement land reform laws paralyzed government action. For example, the Land Reform Act of 1959 sought to discourage large-scale holding of estates through taxation over estates larger than twenty-five *bighas* (a *bigha* is about 2,603.7 square meters). However, the government possessed insufficient records to implement the laws and bureaucrats drawn from the landholding class was less than willing to implement them. As a consequence, the landlords escaped the provisions of the laws through the transfer of titles of landholding within families. While land ownership continued to be concentrated in the hands of few, actual units of cultivation were diminishing in size making the livelihood earned from agriculture much less sustainable for families of poor tenants. More importantly, land revenue collectors, or *zamindars*, sought to produce confusing documents and played a critical role in evicting landless peasants. The moneylenders in the villages also charged higher interest rates and evicted defaulting tenants. As the Land Reform Acts sought to provide rights to tenant cultivators, the rates of evictions of tenants increased, contributing to increased agrarian tensions and landlessness.

Alongside this the government attempt to reform an earlier tenurial structure based on *Birta* system also did not prove to be effective. The *Birta* evolved from tax-free land grants awarded by the state during the earlier Shah Rana period to loyal chieftains. In addition, *Gunthi* land grants had been made to religious institutions. The Land Reform Act of 1959 made a distinction between two types of *Birta* holders. In the case of those *Birta* holders who collected land revenue and retained it entirely, the government proposed nationalization of their holdings with compensation. On the other hand, those *Birta* holders who collected rent from tenant cultivators in their estates were ordered to pay land revenues to the state at a similar rate to the state held land in adjoining areas. Even these modest land reforms were opposed by the powerful class of *Birta* holders and thus the act remained largely ineffectual. More interestingly, these land reform measures were adopted only during the brief tenure of the democratically elected government of the Nepali Congress in the period between 1958 and 1960.

The land reform measures proved to be more successful when they coincided with the state's agenda towards centralization of political power. For example, historically from the days of the Gorkha conquest Nepal had seventeen vassal states called *rajyas* in western Nepal where treaty obligations prevented the government from collecting taxes within their territories, but under new provisions were compelled to pay taxes. When these *rajyas* were abolished, the landed aristocrats agitated against the elected Congress government. The palace establishment used the agitation to dismiss the elected government but did not restore those privileges. The ascendant monarchy sought to control the opposition of the older aristocracy from the Rana period through the Agricultural Reorganization Act, passed in 1963, and the Land Reform Act, passed in 1964. Both these acts aimed at providing security for tenant farmers and placed a ceiling on landholdings. However, the royal government was also making provisions in the act that would enable them to escape many clauses. The purpose was to make these aristocrats realize that the royal government was their best hope. Hence, several loopholes in the acts enabled large landholders to control most of the lands. Nonetheless, the acts operated to some extent to protect the rights of tenant farmers although land redistribution remained skewed. These land reforms provided a new political base for the monarchical state. While the reforms remained cosmetic, it created a new class of rich peasantry in rural areas alongside the older aristocracy. Politically, under the *panchayat* system the monarchy recognized the peasantry as a class although the palace did not recognize their rights. Among the peasantry itself, only the rich peasants, who were the products of these reforms, were accommodated in the framework of governance and became functionaries of the *Panchayati Raj*. Rich peasants who were more organically linked to the village society became the bedrock of *Panchayati Raj* and later the Nepali Congress Party. The royal government's policies, in the name of development, as this discussion has shown, sought to protect powerful landed interest groups and hence ignored those reforms of agrarian relationship that required the most pressing attention.

The fundamental failure to implement land reforms or invest in agriculture in a sustainable way contributed to rural poverty and subsequently environmental degradation. As a result of cosmetic land reforms, a vast majority of the peasantry remained trapped in a situation of small subsistence farming. According to the Human Development Report 1998, the bottom 40 percent of the population own only 9 percent of the arable land whereas the top 6 percent own around 33 percent. This trend is further confirmed by the census of 2001. The census statistics suggest that 25 percent of households own no land or less than two *ropanies* (one *ropani* is equal to two hundred square meters) of land and thus fall into the category of landless workers. Recent statistics show that "the bottom 40 percent of households owns only 9 percent of the total agricultural land, while the top 6 percent occupies more than 33 percent."[38] Jagannath Adhikary asserts that as late as 2004, one million out of 4.2 million families did not own any land at all. Many of them, nearly 45 percent, were cultivating others' land, hoping that they would obtain titles to cultivation under "tenancy rights." In Terai the problem of landlessness was more acute than in the hills. Nearly 18 percent of the population had no access to land. According to Adhikary, approximately 22 percent of the absolutely landless people were from Dalit households, and more importantly a vast majority of Dalit households had only a small piece of land to meet their basic domestic needs. Their dependency on the higher castes resembled the status of bonded workers.[39] In 2001 there took place another amendment of the land reforms act with a stricter ceiling on landholding reducing the legal limit of landholding in Terai to ten *bighas* from twenty-five *bighas* and to twenty-five *ropanies* from fifty *ropanies* in Kathmandu valley and to seventy *ropanies* from eighty *ropanies* in the hills. However, the act could not be implemented in practice.[40] Besides landlessness, there prevailed widespread practice of debt bondage in five districts of western Terai. In these districts, parents promised the service of their children in their employers' households as a form of debt repayment. The Kamayia families were obliged to perform underpaid or nearly unpaid work in the house of their employers for generations in payment for debts incurred. In July 2000 the government also passed an act for the cancellation of debt bondage, but very little progress could be achieved in the interior of five western Terai districts.[41] Alongside the Dalits and certain Janajatis, women also suffered from absence of well-defined land rights. In many cases, as elsewhere in South Asia, women's positions are defined in terms of their marital status, without any coherent well-structured definition of access to ancestral property. A daughter would lose all her rights to ancestral property once she married. Though women provided a crucial amount of labor in agricultural activities, they did not have a decision-making role in selecting crops and the cropping pattern. However, they tended to play a critical role in the preservation of seeds in Nepal, but with commercialization of agriculture and the introduction of high-yielding varieties of seeds in Nepal by powerful MNCs, women also witnessed a decline in their role in agriculture.

ECOLOGICAL FACTORS

Although we do not subscribe to the doctrine of "environmental determinism," which postulates that every activity of the society is governed by the environment, the fact that the environment, particularly ecology, plays a pivotal role in the economic crisis in Nepal and has been a major factor in the impoverishment of many people, and consequently contributed to the insurgency, cannot be overlooked. We are in agreement with Homer-Dixon that "environmental scarcity simultaneously increases deprivation and disrupts key social institutions, which in turns causes 'deprivation' conflicts such as civil strife and insurgency."[42] And Nepal is in many ways an exemplary case in this regard, as Bhurtel and Ali in their seminal study "The Green Roots of Red Rebellion: Environmental Degradation and the Rise of the Maoist Movement in Nepal" have demonstrated.[43] Environmental scarcity in Nepal can be traced to two factors: the fragile mountain environment and population growth.

That many mountain areas are inaccessible and irrigation in the mountains is not economically viable forced the poorer sections of society to move to previously uncultivated lands, primarily the forests causing massive deforestation and soil degradation. The necessity for exploiting previously uncultivated land primarily derived from the high growth rate of the population.

In terms of population growth Nepal shares a common characteristic with other developing countries: rapidly increasing population composed of primarily young adult workers. Internationally accepted census measures have been conducted in Nepal since 1961, although there had been a previous census to enumerate the population. The 1961 census recorded the total population at 9.41 million. The dramatic growth in population began

Table 4. Population Growth and Increased Density of Settlement

Census Year	Population	Percentage of Inter-Census Change in Population	Exponential Growth Rate	Persons per Square km
1952	8,256,625	31.40	2.27	56.10
1961	9,412,996	14.01	1.64	63.96
1971	11,555,983	22.77	2.05	78.52
1981	15,022,839	30.00	2.62	102.07
1991	18,491,097	23.09	2.08	125.64
2001	23,151,423	25.20	2.25	157.30

Source: Population monograph of Nepal, vol. 1, chapter 3, p. 3, table 1.1. (Nepal Central Bureau of Statistics) www.cbs.gov.np/Population/Monograph/Chapter%2001%20%20A%20Perspective%20on%20population%20Census%202001.pdf (12 July 2005).

in 1952 when experiments with new developmental strategies ensued. In 1952 Nepal's population stood at roughly 8.25 million. Thus the population in Nepal has trebled in the last five decades bringing it to the current twenty-seven million.[44] The density of population also increased from 56.10 people per square kilometer to 157.30 in 2001.[45] Table 4 shows the pattern of population growth in Nepal.

The increase in population can be attributed to the expansion in primary health care and the decline of epidemics both of which increased the longevity of the population in Nepal. But population growth is also a result of gender discrimination in society and urban bias in developmental strategies. Abysmally low participation of women in the organized labor market and their relatively poor access to formal education and health care were also the source of population growth. The lack of any decision-making powers of women within the household contributed to population growth. The absence of bargaining power of Nepali women within the family is reflected in the fact that age of marriage in Nepal has averaged roughly around 16.1 to 16.8 years for the last twenty-five years. Most of these young women were unaware of family planning measures or feared the side effects of such measures.[46] Similarly, the absence of adequate family planning programs in rural areas is evident in the discrepancy between the urban and national fertility rate for women. While in urban areas total fertility rate (TFR) for women was 2.1 in 2004, the national rate of TFR was 4.1. The economic insecurity of the rural family has also played a part.

Rapid population growth obviously contributed to a disparity between the economic growth rate and the growing number of young adult workers. The population growth rate often exceeded that of GDP. Between 1965 and 1988 Nepal's economy grew at only 1.59 percent as opposed to a nearly 2 percent population growth rate during the same time period. Only from the middle of the 1980s did Nepal's economic growth rate outperform the population growth rate.

As we noted before, the most direct implication of the population explosion was growing land scarcity. A slower growth rate in the manufacturing sector meant non-availability of non-farm jobs in the rural areas; consequently, pressure increased on land. This contributed to the fragmentation of landholding. Migration to new land has a historical background as well. In the nineteenth century the state encouraged peasants to move into new land through land tax remission. In the middle of the twentieth century a new option opened for land hungry peasants who were looking for strategies of survival. As soon as the government was able to combat malaria in the Terai plain, large-scale migration occurred to Terai. Nepalis migrated en masse, sometimes with government encouragement but more often on their own. This obviously altered the entire demographic distribution of the population in three different regions of Nepal. The changing demographic shift in Nepal's population documented in Table 5 is a testimony to this fact.

As a result of the demographic shift Terai emerged not simply as the economic heartland of Nepal but also as large labor absorbing areas. In conjunction with growing ethnic politics in Terai, this rapid population growth concentrated in agriculture a new form of agrarian crisis. Regional lopsidedness was accompanied by wider deprivation in Janajati communities of the east or peripheral communities accentuating the rift between the regime and marginalized Nepalis.

CONCLUSION

The preceding discussion has shown that the economic strategy of modernization pursued by various regimes during the last five decades has failed to improve the plight of the common people of Nepal. Additionally, it has contributed to the impoverishment of various segments of the society. Modernization and the rise of a bureaucracy-directed market economy institutionalized earlier social inequities in class terms and sharpened economic disparity. While it would be erroneous to imagine that in Nepal different caste and ethnic groups were hermetically sealed communities organized in a hierarchical order, it would be equally erroneous not to recognize how the marginalization of Dalits and Janajatis became institutionalized during the monarchical period. At the same time, the entire system boosted Kathmandu's economy at the expense of the rest of the country. The modernization theory, which was the ideological premise of the new economic model adopted by the country in the 1950s and the 1960s, stipulated that in developing societies, elites who had the ability to absorb modern values would in turn educate a traditional backward population in the art of managing modern economic development. In reality this implied that Kathmandu-based high caste elites would now supervise economic growth and would regard the rest of the rural low caste

Table 5. Demographic Shift in Various Regions (1952–2001)

Year	Mountains		Hills		Hills and Mountains		Terai		Total
	Number	*% Total Population*	*Number*	*Total Population*	*Number*	*%*	*Number*	*%*	*Total*
1952–1954			53,499,988	64.8	2,906,637	35.2	8,256,625		
1961					5,991,297	63.6	3,421,699	36.4	9,412,996
1971	1,138,610	9.9	6,071,407	52.5	7,210,017	62.4	4,345,966	37.6	11,555,983
1981	1,302,896	8.7	7,163,115	47.7	8,466,011	56.4	6,556,828	43.6	15,022,839
1991	1,443,130	7.8	8,419,889	45.5	9,863,019	53.3	8,628,078	46.7	18,491,097
2001	1,687,859	7.3	10,251,111	44.3	11,938,970	51.6	11,212,453	48.4	23,151,423

Source: Population Monograph Nepal, vol. 1, chapter 2, p. 41, table 2.2. www.cbs.gov.np/Population/Monograph/Chapter%2002%20%20A%20Population%20Size%20 Growth%20and%20Distribution.pdf (12 July 2005).

population as backward; the latter would only obtain benefits through a trickle down effect. But, as elsewhere, this was wishful thinking in Nepal. The results were identical to other countries where such a lopsided strategy only increased income inequality between various segments of the society and bred discontent. The process of impoverishment and marginalization occurred in the agricultural sector because of the lack of an extensive reform that would have brought the lands into the control of tillers. It is clear from our discussion that Nepal's agrarian relationship is structured by an ancient property regime whereby the vast majority of the rural population had little access to economic resources. The most significant and long-term impact of these measures has been the perpetuation of external dependency. Although the roots of external dependency can be traced to the geographical location of the country and global politics in the 1950s, the perpetuation of this unequal relationship is a result of policy choices made by the ruling elites of Nepal. These sent the country into a spiral of perpetual economic crisis.

NOTES

1. Asian Development Bank, 2005, "Nepal: Public Finance Management Assessment," *ADB Strategy and Assessment Program* (December 2005): 1.

2. Surendra R. Devkota, "The Politics of Poverty in Nepal: Structural Analysis of Socioeconomic Development from the Past Five Decades," in *Heidelberg Papers in South Asian and Comparative Politics*, no. 25 (Heidelberg: South Asia Institute, Department of Political Science, University of Heidelberg, February 2005): 5.

3. Sangeeta Thapliyal, "Contesting Mutual Security: India-Nepal Relations," in *Observer Research Foundation Analysis* (New Delhi: ORF, 2005): 2.

4. Leo Rose and Roger Dial, "Can a Ministate Find True Happiness in a World Dominated by Protagonist Powers? [The] Nepal Case," in *Protagonists, Power, and the Third World: Essays on the Changing International System*, Annals of the American Academy of Political and Social Science 386 (November 1969): 89–101.

5. Rose and Dial, "Can a Ministate," 92.

6. Clause 5 of the deal is a case in point. The clause stated, "The Government of Nepal agrees to levy at rates not lower than those for the time being in India, custom duties on imports from and exports to countries outside India. The government of Nepal also agrees to levy on goods produced or manufactured in Nepal which are exported to India, export duty at rates sufficient to prevent their sale in India at prices more favorable than those of goods produced or manufactured in India which are subject to central excise duty."

7. S. D. Muni, "Chinese Arms Pour into Nepal," *Times of India*, 1 September 1988.

8. John W. Garver, "China-India Rivalry in Nepal: The Clash over Chinese Arms Sales," *Asian Survey* 31, no. 10 (October 1991): 956–75.

9. Dhruba Kumar, "Managing Nepal's India Policy?" *Asian Survey* 30, no. 7 (July 1990): 697–710.

10. The Monroe Doctrine, expressed in 1823 by the then-President of the United States James Monroe in his annual State of the Union address, insisted that European powers should no longer colonize the Americas or interfere with the affairs of sovereign nations located in the Americas, such as the United States of America, Mexico, and others. In return, the United States offered to stay neutral in wars between European powers and in wars between a European power and its colonies. In the event of European involvement in any wars in the Americas, the United States would view such action as hostile toward itself. The doctrine implies that the United States considers itself the sole protector of the Americas and opposes involvement of any other countries in the region.

11. The Colombo Plan is an international economic organization created in a cooperative attempt to strengthen the economic and social development of the nations of Southeast Asia and the Pacific, which came into being in 1951. Originally conceived as lasting for a period of six years, the Colombo Plan was extended several times until 1980, when it was extended indefinitely. The organization's headquarters are in Colombo, Sri Lanka. "Colombo Plan," *The Columbia Electronic Encyclopedia*, ©1994, 2000–2005, on Infoplease, http://www.infoplease.com/ce6/history/A0812916.html (20 August 2006).

12. Leo and Dial, "Can a Ministate," 89–101.

13. Narayan Khadka, "U.S. Aid to Nepal in the Cold War Period: Lessons for the Future," *Pacific Affairs* 73, no. 1 (Spring 2000): 77–95.

14. Library of Congress, "Nepal," http://www.country-data.com/cgi-bin/query/r-9115.html (20 August 2006).

15. Narayan Khadka, "Nepal's Stagnant Economy: The Panchayat Legacy," *Asian Survey* 31, no. 8 (August 1991): 694–711.

16. Library of Congress, "Nepal," http://www.country-data.com/cgi-bin/query/r-9115.html (20 August 2006).

17. Devkota, "The Politics of Poverty," 12.

18. Narayan Khadka, "Foreign Aid to Nepal: Donor Motivations in the Post-Cold War Period," *Asian Survey* 37, no. 11 (November 1997): 1044–61.

19. Asian Development Bank, "Nepal: Public Finance," 7.

20. World Bank, *World Development Report 2000/2001: Attacking Poverty* (Washington, DC: World Bank, 2001).

21. Auditor General's comment in the *Kathmandu Post* of 1 October 2001, quoted in Devkota, *The Politics of Poverty*, 12.

22. World Bank, "Poverty in Nepal At the Turn of the Twenty-First Century," report no. 18639-NEP (Washington, DC: The World Bank, 1998): 1.

23. Werner Levi, "Government and Politics of Nepal: I," *Far Eastern Review 21*, no. 18 (December 1952): 190.

24. Nanda R. Srestha, *Landlessness and Migration in Nepal* (Boulder: Westview Press, 1990), 10–16.

25. For example, the transportation network in Nepal in 1951 comprised only one hundred kilometers of railway track, about fifty kilometers of ropeways and approximately four hundred kilometers of motorable roads of which only five kilometers were paved. (See: Sukhdev Shah, "Developing an Economy—Nepal's Experience," *Asian Survey* XXI, no. 10 [October 1981]: 1062).

26. M. C. Regmi, *An Economic History of Nepal, 1846–1951* (Varanasi: Nath, 1988), 26.

27. 39 percent of the total 615 million rupees allocation of the second plan went to the transportation and communication sector. Industry, tourism, and social services cumulatively received second priority. Agriculture was at the bottom of the list of priorities. During the third five-year plan (1965–1970) the transportation and communications sector received priority although industrial and agricultural developments drew the attention of planners and the targeted expenditure was more than 1.6 billion rupees. In the fourth five-year plan (1970–1975), nearly 41.2 percent of targeted expenditure amounting to 3.3 billion rupees was allocated for the infrastructure sector. On the contrary agriculture received 26 percent of the budget.

28. Aran Schloss, "Stages of Development and Uses of Planning," *Asian Survey* 23, no. 10 (October 1983): 1115–27.

29. For example, Blaikie, et al. observe that road construction did not always improve the productive base of the economy (Piers Blaikie, John Cameron, and David Seddon, eds., *Nepal in Crisis: Growth and Stagnation at the Periphery* [Oxford: Clarendon Press, 1980]: 3–4).

30. Stacy Leigh Pigg, "Inventing Social Categories Through Place: Social Representations and Development in Nepal," *Comparative Studies in Society and History* 34, no. 3 (July 1992): 419–513.

31. T. Jamison and Marlaine E. Lockheed, "Participation in Schooling: Determinants and Learning Outcomes," *Economic Development and Cultural Change* 35, no. 2 (January 1987): 279–306; p. 281.

32. Sukhdev Shah, "Developing an Economy—Nepal's Experience," *Asian Survey* XXI, no. 10 (October 1981): 1062.

33. Merrill Goodwill, "Bureaucracy and Bureaucrats: Some Themes Drawn from the Nepal Experience," *Asian Survey* 15, no. 10 (October 1975): 892–95.

34. Library of Congress, "Nepal Education," http://countrystudies.us/nepal/34 .htm (12 August 2006).

35. Shanta Dixit, "Nepal Education in Crisis," *Harvard South Asian Journal* 3, no. 1 (Spring 2005) http://www.harvardsaa.org/saj/news.php?nID=7&pgID=1 (12 August 2006).

36. Kumar, "Managing Nepal's India Policy?" 697–710.

37. M. C. Regmi, "Recent Land Reform Programs in Nepal," *Asian Survey* 1, no. 7 (September 1961): 32–37 (p. 32).

38. SAAPE (South Asia Alliance for Poverty Eradication), *Poverty in South Asia 2003: Civil Society Perspectives* (Kathmandu: SAAPE, 2003): 126.

39. Jagannath Adhikari, "Farmers' Rights to Land: A Crucial Dimension on Livelihood Security," *South Asia Partnership Canada*, 22 November 2004, http://action.web .ca/home/sap/nepal_resources.shtml?x=69984 (6 August 2006).

40. Gorkhana Raj Aryal and Ghan Shyam Awasthi, "Agrarian Reform and Access to Land Resource in Nepal: Present Status and Future Prospective Action," *CERAI (Center for Rural Studies and International Agriculture)*, Valencia, Spain, http://www .cerai.es/fmra/archivo/nepal.pdf (28 July 2006).

41. Shiva Sharma and Bijendra Basnyat, "Nepal: Bonded Labor among Child Workers of Kamaiya System: A Rapid Assessment," International Labor Organization, International Labor Program on the Elimination of Child Labor 2001, http://

www.ilo.org/public/english/standards/ipec/simpoc/nepal/rap/bonded.pdf (15 July 2006).

42. T. Homer-Dixon, "On the Threshold: Environmental Changes as Causes of Acute Conflict," *International Security* 16, no. 2 (Fall 1991): 76–116, quoted in Jugal Bhurtel and Saleem H. Ali, "The Green Roots of Red Rebellion: Environmental Degradation and the Rise of the Maoist Movement in Nepal," 2003, www.uvm.edu/~shali/Maoist.pdf (22 October 2005).

43. Bhurtel and Ali, "The Green Roots of Red Rebellion: Environmental Degradation and the Rise of Maoist Movement in Nepal," 2003, www.uvm.edu/~shali/Maoist.pdf.

44. Ritu Pantha and Bharat Raj Sharma, "Population Size Growth and Distribution," *Population Monograph* 1 (Kathmandu: Central Bureau of Statistics Report, Government of Nepal, 2002).

45. Tunga Bastola and G. C. Radhakrishna, "A Perspective on Population Census 2001," *Population Monograph* 1 (Kathmandu: Central Bureau of Statistics Report, Government of Nepal, 2002).

46. "Nepal and Family Planning: An Overview," *World Health Organization Report*, 2001, http://w3.whosea.org/LinkFiles/Family_Planning_Fact_Sheets_nepal.pdf (12 August 2006).

4

Maoist Insurgency and the Militarization of the Nepali Polity and Society

By any standards, the rise of Maoists as a political force in Nepal between 1996 and 2005 is spectacular. In the first general election of 1991 after the restoration of multiparty democracy a coalition of Maoist forces contested the poll under the banner of the United National People's Front. Only nine out of their seventy candidates were elected. The UNPF emerged as a distant third force in the Nepali parliament with the Nepali Congress and the Communist Party of Nepal (United Marxist-Leninist) emerging as the two largest parliamentary parties securing 110 and 69 seats respectively in a house of 205 representatives.[1] Soon after the electoral debacle, the United People's Front and its underground party organization, the Communist Unity Center, underwent a bewildering process of splits and counter-splits. From among the debris of the Unity Center there emerged a small fraction of Maoists who advocated people's war and subsequently gave a call for insurgency in 1996.[2] Before long they led one of the most successful Communist insurgencies in the world in an era when revolutionary Communism was believed to be safely buried in the quicksand of history.

This chapter explores the reasons behind the spectacular success of such a small fraction of Maoists. Why were they so successful in establishing their political presence? What was their political agenda? What strategies assisted them in spreading their influence and popularizing their political agenda? To what extent would they be successful in achieving their goals? The contemporary political history of Nepal, especially since the beginning of the democratic era in 1991, will be assessed in detail in this chapter to explain the trajectory of the Maoist insurgency.

DEMOCRACY IN NEPAL AND
THE MARGINALIZATION OF MAOISTS (1949–1996)

Comprehending the Communist movement in Nepal requires an understanding of the factional feuds—an ironic but perennial feature of Nepali Communist parties and their leadership. This is so much so that one can paraphrase Marx and write with confidence that the history of hitherto existing Communist politics in Nepal is a history of factional squabbles for the correct political path and ideological purity.[3]

The origin of ideological disputes over the strategy of revolution within the Communist movement of Nepal may be traced back to the political circumstances surrounding the birth of the party. The Communist Party of Nepal came into existence during a clandestine meeting in Calcutta, India, in 1949. At the time of the birth of the Communist Party of Nepal, the Indian Communist movement was passing through a radical revolutionary phase. At the all-India level in 1948, B. T. Ranadive, the newly elected secretary of the Communist Party of India (CPI), gave a call for a revolution. He counseled a strategic combination of peasant insurrection in the countryside and mass insurrection in the cities led by workers. Indian Communists were particularly successful in Telengana, a region located in the largest princely state of British India—namely, Hyderabad—where they developed a strategy of peasant rebellion following from the recently concluded successful Maoist guerilla war in China.

As Communists were planning to organize a revolution from below, the newly independent Indian state, under Nehru and Patel, was slowly recovering from the wounds of partition. Patel and Nehru began consolidating their newly gained power, inherited from the departing British Raj. They could hardly afford to tolerate a Communist revolution in the country and suppressed it violently by deploying Indian troops in Telengana and banning the Communist Party of India until it returned to parliamentary path in 1950.

The Indian experience in 1949 was not an exception. In the immediate aftermath of World War II the whole of Asia experienced unprecedented political turmoil. Old colonial orders were collapsing rapidly. Everywhere Communists were confronting not only their former colonial masters, but also local nationalists in the struggle to capture state power. From China to Korea, Vietnam to Malaysia, Indonesia to India, Communists were participating in or providing direction to peasant revolutions.

These revolutionary movements all over Asia in general, and India in particular, left indelible marks on Nepali Communist politics. In the wake of the collapse of colonial rule in South Asia in 1947, Nepal was also going through a massive political upheaval. The Nepali Congress Party, a centrist political formation, committed to multiparty democracy and ideologies of democratic socialism, was planning political insurrections against the Rana regime. The Nepali monarch, who was practically a prisoner in the hands of his hereditary Rana prime minister, was openly with the rebels (see chapter 1 for details). However, the geo-strategic location of Nepal is such that no Nepali revolution could succeed without the tacit or active support of the Indian government.

The government of India was keen on promoting stability in this crucial buffer state between India and China. For India, this strategic need became particularly pressing at the beginning of 1950 as Communist China was expanding its hold over Tibet—a former quasi-independent vassal state of imperial China. The Indian government thus offered lukewarm support to the Nepali Congress and negotiated with the ruling Rana regime for a power sharing deal between the Ranas, the king, and the democratic forces. This came to be known as the Delhi Accord of 1951.

The emerging Communist movement in Nepal witnessed ideological differences within its rank and file on the most fundamental issue: how to develop a clear Marxist identification of the political power configuration of the state in Nepal. This involved an analysis relationship among three crucial political forces in Nepali politics: the monarchy, the Nepali Congress Party, and Indian influence.

Nepali Communists were distrustful of the Indian government. As soon as the Delhi Accord was announced, the Communist Party of Nepal denounced it as a betrayal of revolution. The Communists soon raised the demand for the formation of a constituent assembly elected on the basis of universal franchise by the people of Nepal. The monarchy was lukewarm in its approach to the subject despite their formal commitment toward such an arrangement in the royal declaration on 14 February 1951.

In the early 1950s, soon after the restoration of monarchy, following nearly a hundred years of patrimonial rule, Nepal experienced an emerging power struggle between the monarchy and nascent party political formations. The king/monarchy evaded the issue of transition toward a formal constitutional democracy while the largest political party, the Nepali Congress, demanded a clear constitutional framework for this transition. However, the Nepali Congress would be hopelessly mired in factional disputes between two brothers, M. P. Koirala and B. P. Koirala, jostling for the leadership of the party and the cabinet formed by the crown.[4]

Unlike the Nepali Congress, the Communists could develop a coherent response to the situation. In 1950 they formed a United Front with like-minded political formations and peasant associations. They even supported the sudden military putsch led by K. I. Singh, a leader of the peasant association in 1951, but could hardly play an effective role in that rebellion. For this rather adventurist posturing, the Communist Party faced a political ban by the monarchy. By this time a critical ideological fault-line was already

emerging within the Nepali Communist movement, which became evident
in their first clandestine party conference in Nepal in January 1954. In the
conference Communists announced their uncompromising struggle against
the "feudal regime" in Nepal but could not effectively formulate a political
strategy of revolution. The CPN (UM-L) party's official website frankly
states that "the First Party-Congress could not concretize political goal and
working-orientation (Karya Disha)" as Pushpa Lal and Keshar Jung Rayamajhi proposed two conflicting party lines.[5]

In 1956 the Nepali government withdrew the ban when the Communists formally agreed to work within a political system headed by the
monarchy. Soon the party faced serious debates over its political programs
and line of action. While the new secretary of the party, Keshar Jung Rayamajhi, was in favor of cooperation with the political regime, Pushpa Lal, a
radical founding member of the party, argued for uncompromising struggle against the monarchy in alliance with other democratic forces. The
party sought to remove these differences in 1957 in their first open conference in Kathmundu. However, the conference produced an odd compromise. It allowed Keshar Jung Rayamajhi to continue as the secretary, but
adopted Pushpa Lal's radical slogan of establishing a republic with the immediate aim of installing a constituent assembly. This was really a superfi-
cial patch-up as discontent over party leadership simmered within the rank
and file.[6]

This disunity within the party and the lack of direction in spreading its
message became tellingly evident when King Mahendra called for elections
on 1 February 1958. Although the party's official resolution was for a constituent assembly and not a monarchical parliament, the central committee
of the party decided to participate in the election. It performed poorly in
the election, winning only four seats out of the forty-seven it contested. The
Nepali Congress swept the poll and the king invited its leader, B. P. Koirala,
to form the government.

Throughout the brief spell of parliamentary government, the Communist
Party of Nepal steadfastly opposed the Congress government. It constantly
campaigned against the supposed pro-India orientation of the Congress
government. For example, when on one occasion the government imported
vegetable oil from India, the CPN argued that this was a ploy to destroy the
independence of Nepal through mass poisoning and an attack on the indigenous ghee industry. The party followed a policy of highlighting the
achievements of Communist China and suffered a political setback when a
border clash between Nepal and China resulted in the death of a Nepali officer.[7] Although the party emerged as a coherent opposition, it could not
decide on a clear political program. Indeed, when the king dismissed the
Nepali Congress government, General Secretary Keshar Jung Rayamajhi,
who was in Moscow to attend a conference of sixty Communist parties, wel-

comed it in a political statement. In contrast, Pushpa Lal called for a convention of all democratic parties for the end of what he described as military terror.[8] In March 1961, the party held a conference in Darbhanga, India. The conference witnessed the emergence of three different political strategic lines. The party leader Keshar Jung Rayamajhi proposed to accept the dissolution of parliament and the establishment of royal-guided democracy. Pushpa Lal and his faction argued for the restoration of the parliament and a joint movement with the Nepali Congress. Mohan Bikram Singh, a radical leader, called for the election of a constituent assembly. The majority of the party members voted for this proposal but the plenum adopted Keshar Jung Rayamajhi's thesis as official policy. This obviously meant that there emerged two irreconcilable differences within the party. These different ideological camps went ahead with their own programs.

Keshar Jung Rayamajhi decided to launch a civil disobedience program in the country for the restoration of fundamental rights of citizens, but did not endorse the demand aiming at the removal of monarchy from power. His opponents planned a third convention of the party at Varanasi. In this convention, three theses were proposed for future political action. While Pushpa Lal and Mohan Bikram Singh stuck to their respective earlier proposals, Tulsi Amatya, the new general secretary of the party, called for "supreme sovereign parliament." The party accepted Tulsi Amatya's proposal, but with the idea of national democracy as the ultimate goal of the party. Pushpa Lal disagreed and called for a people's democracy.

In Nepal, the Communist movement witnessed further fragmentation based on these conflicting ideological lines. By 1968, Pushpa Lal left the original party and formed his own party with the aim of establishing a disciplined revolutionary organization dedicated toward abolishing the "feudal military aristocratic" monarchical regime. This party could hardly become an effective political force in Nepal. In 1971, there took place an attempt by the leadership of the party to establish a central nucleus to unite several Communist groups but it resulted in more fundamental splits within the party. Pushpa Lal refused to join the effort. He invited others to join his party. He also favored cooperation with the Nepali Congress in the struggle for a democratic regime. Meanwhile two other leaders—Manmohan Adhikary and Mohan Bikram Singh—could not agree with each other on ideological grounds. Mohan Bikram Singh argued that these differences arose because of their divergent approaches toward the applicability of Mao's thought in Nepal. Manmohan Adhikary claimed that Maoists refused to accept his proposal of a struggle for a constituent assembly.

The move toward a united party came from outside the central leadership. On 22 April 1971, a Jhapa district committee in eastern Nepal, inspired by Naxalites in the neighboring districts of Bengal, adopted a political resolution of launching a movement for the capture of state power.

These young Communists could hardly find support among established Communist politicians. Indeed, the established Maoist politicians such as Mohan Bikram Singh condemned their political action as "terrorist anarchism."

While their rebellion was ruthlessly suppressed by the state, Jhapali Communists, as they were known, in June 1974 gave a call for coordination among Communist revolutionaries. In June 1975, they organized a party conference of all district level workers and established the all Nepal Communist Coordination Committee. Gradually, these Communist coordination committees gained support from other localized movements and in 1978 they were able to establish the Communist Party of Nepal (Marxist-Leninist) [CPN (M-L)] in December 1978.[9]

The CPN (M-L) attracted most of the localized Communist movements in Nepal. Learning lessons from their rather romantic political adventure in 1974, the CPN (M-L) combined underground movements with opposition within the "partyless" *panchayat* system through participation in *panchayat* elections. They adopted a flexible political strategy of contesting elections for *panchayats* on an individual basis and then providing a coherent opposition within the national *panchayat*. Indeed, the party also broadened its struggle by linking everyday movement of the people with wider political questions.[10] Thus the party sought to practice politics that would combine electoral politics with underground resistance.

In 1989 at the party conference it was decided to develop further unity among Communists to launch a struggle for multiparty democracy. This process led to the formation of the United Left Front. The United Left Front comprised various factions, including the CPN (M-L), CPN-Marxist, CPN (Fourth Congress), Nepal Worker and Peasant Party, CPN-Varma, CPN-Amatya, and CPN-Manandhar. These last two factions were loyal to two individual charismatic Communist leaders Amatya and Manandhar.

The United Left Front played a pivotal role in organizing the pro-democracy "People's Movement" (*Jana Andolan*) in Nepal in 1990. As this movement gained widespread popularity, the process of unification of Communist parties gathered further momentum. In January 1991 the CPN (M-L) and CPN-Marxist came together and a new unified Communist party named CPN (UM-L) came into existence.[11] After the formation of the CPN (UM-L), another smaller fraction, the CPN-Amatya, joined the unified platform. As a consequence the CPN (UM-L) emerged as the largest parliamentary Marxist outfit. In the 1991 general election the CPN (UM-L) became the second largest political platform in Nepal, and in 1994 the CPN (UM-L) was the first Communist party to form an elected government under a constitutional monarchy. Thus the bitter experience of political failure of the revolutionary line in 1974 slowly pushed the largest segment of Nepali Communists to move toward open democratic politics. Indeed, the idea of a multiparty people's democracy appeared to be a coherent political thesis that the party developed in order to formulate its strategies in the post-Cold War political situation. In line with this thesis, many within the party now favor renaming the organization simply as the Communist Party of Nepal.[12]

While the process of unification of non-Maoist or post-Maoist Marxist political groups led to the birth of a wider mass-based Marxist parliamentary party, this should not be viewed as the only effort of the Communists to expand its influence within the populace. Since 1974 the Maoists had also sought to form a viable political party based on a sustainable programmatic unity. Maoists under the leadership of Mohan Bikram Singh and Nirmal Lama formed a new party called the Communist Party of Nepal (Fourth Convention) at that time. They sought to develop a wider popular movement against the monarchical regime with the aim of transforming the movement into an open armed insurrection. In 1979 when the king announced a referendum for a transition to multiparty democracy, this party played a crucial role in bringing left unity to defeat the monarchy-sponsored *panchayat* regime. Indeed, all factions of the Communist movement in Nepal and the Nepali Congress worked together to defeat the royal *panchayat* regime.

Nonetheless, as the *panchayat* regime emerged victorious through controversial methods in the referendum, the democratic movement suffered a setback (see chapter 1). The defeat led to an inner party feud whereby the general secretary of the party, Nirmal Lama, had to quit for his views in favor of participating in electoral process.[13] Nirmal Lama continued to argue in favor of penetrating the newly reformed *panchayat* system constituted through secret ballot and adult franchise. Mohan Bikram Singh was in favor of shunning the path of electoral battle. Their differences became more pronounced in 1979 as a consequence of changes within the leadership in the Chinese Communist Party, following Den Xiao Ping's assumption of the leadership of China. Nirmal Lama recognized this new Chinese leadership but Mohan Bikram Singh branded it as revisionist. In such circumstances, with the deepening of ideological divisions, the party split in 1984.

These fractional feuds between Maoists did not stop with this split. Indeed, soon after Mohan Bikram Singh formed his own party, CPN (Masal), Mohan Vaidya (*nom de guerre* Kiran—"sun rays"), a colleague of Mohan Bikram, moved ahead and floated a new forum called Mashal. In Nepali, both these words mean "torch," but they were spelled differently by different groups of Maoist revolutionaries in order to distinguish one group from other. Interestingly, two significant proponents of the current people's war came from these two different parties called *Masal* and *Mashal*. While Baburam Bhattarai, the ideologue of the current people's war group, was with Mohan Bikram Singh, the current party chairman Pushpa Kumar Dahal (*nom de guerre* Prachanda—"mighty") was with Mohan Vaidya's Masal. In

1984, Nepali Maoists in the Mashal group became members of the Revolutionary Internationalist Movement (RIM)[14] that actually brought them into contact with a global conglomeration of Maoist forces including the Communist Party of Peru later known as Shining Path. This relationship obviously impacted upon the later ideological formulation of the CPN (M).

In 1990, when a mass upsurge against the monarchical regime began, these Maoist factions came together in a new political formation called the Communist Party of Nepal (Unity Center) under the leadership of "Comrade Prachanda." Mohan Bikram Singh retained his party identity, but his former comrade Baburam Bhattarai joined the new party. More importantly, they formed a wider political front that came to be known as the Samyukta Rastrya Jana Andolan (or the United National People's Movement—UNPM). The UNPM joined the pro-democracy movement once it gained momentum, but rejected the new constitution as surrender to the crown.[15]

This new political formation the CPN (Unity Center) fought the 1991 election under the banner of the UNPM, their open legally recognized organization and secured nine seats with 352,000 votes (4.83 percent of polled votes).[16] They carved out a base in mid-western Nepal comprising Rolpa and Rukum districts where they won two seats. In May 1992 the party promoted a violent but successful general strike in Nepal. Yet as they started experimenting within the newly created democratic set-up, the Nepali Congress government unleashed a process of massive repression on the Maoist cadres in their core areas of influence in Rolpa and Rukum.

As the repression of the ruling party took a serious form, it triggered inner party debates over the correct political strategy. While a faction of Maoists supported participation in the parliamentary election, radicals based on their Rolpa and Rukum experiences stuck to the line of people's war. Soon the CPN (Unity Center) and the UNPM witnessed a further split and from its debris emerged the new political party, which named itself the CPN (Maoist) under the leadership of Prachanda, while the UNPM under the leadership of Baburam Bhattarai functioned as its open public forum.[17]

This new name of CPN (Maoist) was an ideological departure from earlier revolutionary Marxist tradition. Previous revolutionary political formations referred to their ideology as Marx, Lenin, and Mao's thought. By borrowing from the new political tradition of the Shining Path movement in Peru through the RIM, Nepali Communists rechristened themselves as Maoists. This new political tradition privileged Mao over previous ideological founders of Communist politics and at the same time considered the military strategy of conducting guerilla warfare as fundamental to the revolution in Nepal. Under the new Maoist theoretical formulation, political transformation in Nepal could only be achieved through a violent, protracted people's war. In this context they could draw upon an existing tradition of armed rebellions and revolutionary Communist movements in Nepal.

Yet this adoption of a radical line was a reflection of a politically desperate act by the leaders trapped in a hopeless situation. The UNPM under Baburam Bhattarai sought recognition from the election commission as the inheritor of the earlier organization. But the election commission denied this recognition. In such a desperate moment of political isolation, with the ongoing repression in their base areas, the new party decided to adopt a policy of protracted people's war in 1995.

Thus there came into existence two different strands in the Nepali Communist movement ranging from support and consolidation of the parliamentary Marxist movement on the one hand to people's war launched in the mid-western region of Nepal on the other. Both these strands were products of specific historic circumstances. The suppression of radical revolutionary insurrections actually compelled the CPN (UM-L) to move toward open democratic politics, while political isolation in democratic political circumstances compelled Maoists to move toward their desperate political gamble called the people's war.

There exists a third force within the Nepali Communist movement. There were individual Maoists who ideologically supported the concept of people's war but argued that the timing was wrong. However, many would describe their dilemma as that of those who could not join the people's war due to personal rivalries and were outsmarted in their own political game.

THE CRISIS OF GOVERNANCE AND THE ORIGINS OF THE PEOPLE'S WAR

In 1995, when a group of Communists decided to gamble their political fortunes and pursue the violent path of the people's war, no one thought this desperate strategy would pay off so well. If their capacity to articulate the yearnings of a segment of the marginalized Nepali population can be credited as a factor in their success, the other, and perhaps the more important factor, lies within the political establishment in Kathmandu—namely, the intense power struggle and the consequent crises of governance at various levels of state. The coming of quasi-monarchical democracy was thus marked by confusions within the Nepali political establishment. This became more pronounced as no social ideology existed that could legitimize the ruling authority. The notion of the crown as the guarantor of a unique Nepali Hindu identity—represented by a constructed ethno-religious hierarchy—had already collapsed on the quotidian reality of social and political modernity in Nepal. Yet it lingered on as a political institutional structure because of the hasty compromise negotiated by political parties with the palace establishment at the end of the movement for democracy in 1990. More importantly, the constitution left too many emergency powers in the hands of crown. The king also remained the supreme commander of the army. This transformed the constitution into a quasi-monarchical democracy rather than full-fledged democracy.

The retention of the power in the hands of monarch was an anachronistic compromise as the movement for democracy in 1990 further removed the legitimacy of the crown as ruler in Nepali society. However, the constitution that replaced the crown's authority could hardly include in the new political system those who were on the wrong side of deeper social faultlines in Nepali society. Indeed, as has been pointed out, the "first past the post system" has created a majoritarian ethos in politics that benefited only larger parties headed by upper caste elites.[18] Similarly, the unitary system of governance has failed to provide representation to the complex social mosaic of Nepal. The emphasis on Nepali as a national language has alienated many who speak local languages. While these grievances matured into political movements, in the absence of a defining hegemonic ideology of the political system, ruling elites often used violence to intimidate political opponents and even those who were in parliamentary opposition. This situation has prevailed in Nepal because of the clashing political agenda of powerful actors in the Nepali political system.

From the beginning, among different actors involved in the growing power struggles within the political establishment, the palace had a clear political agenda. It was reluctant to surrender its political power and if given an opportunity it would have preferred to return to the older political system where the crown was the active sovereign political authority. Political parties had to keep an eye on the palace so that they could prevent such a relapse into monarchical authoritarianism. However, political parties, quite naturally, were divided among themselves in terms of ideological orientations. Two principal political parties—the Nepali Congress and the CPN (UM-L) were separated by vast ideological differences in their understanding of multiparty democracy. For the Congress, a constitutional multiparty democracy was an end in itself. To the CPN (UM-L), despite its declared commitment to multiparty democracy, it was the first step in the transitional process toward people's democracy. This ideological difference toward multiparty democracy had wider ramifications for the respective political activities of two parties.

The commitment to multiparty democracy on the part of the CPN (UM-L) produced a serious ideological crisis for the party. The CPN (UM-L) officially proposed to work within multiparty democracy under a constitutional monarch. This meant that the party had to gradually restrict its underground political activities that constituted a critical aspect of the party's activity from the Jhapa movement in 1974 to the people's movement in

1990. This revolutionary activism had once attracted young radicals to the party, yet such revolutionary tradition now proved to be a liability. Despite their tradition of participation in electoral process, the contradiction between the rhetoric of revolution and the quotidian reality of professing loyalty to the constitutional monarchy could hardly be resolved by the CPN (UM-L). In spite of being the largest Marxist political party in Nepal with a wide network of politically committed cadres and persistent pro-poor orientation, the CPN (UM-L) is hard-pressed to preserve its mass base and convince the cadres of the need to work within the multiparty democracy to achieve their long-term goals of a socialist people's democracy.

As a consequence, in the initial stages they had to combine a strategy of parliamentary politics and street-level extra-parliamentary agitations marked by strikes, *bandhs* (forced shutdown of normal life), and sit-ins. This created a political culture of street protests that had potentialities of degenerating into violence. This also created a political space for extra-constitutional politics espoused by Maoists. Indeed, during street-level agitation Maoists had an advantage over the CPN (UM-L). Maoists could potentially win the CPN (UM-L)'s mass base by adopting the course of direct action without caring for its law and order implications. The CPN (UM-L) had to stave off the Maoists' threat from below, while at the same time they had to contend with the Nepali Congress within the parliamentary system and defeat them in elections. This was a hard task because the Nepali Congress quite justifiably claimed that they had achieved multiparty democracy through long struggle.

Nonetheless, the Nepali Congress had its own problems. It was internally weakened by inner-party personal rivalries and factional feuds. Since the restoration of a democratic political system, the party witnessed unsavory fights among K. P. Bhattarai, Girija Prasad Koirala, and Sher Bahadur Deuba, three stalwarts of the Nepali Congress. These rivalries were products of the clientelist political processes, which are often the characteristics of weak states. In such cases, politics is primarily concerned with the distribution of patronage among putative client bases in return for political support. It would be wrong to suggest that ideology did not play a critical role in the movement for democracy. More importantly, it would be cynical to perceive the Nepali Congress and parliamentary Communists as people devoid of ideological orientation. However, almost all observers of Nepali politics agree that the political culture of governance in Nepal under the Nepali Congress took a critical turn towards a clientelist pattern of mobilization. Borrowing from political analysis of Mexico by Brachet-Marquez,[19] the term clientelism is used here to refer "to the structuring of political power through networks of informal dyadic relations that link individuals of unequal power in relationships of exchange. In clientelistic structures of authority, power is vested in the top individual (the boss, sovereign, or head of clan) who personally decides how to distribute resources according to personal preferences." This clientelist mobilization had its roots in the history of state formation in Nepal.

For many years Nepal was under a patrimonial political system. Nepali rulers divided opposition by distributing favors through patron-client networks and thus creating a tradition of competition among powerful political entrepreneurs for access to the resource distribution mechanism of the state. Locally dominant elites generally supported the ruling powers in return for access to governmental resources. Among ruling powers, dominant figures, while competing for more power, tended to reward their followers by distributing favors—often transgressing limits of officially allocated funds. Therefore personalized networks of influence and intense competition for resources characterized the system. The Nepali Congress as a political party was integrally related to this political culture of the patrimonial state. Once the Nepali Congress leaders gained access to political power, party stalwarts clashed with each other and tried to expand their personal bases in competition for the position of prime minister. How did this power struggle endanger the nascent democracy? The answer may be found in the political practice of the Nepali Congress and its attempt to penetrate local politics in order to compete with the well-organized cadre-based CPN (UM-L).

In local politics the Nepali Congress inherited the legacy of an authoritarian *panchayat* regime. The *panchayat* regime in practice recruited powerful local political entrepreneurs to run the system. These leaders constituted local elites who, in many instances, belonged to economically and socially dominant families in the villages. As a change of guard at Kathmandu took place, these leaders looked toward the new regime of the Nepali Congress for support and accommodation within the patronage distribution structure. The party leaders heartily embraced these local power brokers. The party collectively and party leaders individually tried their level best to recruit former leaders of the monarchical *panchayat* system at the grassroots level. As local elites and former supporters of the *panchayat* system switched loyalties, leaders of the Nepali Congress not only expanded their mass base, but also entered into the complex politics of localities. They unwittingly intervened in favor of rural elites against the rural poor who had suffered under the same elites during the *panchayat* period. It must be noted here that we use the terms *elite* and *poor* deliberately in order to avoid giving the impression of rigid social stratification along rich/poor lines.

This policy generated new tension in the Maoist strongholds of Rolpa and Rukum districts. Soon after the formation of the Nepali Congress government, local politicians allied with the Nepali Congress in Rolpa did not allow the opposition to file nominations for local development committee elections. They captured positions in these institutions through the coercion. Any opposition to their activities was suppressed by the police, who arrested local youths indiscriminately and made little distinction between regular party political activities and violent confrontations.[20]

For Maoists, this was their battle for survival. In the early 1990s Maoists were a desperate political group on the verge of extinction. Their situation became even more difficult when they were denied the opportunity to consolidate their bases in Rolpa and Rukum through the democratic process. Not surprisingly, Maoists found the path of people's war a more attractive proposition. Indeed, the combination of repression and the indiscriminate use of force by local elites affiliated with the Nepali Congress slowly drove Maoists toward violent political struggle.

By early 1995 the Maoists were preparing themselves for sustained guerilla activities. This was reflected in the internal political transformation within the party. The third plenum of the Maoist political formation in March 1995 adopted the new name CPN (Maoist). Even under Mao in China, the government and the party styled its revolutionary thoughts as Marx-Lenin-Mao's thought. The locution "Maoism" was earlier used as a descriptive category by people external to the movement. Non-Maoist Marxist critiques often used the word as a pejorative label. Hence the use of the word "Maoist" in the official nomenclature of the party reflects the ideological influence of Shining Path of Peru—a self-styled Maoist political configuration.

As Nepali Maoists embraced ideologies of the Shining Path in Peru in September 1995, they prepared a document entitled "Plan for the historic initiation of the people's war."[21] They started a political campaign to reeducate their party members along this line, which was code-named the Sija campaign after the two mountain peaks in Rolpa and Rukum called Sisne and Jaljala.[22] A critical component of Maoist preparation for people's war was the readiness to sanction violence to secure a political goal. Maoists ideologically glorified violence as a means to end an exploitative social system. Not surprisingly, as they developed this ideological campaign, throughout the second half of 1994, local Maoists clashed with supporters of the Nepali Congress in Rolpa.

In order to suppress the Maoists, Nepali Congress leader and home minister Khum Bahadur Khadka, noted for his own violent predilections, ordered a massive police operation named "Operation Romeo" in 1995. The Nepali Congress used such police operations for several reasons: first, to assure their local supporters that they were powerful enough to provide protection; secondly, they were mindful of the fact that the crown controlled the army and thus their best bet was the police which were now being infiltrated by the Nepali Congress supporters; and finally, the leaders of the Nepali Congress wanted to demonstrate that a Maoist challenge to their political position would not be tolerated. Individuals also played a crucial role in accelerating such conflicts. Beside the home minister Khadka, Prime

Minister Girija Prasad Koirala was a noted anti-Communist. Both of them were the architects of police repression. Police violence was a heaven-sent opportunity to Maoists. The wanton atrocities by police against rural people enabled Maoists to recruit local youth. Maoist leader Baburam Bhattarai, in an interview with a Nepali newspaper in December 1995, claimed that fifteen hundred policemen and a specially trained commando unit had "let loose a reign of terror against the poor peasants." He also alleged that thousands between the age of twelve and seventy had been arrested and "most of them have been subjected to inhuman torture." Furthermore:

> An eighteen-year old girl from Gam VDC was raped in Sulichour police station; eight girls from Oowa VDC were stripped to nudity and tortured with Sisnu Pani. Numerous houses of poor peasants in Kotgaon VDC have been set ablaze and there has been indiscriminate ransacking and looting of properties of common people by the ruling party hoodlums under the protection of the police force. More than ten thousand rural youths, out of a population of two hundred thousand for the whole district, have been forced to flee their homes and take shelter in remote jungles.[23]

Maoists survived the local turf war. This is largely due to the topography and demographic composition of Rukum and Rolpa. Surrounded by hills and forests, this region constituted an ideal location for guerilla struggle. Demographically, these areas were primarily inhabited by Janajatis mainly belonging to Kham Magar communities. They resented the domination of upper caste elites of Kathmandu and at the same time reformists and ethnic activists among them sought to emulate their practice. Prior to the rise of the Maoists, an ethno-cultural movement was present in the region. The movement was weak, but this sense of distinctive identity provided the Maoists with a background upon which they could build their propaganda. The use of regionally specific ethno-religious cultural traditions by Maoists had enabled them to strike a sympathetic chord among Magars. The very adoption of Sija as the code-name of their operation and their erection of the martyrs' column actually indicated Maoists' ability to appropriate local cultural idioms.[24]

The Communist Party of Nepal (Maoists) identified the mid-western hills of the Rolpa and Rukum districts as the critical geo-strategic landmass where they could form their base area. However, they also sought to orchestrate an all-Nepal action as a diversionary tactic in order to avoid the attention of the police and central state. As Pushpa Kumar Dahal noted in an interview:

> [the] West (i.e., the mid-west of the country) is the key region for the People's War. But we also recognized that we cannot wage the People's War only in the Western part, because the ruling class is very powerful. They have a powerful

army, powerful communications system and all these things. . . . Therefore, we concluded that we should initiate "People's War" from different parts of the country.[25]

In accordance with this plan on 4 February 1996, Baburam Bhattarai, the leader of the UNPF, the public wing of the party, submitted a forty-point memorandum to Prime Minister Sher Bahadur Deuba, along with two other members (see appendix 2). The deputation warned that if appropriate steps were not taken to meet these demands before 17 February, his party would declare people's war. Sher Bahadur Deuba ignored these demands and went on an official tour to India. This obviously provoked the CPN (Maoist) party and they started their insurgency on 13 February 1996. It may also be the case that the submission of demands was a propaganda ploy, and that Maoists had already decided on their course of action.

From the perspective of political propaganda, the forty-point memo was not a wish list of Maoists. Rather, the manifesto sought to weave a patriotic consensus and a multiclass alliance of cross-segments of the population behind their political agenda. The demand list submitted by Baburam Bhattarai was a rehash of the election manifesto of the UNPF in the 1991 general election. In many ways, these demands were also those of the broad spectrum of leftist political activists in Nepal and thus Maoists could create a wide-ranging program through which they could communicate their ideas to ordinary Nepali citizens.

The first section of the demands charter was highly nationalistic and called for revision of various treaties with India, the adoption of a policy of economic self-reliance, and the preservation of the cultural distinctiveness of Nepal. Maoists repeatedly claimed that "Indian expansionist designs" were the most crucial factor in the underdevelopment of Nepal. Baburam Bhattarai articulated this in no uncertain terms when he decried "Indian expansionism" as the "agent of various forms of higher imperial power" in South Asia.[26] This emphasis on India as the arch-villain is not surprising. In Nepal, all political actors, with the exception of the Nepali Congress, periodically indulged in anti-Indian political propaganda. Maoists were thus trying to tap in to the existing political culture of India-bashing. Maoists also apprehended that India could intervene if the CPN (M) appeared to be winning their people's war. So they were ideologically and psychologically preparing the ground for such resistance.

The second section of the manifesto was a criticism of the government and contained the most serious proposals for political reforms, such as the creation of a constituent assembly, adoption of secularism, bringing the army and bureaucracy under the control of an elected representative of the people, the release of political prisoners, and regional autonomy for ethnic minority areas. This section proposed sweeping reforms in the Nepali political system aiming at the establishment of a republic. Secularism as an ideological tool was adopted to end the domination of a Hindu monarchical government that had initiated and sustained the constructed caste structure of Nepali society. This demand obviously had the potential to endear them to Dalits and ethnic minorities. In a poly-ethnic plural society like Nepal, the politicization of ethnic divisions had occurred with the expansion of democracy. Indeed, Janajatis had already started demanding the end of what they termed *Bahunbad*, or Brahminical Hindu domination. By raising the demand for territorial autonomy for "oppressed nationalities," Maoists were trying to address ethnic grievances by promising to create autonomous regions within a greater Nepal. In so doing, they planned to win over Janajatis to the support of a people's war.

The third section contained their economic ideas, and highlighted radical land reforms under the slogan "land to the tiller," state-led rapid industrialization, a minimum wage for workers and subsidies for farming implements, proper compensation for natural disasters, universal health care, and free education. This section was not especially innovative, since most left parties in Nepal had proposed such changes, which they failed to implement due to international pressure and inbuilt structural constraints within the Nepali society and polity.

Yet it would be wrong to assume that the Maoists were successful because of their ability to interpret the political mood of Nepali society, although that played its part. Maoists had an advantage both ideologically and strategically. Ideologically they rejected the system, and strategically they sought to undermine it by organizing armed insurrection against political elites badly divided among themselves. This insurrection gained ground among those who felt they had been left out of the system. To the disenfranchised population violence was not a new phenomenon but an everyday reality. However, undoubtedly in the course of counterinsurgency measures violence became an institutionalized mode of political transaction in Nepal in which it was the poor who suffered most.

THE LANDLORD-POLICE ALLIANCE AND THE POPULAR CULTURE OF PEASANT RESISTANCE

Nothing would be farther from the truth than to represent Maoist insurgency as a successful plot implemented by a handful of Communist revolutionaries. Such analyses would deny agency to various segments of peasant participants in the movement in making their political statements. Indeed, the peasant perception of the state critically informed their opinion about Maoists too. From 1951 onward the Nepali peasantry encountered the apparatus of the state in everyday life through the development bureaucracy. Nepal experienced a rapid expansion of the centralized bureaucracy after 1951 when the first phase of experiments with democratization began in Nepal. Since then the bureaucracy has been used for the purpose of modernizing the economy and the restructuring of rural society. These bureaucrats ran everyday administration from district headquarters and implemented development projects in the countryside.[27] During the *panchayat* era, bureaucrats enjoyed a wide range of powers that affected the everyday life of peasants. The peasant experience of interaction with bureaucrats had not always been free from the undercurrent of tension. This has often to do with the way bureaucrats exercised power. Noted Nepali ethnographer, Kamal R. Adhikary, then a researcher at University of Texas–Austin, records in his fieldnotes a typical incident during his visit to a village with a *panchayat* secretary—a rather formidable local official—in 1987–1988:

> When I went to Madanpur with the Panchayat Secretary we ate our morning meal at a Magar house. Before leaving the house I asked the host if I could pay for the food. The host did not say anything and I gave Rs. 5 as a token payment. At this Panchayat secretary was very annoyed. He told me that I did not have to pay. He added that I was there just once, it was easy for me to pay, but he would go to the village again and again and it would not be possible for him to pay. I could not understand his reasoning. He was given a salary for his job, and on the top of that per diem. He wanted to save that by not paying his meal.[28]

Adhikary noted that it was a common custom for officials to take advantage of the village population. Such behavior, coupled with the non-implementation of government programs and false claims and reports about the completion of programs, generated skepticism and latent hostility among the rural population about the state and its representatives. Adhikary himself notes that the stoic silence of villagers about such abuse was gradually changing into active criticism.[29] In other words, rural peoples' awareness of such abuse was changing. In collective popular consciousness bureaucrats were increasingly appearing as burdensome outsiders whose actions were detrimental to rural interests.

In our description here, the tension between the rural population and government officials refers to two different actors: villagers and bureaucrats. Neither are homogenous categories. Both bureaucrats and villagers were highly internally stratified categories. Within rural societies there were latent tensions between relatively affluent and poor, between social groups marginalized on the basis of caste, ethnicity, and gender. Everyday life in rural areas thus encompassed a complex negotiation of power on behalf of marginalized social groups.

A sizeable section of rural poor in Nepal belong to ethnic minority, or Janajati and Dalit communities. These groups had to bear the triple burden of social, economic, and political marginalization. This had obviously impacted upon these people in such a manner that once radical political parties, NGOs, and social movement groups became active on such issues, the popular consciousness developed a new mode of resistance.

These identities involving class, ethnicity, caste, and gender are complex. It would be wrong to imagine such identities as sharply defined and thus waiting to be mobilized by outsiders. Rather, these identities assume different shapes in interaction with various forms of ongoing political, social, and cultural exchange of ideas at local, national, and global levels to which these villagers were increasingly exposed during the democracy era.

The documentation of the *Kamaiya* liberation movement is a case in the point. Debt bondage is a crucial phenomenon of agricultural labor service in the far western regions of Terai in Nepal. *Kamaiya* is a Tharu word, which, according to Tatsuro Fujikura, indicates the position of a man in the intrahousehold division of labor where he carries out physically demanding work. Despite the complexity surrounding the real use of the term in Tharu, it became synonymous with debt bondage in Nepal. Most of these bonded workers belonged to Tharu Janajatis and in many instances worked for high caste Hindus. Indeed, in many ways the Tharu identity had been constructed out of morass of diverse sociolinguistic groups inhabiting the region centering on the notion of loss of land to hill immigrants.[30]

According to local Tharu oral tradition, in the early 1960s, when high caste Hindu migrants from the hill areas began settling in the rich fertile lands of the low plains, known as the Terai, they evicted Tharus from their land. In five districts of Dang, Banke, Kailali, Bardiya, and Kanchanpur, about 450 km west of the capital, Kathmandu, the Tharu activists claim that false loan documents were prepared and procured which showed land as collateral. In the process, many Tharus lost the land they had farmed for generations. These Tharus were now compelled to work on the agricultural land they used to own until they had repaid the supposed loans. Few could clear their debts as the landlords kept increasing the rate of loan interest every year. Thus the *Kamaiya* system kept many Tharu men and women in perpetual debt. This obviously did not imply that all Tharus were transformed into bonded workers but many within the community became so, and they were led by Tharu activists from elite backgrounds.

From 1990 a new movement for the abolition of *Kamaiya* practices emerged. This movement, popularly known as the Kamaiya Liberation Movement, was led by the organization known as Backward Society Education or BASE in 1985. From 1990, it operated as an NGO and established nearly 130 branches throughout Nepal. The leaders of the movement also organized a separate outfit known as the Kamaiya Mukti Parichalan Samity. Soon after the restoration of formal democracy in Nepal, the International Labor Organization (ILO) and the U.S. Department of Labor tried to organize target projects among bonded workers. The U.S.AID-led Rapti Integrated Rural Development Project played a crucial role in establishing a connection between the movement and the outside world. Though it did not remain under the tutelage of the U.S.AID for long, this connection provided a platform for the movement to articulate its views at an international level. The movement's leaders were exposed to wider ideas, and local grievances now became part of the wider anti-slavery movement in contemporary South Asia and the world.

By 1 May 2000, when movement leaders planned to free nineteen *Kamaiyas* from the landlord and a former minister Shiv Raj Pant, it became a mass movement that attracted international attention. In early July they held a two-day meeting in Nepal Gunj. Soon representatives from anti-slavery organizations flocked to the area and demanded the immediate liberation of *Kamaiya* people. A mass sit-in of 150 *Kamaiyas* in front of the district government office in Bhadrakali took place. As the movement gained momentum, it attracted media attention. Finally, on 17 July the government announced the liberation of two hundred thousand *Kamaiyas* in western Nepal. However, soon these liberated Tharus were evicted from their homes and plots of land by the landlords and the condition of former *Kamaiyas* deteriorated rapidly. Even today the situation has not improved much.[31]

The story narrated here reflects the close connection between self-mobilization by Tharus and the impact of the opening of society in the post-democracy era. The transformation of popular consciousness among former bonded workers and their ability to negotiate with the state and landlords through a popular movement was clearly a product of this process. Two important observations may be drawn from this event: first, popular consciousness during the democracy era changed rapidly; and secondly, this created a new popular consciousness of resistance. The socially excluded were not ready to wait for the benevolent action of the state. Rather, they were prepared to use their own organizational techniques to bargain with the state.

The resistance of Dalits also proved to be a case whereby popular consciousness had transformed from subservience to oppression to gradual assertion of defiance. The status of Dalit was not simply the result of social evolution of the caste hierarchy—rather it was part of the process of state formation in Nepal. Indeed, King Jayasthiti Malla issued the first edict against artisan service castes in the Kathmandu valley in the fourteenth century (1380–1394). In the nineteenth century in 1854 under *Muluki Ain* proclaimed by Jang Bahadur Kunwar Rana, a particular group of service castes were declared *Pani nachaine-chhai chitta halnu parne*, i.e., whose touch required purification by sprinkling of water. Even though untouchability was banned by a government edict in 1963, Dalits hardly experienced any improvement in their social status during the *panchayat* era. Ironically, their situation did not undergo radical change in the post-democracy era either except for new forms of popular mobilization.

Indeed, the very size of the Dalit population is not above controversy as the national census has failed to account for many Dalit castes within the Newar community or in Terai. The 2001 census has put the figure of Dalits at around 12.9 percent of the population or some 2.9 million people. Dalits also do not constitute a homogenous category. Not only are they internally stratified in terms of caste ranks but there also exist differences between hill and Terai Dalits and obviously between men and women. Yet three factors stand out about Dalits that obviously characterize their status as a discriminated-against minority. First, economically their per capita income is the lowest in Nepal and they also hold the lowest amount of per capita land, with nearly 50 percent suffering from food deficiency. Most of them had little access to jobs in the organized labor market and many performed traditional artisanal occupations. Social exclusion remained acute in the case of Dalits. Dalit children face discrimination in school. An ambiguous ruling by the Supreme Court has practically barred them from entering temples. Among Dalits, women were the least privileged group. They suffer enormously for being Dalit and for being women. For example, the literacy rate among Dalit women is only 7 percent in comparison to 66 percent literacy rate among general population of Nepal. They also have the lowest life expectancy of any social group in Nepal.[32]

Political exclusion of Dalits from the highest decision-making power under democracy was acute. There was only one Dalit member of parliament and no government appointed any Dalit minister. The bureaucracy and army did not have any high-ranking Dalit officer. The state remained a passive spectator, or, in many instances, personnel of the state would act as the custodians of the existing social order rather than displaying any commitment to change this situation. Yet democracy transformed the Dalit experience in a different way. With democracy a number of Dalit organizations came into existence to espouse their causes. Each of the major political parties had Dalit organizations, but Dalit NGOs organized under the banner of the Dalit NGO Federation, Dalit Welfare Organization, Feminist Dalit Organization of Nepal, Lawyers' National Campaign against Untouchability or Literary Academy for Dalits of Nepal, and the National Dalit Intellectuals' Association were more effective.[33]

Many of these organizations had connections abroad with the United Nations, human rights advocacy groups, and international NGOs such as Action Aid. These organizations played a critical role in supporting the activities of the Nepali Dalit organizations and permitted the exchange of ideas across the globe. While these organizations played an increasing part in creating a political platform and providing a voice for the Dalit population, the increasing political awareness among Dalits also played a crucial role in attracting many to the Maoists.

In what way and how were such complex movements of various segments of the oppressed population linked with Maoist insurgency? We shall try to provide the answer to this question more elaborately in the next section, but a brief answer is in order. While democracy enhanced the critical ability of the people to engage with social and political hierarchy, the quasi-monarchical state failed to respond to their new expectations in an innovative and constructive way. Instead, they moved slowly to resolve outstanding and accumulated social grievances. In many crucial areas of life the state was absent or functioned in a perfunctory manner. Maoists provided this accumulated anger with a political outlet in various ways. Ironically, while the state had failed in the delivery of public goods, its law enforcement agencies functioned rudimentarily in rural areas but in a partisan manner in alliance with local landlords. Thus the police symbolized a rather repressive face of the state to the local population. This is evident in several incidents concerning police operations in rural areas. Sarah Shneiderman's ethnographic study on social mobilization in Piskar provides an excellent example of this.

On 15 January 1984, approximately two thousand villagers from Piskar and other villages in the area gathered in the local temple for their annual *jatra*, or folk theater performance. The program included songs and skits critical of local landowner Devi Jang Pandey's treatment of the local poor. Devi Jang Pandey, with the help of the district police officer, surrounded the festival ground, opened fire, and killed at least two people on the spot and nearly five others who died later from their wounds. Hundreds of people were arrested. At that point, parliamentary Marxists organized the local population around the demand for universal franchise and voting rights. This event entered into the collective memory of the local population as the signifier of police and landlord collusion. Dead villagers became celebrated folk heroes. Nothing happened to Devi Jang despite the fact that the parliamentary Marxists came to power in Nepal in 1994. In the late 1990s, Maoists no doubt gained popularity when they murdered this landlord. Today, Piskar village is a Maoist stronghold. Thus Maoists filled two different kinds of political voids. They built up an institutional presence that addressed the political void left by the state's identification with rural elites and through their agitations they also stepped into the political void created by the increasing isolation of parliamentary Marxists.

This interpretation of the story may invite a charge of simplification of many complex strands in popular consciousness. We shall not suggest any linear evolution of a popular peasant consciousness. However, there is little doubt that in a situation of a rapidly growing political consciousness among a marginalized rural population who sought to address their marginality through local social coalition building and collective action, Maoist politics registered a favorable presence in their mind when they offered resistance to the state's repressive actions. We shall of course note here with caution that this does not represent an endorsement of Maoists and their politics of terror. Maoist politics obviously employed terror as a weapon that enabled them to silence their opponents and even compelled them to leave their homes. As a Maoist political organ noted in a chilling matter-of-fact way:

> In Rolpa district about a dozen local goons and six police informers were punished with amputation of their limbs, which spread a reign of terror among the reactionaries throughout the district and adjoining districts. In Rukum district the house and rice mills of several tyrants including a notorious feudal tyrant and currently an Assistant Minister, Gopalji Jung Shah, were blasted and properties seized.[34]

Violence begets violence, and as the centralized state descended into a whirlpool of violence in local politics, violent political actors locally sought to retaliate against the state. In a situation of growing awareness of political rights they enjoyed a degree of support from among marginalized rural groups. In many instances, the access to weapons and violence provided a sense of empowerment, but at the same time for most working poor in rural Nepal this situation gradually developed into a nightmare. Yet the Maoists now exercised control through a new form of state structure in rural Nepal.

MILITARY STRATEGY AND THE CONSTRUCTION OF PARA-STATAL INFRASTRUCTURE

The strategic advantage of Maoists over other parties was that they were planning a protracted revolutionary war to achieve their goals. They had the ideological determination and commitment to build an underground army to enforce their political action. They analyzed Mao's ideas of conducting a long people's war. For Nepali Maoists, people's war entailed three different stages through which revolutionaries hoped to achieve strategic victory. These stages were the strategic defensive stage, stalemate stage, and strategic offensive stage. The strategic defensive stage involved three phases: the preparatory phase, continuity phase, and base area formation phase.[35]

Maoists claimed to have completed their preparatory phase when they ideologically retrained their cadres in Rolpa and Rukun to launch the people's war. Once the preparatory phase was over, Maoists concentrated on their strategy of continuing attacks with the aim of forming base areas. In the initial phase Maoist strategy consisted of attacking the police stations and communication infrastructure.[36] Their primary target was the rural police force, the most important symbol of the central government's authority in the countryside.

From a Maoist perspective, the attack on the police force had a clear rationale. Historically, the Nepali state relied upon local elites to maintain law and order in the country. These elites were backed by a thinly spread police force. Under the monarchy this system worked because the armed threat to the state was contained partially through the ideology of distinctive Nepali identity that presented the monarchy as the divine head of a Nepali Hindu ethno-religious order. With the heightening of political activities in rural areas and the expansion of rudimentary literacy, the legitimizing role of this political ideology had eroded in Nepal. More importantly, in the absence of this legitimizing ideology, many in the rural population came to view the police not as enforcers of the rule of law, but as an ally of vested interests and powerful local social and economic elites. As a consequence, the police faced political isolation.

Under such circumstances, when Maoists launched systematic hit and run attacks on police stations in remote countryside areas, the ill-equipped, underpaid, and in some instances corrupt police forces found it difficult to deal with committed Maoist guerillas. Postings in Maoist areas came to be regarded as punishments. Many police officers deserted their posts.[37] Thus, by 1998 Maoist attacks, in Rukum and Rolpa districts in particular, had destabilized police forces.

Increased attacks on police stations so alarmed the government that by June 2000 isolated police stations in rural areas of Rolpa and Rukum were closed. The police were increasingly concentrated in the district headquarters. This situation enabled Maoists to move freely in the countryside and establish their own political control over villages. It also gave them the opportunity to experiment with Maoist political ideas. They soon started collecting taxes, extorting money from relatively affluent government employees, and compelling the local youth to join them. In a situation of scarce employment opportunities, participation in guerilla activities provided an escape route from rural poverty. Frustration with the current political situation also motivated many rural youths to join the Maoists.

As the centralized Kathamandu-based state retreated from the interior in the face of determined attack by insurgents, the Maoists utilized this opportunity to constitute a base area. Although this base did not fully match the Maoist expectations of liberated zones, the political void in these districts enabled Maoists to build up a para-statal apparatus within a state. By the end of 2005, Maoist-dominated core areas comprised Rolpa, Rukum, Jajarkot, and Salyan districts in the mid-western administrative development region. The state building efforts of Maoists centered on three different institutions: the party, united front, and the army.

The party provided the ideological and political leadership to the insurgency. It was headed by a standing committee of ten members. Below the standing committee was the political bureau followed by the central committee, which coordinated wider party activities. Five regional bureaus comprising eastern, central, Kathmandu valley, western, and international departments looked after party affairs at the regional level and in relation to foreign policy matters. Finally, sub-regional and special regional bureaus were set up in some areas. These regional committees directed the activities of district committees and area committees. At the bottom of the party hierarchy was the cell committee. This organizational infrastructure comprised approximately forty-five hundred party cadres recruited precisely for their dedication to the cause of revolution. The party cadres constituted the organizational core of the Maoist political infrastructure. The hold of the central committee over the ordinary workers is partially reflected in the BBC interview of a party worker, Akash, who unambiguously stated, "We are the property of the Maoist party machine. . . . The central committee decides which machine part fits where. I am a political person."[38] Yet it would be wrong to presume that the central committee could function without support from local party cadres.

The Maoist party has been assisted by the expanding organization of the people's army run by a Central Military Commission formed in February 1998. Regional military commissions, sub-regional military commissions, and district military commissions provide direction to military activities at their respective levels. They have military units comprising platoons, companies, and battalions, and by July 2002 Maoists claimed to have formed several brigade level units. In terms of everyday military operations, the Politburo sends directives through an approximately twenty-five-member central committee. Chief Commissars, who are central committee members, instruct the combat operation on the field. The Politburo and standing committee reportedly formulate most of the political and strategic policies.[39]

Beside party organizations and military formations, Maoists have wider organizations comprising different segments of the population representing various sorts of ethnic minorities, or social groups such as students, women, workers, and intellectuals, including organizations in India comprised of expatriate Nepali residents and students. The idea behind such dense organizational networks of unions and associations is to build a wider ring of supporters who are not essentially members of the party. These quasi-legal organizations provide a channel for political propaganda work and enable them to influence civil society in Nepal. The party has thus built up a corporate institutional structure of organizations that enable it to coordinate non-military political activities and build up a wider support base. At the same time, active workers graduate to party membership and move up through the party bureaucracy.

Maoists have also started setting up an infrastructure of governance through a united people's revolutionary front comprising United People's Revolutionary Committees from district, area, village, and ward levels. Maoists claimed that these committees were elected from among the people on an individual basis. But several journalistic accounts of base areas confirmed that the elections were one-sided and that candidates were often selected by Maoist leaders with the enforced consensus of the local population. Though many of these members of people's revolutionary committees were selected from people of diverse political backgrounds, their political loyalties were enforced by the People's Liberation Army and the party. As journalist Suman Pradhan noted:

> I kept thinking about the similarities between the Panchayat-era elections and this election. Both had approved candidates. Both could have independent candidates. But both were conducted under an overarching self-righteous political setup that seemed to say: "We know best, what is good for the people."
>
> That is when you notice the second thing: the expression on the locals' faces. It's not fear or even concern, but rather stoic acceptance, even resignation. They all seem to say: The satta (people's government) stay[s]. You can't fight it, so accept it and carry on with your lives.[40]

These state-building efforts of Maoists were part of their wider drive to constitute base areas and consolidate their position within. Maoists also created directives for the local new people's government to run local level administrative, economic, social, educational, and cultural affairs. These committees introduced partial land reforms by trying to establish tillers' rights. According to an assessment made by Robert Garsony of U.S.AID, Maoists have imposed a tax of ten kilograms each on two yearly harvests, and compelled teachers and health workers to pay 5 percent of their salary as tax. In many areas teachers abandoned their schools or complained about Maoist coercion.[41] In what ways then could the Maoist para-statal structure be perceived to have incorporated grievances of marginalized social groups?

The clear impact of Maoist people's government committees has been felt on social issues, particularly women's conditions. These committees encourage widow remarriage and inter-caste marriages. They have banned gambling, alcohol consumption, and domestic violence. For many years, women had complained about such activities. The fact that Maoists were able to deal with this situation so effectively may also be attributed to the preponderance of women in the guerilla force. It has been estimated that women constituted nearly one-fifth to one-third of Maoist cadres and combatants. The Revolutionary Women's Organization has a presence in most of the rural areas. *Jane's Intelligence Review* reported in October 2001 that typically two women were stationed in each unit of thirty-five to forty men. These women play a crucial role in gathering intelligence or dispatching news. Baburam Bhattarai was quoted as saying in *Spacetime* on 18 April 2003 that 50 percent of cadres at the lower level, 30 percent of soldiers, and 10 percent of members of the central committee were women. Durgha Pokhrel, Chairwoman of the National Women's Commission, who visited more than twenty-five Maoist-affected districts, stated on 3 July 2003 during a talk delivered at the Nepal Council of World Affairs, that the percentage of women cadres could be as high as 40 percent. A women's group, the All Nepal Women's Association (Revolutionary), constitutes a front of the CPN (M). Nevertheless, it would be wrong to conclude that the Maoists' treatment of women was exemplary. There have been allegations about sexual exploitation of women in the people's liberation army. A high-ranking leader named Alok was chastised for his transgression of moral codes in the army and the party. This situation could also be a reflection of new developments in Nepal countryside whereby men, in order to avoid being caught in crossfire, had left their villages to work in the Kathmandu valley or across the border in India. Women tended to be left behind to look after rural property, rear children, and bear the burden of war on their own. In such circumstances, in the initial stages, Maoists' demands for property rights for women, their promise of land reforms, and their readiness to accommodate women in the middle and top level of party hierarchy actually prompted them to join the movement. Many scholars have, however, argued that women were more confined to the middle level of the party leadership rather than being promoted to the top leadership.[42] The inclusion of women in the political activities of Maoists indicates two critical developments: 1) the ability of Maoists to develop from below political infrastructure of para-statal organizations that could effectively govern rural areas in the absence and retreat of the centralized state; and 2) the incorporation of marginalized social constituencies within the fold of state-building efforts.

At the societal level, Maoists also embarked upon ideological retraining of the rural population through educational reforms. Recently in the Maoist-controlled areas a new alternative school curriculum, known as People's Democratic Education, or *Janavadi* education, has been introduced. This education system emphasizes vocational training to enable poor students to earn a livelihood. Maoists now claim to have established thirty-five schools in their base areas. Their aim is to establish a model *Janavadi* school in each district under their control. The most prominent among these schools is the Thawang model school, supposedly housing forty students studying between grades one and three. This school caters to the needs of the children of dead Maoist activists. They even finalized *Janavadi* curricula with prescribed books.[43] According to a recent report by Charles Haviland of the BBC, Maoists have also started training teachers in the interior of Nepal. Rajan Rota, a thirty-six-year-old teacher, told Haviland that "the old educational system is a farce—it's all about praising kings and gods." He went on, "Our new system is practical—if you want to do farming, it helps you do farming. It's about making a community without class or caste." In general the Maoist insurrection contributed to a serious crisis in the education system as the insurgents banned elite private schools and abducted many teachers. However, the establishment of an alternative educational structure solved two problems for Maoists: firstly, the ideological retraining of rural youth; and secondly, the inclusion of children within their paramilitary organizations.

Through the village government mechanism, Maoists also sought to reinforce their economic concepts of local self-reliance, encourage local small industrial enterprises, raising livestock and poultry collectively, and provide effective relief distribution during natural disasters. These committees also engage in constructing martyrs' columns and triumphal gates commemorating Maoist victories. The international media has provided widespread coverage of Maoists' attempt at road construction. Many, however, complained that such works involve coercive labor practices rather than voluntary work. Nevertheless, these activities have enabled Maoists to reach the rural poor and involve them in the local state building and economic activities in the country.

The greatest political success of Maoists was to create a political language that familiarized this coercive grassroots-level state to the rural poor. Pankaj Kapoor reported in the *London Review of Books* (in June 2005) that a disillusioned young Maoist from a rural area held a political discussion with him by frequently employing terms such as comprador bourgeoisie or bureaucratic capitalist class. The wider usages of such terms among the Nepali rural people indicate how Maoists have impacted upon the rural population's commonsensical perception of politics.[44] This is also reflected in the interviews of cadres by Li Onesto, an American political activist, definitely sympathetic to the Maoists, who has quoted a rural woman who supposedly said to her:

> We are illiterate. Due to our traditional customs, we did not learn to read and write, because it is said daughters should not be educated. But now we are beginning people's education. Before we only passed the time working in the fields, bringing fodder and grass to the cattle, and doing other household work. The main thing that we have to know is that all the oppression we are facing today is due to the reactionary state power. We have come to the conclusion and what we are doing here has made us clearer about the exploitative nature of the reactionary government.[45]

Many scholars have expressed their concerns about Onesto's readiness to accept Maoist interpretations without subjecting them to thorough scrutiny. Without entering into such debates one can safely say, as this statement reveals, that Maoists have tapped a responsive chord among many rural women in Nepal. Thus, even though Maoist military success is highly constricted, as they have been unable to fully consolidate their position, they have gained a political influence that cannot be erased immediately.

This is evident in the expansion of political areas under the control of Maoists. By 2001 the government had developed a clear classification of districts based on the presence of Maoist guerillas in a region. These categories were: category A (most affected), which included Jajarkot, Rolpa, Rukum, and Salyan districts; category B (affected), covering the districts of Dolkha, Gorkha, Jumla, Kavre, Khotang, Pyuthan, Ramechap, Sindhuli, and Sindhu Phulchowk; and category C (ordinarily affected), including Argakhanchi, Bardiya, Bhojpur, Dailekh, Dang, Dhading, Dolpa, Gulmi, Lalitpur, Lamjung, Makwanpur, Nuwakot, Okhaldhunga, Surkhet, Syangja, Tanahu, and Udaypur districts. By late 2002 Maoists held about a quarter of the country and were expanding their control of rural areas. While the royal government in Kathmandu controlled all seventy-five district centers, the Maoists had extended their zone of action over seven of Nepal's seventy-five districts. In these districts, they have declared people's governments, established people's courts, and control basic health and education services. Maoists have a significant presence in seventeen additional districts and have carried out violent activities in seventy-four out of seventy-five districts.[46]

It had often been pointed out that the economic backwardness of the mid-western region played a crucial role in the rebellion in this part of Nepal. While poverty and underdevelopment no doubt constitutes a critical backdrop for the current insurgency and possibly constitutes part of wider political phenomena, its immediate causes have to be sought elsewhere. The immediate cause of rebellion was the failure of the state to address the Maoist movement in a political manner within the framework of a democratic political setup. Indeed, in a complex political environment where the political system was transitional in nature and constitutional democracy was erected on the shaky panoply of uneasy monarchical tolerance, violence became an easy shortcut for political parties to carve out their base. Institution building and accommodation of political diversity was not a priority for the new managers of the Nepali government.

Divorced from the local political situation, members of the ruling Nepali Congress showed very little consistency in terms of political policies. It sought to dismiss Maoist rebellion as a conspiracy of a radical political cult in Nepal. Indeed, in 1996 Maoist guerillas were hardly a serious threat to the Nepali state, and the people's war made little impact on national headlines. Events in remote districts of mid-western Nepal were dismissed as troubles in the fringe areas. The fact that government could not evolve an effective political strategy was not so much due to the correct political paths followed by Maoists, but rather to the absence of a coherent political program to resist the Maoist rebellion from below and consolidate a democratic political system which could accommodate various sorts of political challenges and yet retain the legitimacy of the system in the perception of ordinary citizens. The absence of a local infrastructure of governance that had enabled Maoists to set up their political institutions further allowed them to spread their political activities through dense networks of parastatal organizations. The failure of the centralized state to establish democratic political institutions at the grassroots level enabled Maoists to extend their state-building activities from below and thus reach a marginalized segment of rural population.

THE MONARCH AS A MAOIST HERO: POWER STRUGGLE AMONG POLITICIANS AND ROYALIST AGENDA

In the period between 1996, when the Maoist insurgency started, and 2005, when King Gyanendra organized a political coup sidelining the democratic political process, Nepali politics witnessed a ferocious power struggle between diverse elements of political establishment. These power struggles soon became a game of musical chairs among political leaders of Nepali Congress and various other center right parties to occupy the prime minister's seat. The initial source of this political instability was the uncertain verdict of the 1994 election, which produced a hung parliament (Table 6).

In 1994 the CPN (UM-L) emerged as the largest political party but was short of a majority and thus formed a minority government. The CPN (UM-L) remained in power for a brief period between 30 November 1994 and 12 September 1995. Though the CPN (UM-L) did not make a radical breakthrough during their stint in power, they introduced a popular rural development program by providing money directly to villagers for rural development. However, they formed a minority government. Following a no-confidence motion against Prime Minister Manmohan Adhikary, a Supreme Court ruling prevented him from seeking a fresh mandate from the people. This obviously led to the situation whereby five governments were formed in five years with no clear indication of consistent policies (see chapter 1).

The UML was replaced by the Nepali Congress, which formed an alliance with the National Democratic Party (NDP), a party of the supporters of the former *panchayat* system, and a regional organization of Terai, namely Nepal Sadbhavana Party (NSP). But this coalition under the leadership of Sher Bahadur Deuba failed to provide political stability during its brief

Table 6. Compositions of Parliament 1991–1999

Parties/Independents	1991 Seats Secured	1991 % of Votes	1996 Seats Secured	1996 % of Votes	1999 Seats Secured	1999 % of Votes
Nepali Congress	110	37.75	83	33.38	113	36.14
Nepal Communist Party (UML)	69	27.98	88	30.85	68	30.74
Rastriya Parjatantra Party (Chand)	3	6.56	—	—	—	3.33
Rastriya Prajantra Party (Thapa)	1	5.38	—	—	—	—
Rastriya Prajantra Party	—	—	20	17.93	12	10.14
Nepal Sadbhavana Party	6	4.10	3	3.49	5	3.13
Nepal Majdoor Kisan Party	2	N/A	4	0.98	1	0.55
Samyukta Janamorcha, Nepal	9	4.43	—	1.32	1	0.84
Communist Party of Nepal (Democratic)	2	2.43	—	—	—	—
Rastriya Janmorcha	—	4.83	—	—	5	1.37
Independent	3	2.43	7	6.68	—	2.38
Voters	Year 1991		Year 1994		Year 1999	
Turnout Percentage	65.15		61.86		65.79	

Source: Nepal Election Commission, Previous Elections Results. www.election-commission.org.np/prev_ele.php (17 July 2005).

reign from 12 September 1995 to 12 March 1997. It was during this period that Maoists launched their people's war. As the Deuba government stumbled from one error to another, dissent gathered storm. Soon Lokendra Bahadur Chand of the National Democratic Party (NDP) came to power on 12 March 1997. The Chand government ruled up to 7 October 1997 with the support of the Nepali Congress and the NSP. On 7 October 1997, S. B. Thapa, a fellow member of Chand's NDP, snatched power from Chand through intrigues and ruled for the next eight months until 15 April 1998.

On 15 April 1998, G. P. Koirala of the Nepali Congress managed to appoint himself as the prime minister of Nepal. He displayed strong anti-Maoist attitudes despite his alliance with the parliamentary Marxists. It was during his brief tenure that the government initiated a brutal police operation called "Killo Sierra" in May 1998 and temporarily halted the process of Maoist expansion. But, in the long run, police brutality also enabled the Maoists to recruit new soldiers and cadres in rural areas. Moreover such measures were short-lived and had temporary objectives. The "Killo Sierra" initiative was undertaken with an eye on the election in 1999. The main purpose of the operation was to hold elections relatively undisturbed. The Congress government could hardly sustain their efforts and the party was deeply divided along factional lines.

In the 1999 election, the Nepali Congress won a massive majority (see table 6) and formed the government under K. P. Bhattarai. Bhattarai initiated a peace talk with the Maoists, but before Bhattarai could move ahead in these negotiations, he was outsmarted by Koirala in inner party intrigues. After barely ten months of rule, Bhattarai was compelled to transfer power to Koirala. Immersed in severe factional wars within the party, Koirala could hardly bring peace, although reportedly he received assistance from "undisclosed" western mediators. More critically, as the Nepali Congress witnessed severe power struggles between Koirala, Bhattarai, and Deuba, the palace seemed to follow its own political agenda (see chapter 1).

The role of the palace became clear when the king refused to involve the army in the ongoing insurrection. Indeed, to their credit, the Congress government sought to form an Integrated Security and Development Plan that would involve the army in providing security in insurgency-affected areas. However, the army chief demanded a consensus from the political parties in using the army and also asked for a clear guideline of action. It was clear that the monarch, who also happened to be commander in chief of the army, was responsible for any such counterinsurgency military operation.[47] This obviously revealed a strange political calculation of the crown.

By declining Prime Minister Koirala's request to make use of the army, the palace was acting beyond the constitutional role assigned to the monarchy. The palace establishment was calculating its time to make a return to the center stage of Nepali polity. The political gamble was self-evident: as the

Maoist insurgency would weaken democracy and foment chaos, the yearning for strong centralized government would increase. The army was the trump card of the monarch. He could hardly use it to bolster weak democratic politicians who would then encroach upon the crown's prerogatives. The unfortunate death of the monarch on 1 June 2001 further revealed a bizarre respect for him among Nepali Maoists.

After King Birendra's assassination, on 6 June 2001 Maoist leader Baburam Bhattarai wrote in a letter to the Nepali newspaper *Kantipur Daily* that

[w]hatever your political ideology might be, one thing every honest Nepali nationalist has to agree with is this: King Birendra's liberal political ideology and his patriotism were seen as his weakness and had become a crime in the eyes of the expansionist and imperialist powers. Later, his unwillingness to mobilize the army—which has a tradition of loyalty towards the King—to curb the People's Revolution taking place under the leadership of Nepal Communist Party (Maoist) became his biggest crime in the eyes of the imperialist and expansionist powers. . . . we can now say that we—NCP (Maoist) and King Birendra—had similar views on many national issues and this had created in fact an informal alliance between us.[48]

There is no doubt that Baburam Bhattarai was trying to play on the emotion of the people to exploit the tragedy. He made these claims more explicit in an interview to the *Nepal Times* published on 13 July 2001. During the interview Bhattarai stated explicitly:

Yes, Dhirendra Shah had approached us on behalf of his brother King Birendra, to express concern about the impending danger from Indian expansionists and to try to build an understanding among the patriotic forces in the country. Our Party representatives had several rounds of talks with him. It would be historically important to record it publicly that, in his last meeting with our representatives just weeks before the royal massacre, Dhirendra Shah had expressed danger to his and other royalties' life. This is one of the concrete proof we have about the larger conspiracy for the royal massacre on 1 June 2001. History will definitely unfold the real truth some day.[49]

Even Pushpa Kumar Dahal (*nom de guerre* Prachanda), the chairman of the CPN (Maoist), described King Birendra as a liberal. Drawing upon Cambodian experience he wrote:

King Birendra's relative political liberalism is not hidden to anybody. Instead of killing thousands of people in the street (who were opposing the system), it was his specialty to try to find a way out. Despite his class limitation, his proclamation of the referendum in 1979, his acceptance of multiparty system in 1990 and his "soft" policy towards the Maoist People's War are some of the examples that demonstrate his political liberalism. On the other hand, this type of characteristic of his also made us think that with the development of

"People's War" at some point, Birendra will play the role of Sihanuk [of Cambodia].[50]

It is indeed interesting that Maoists and the palace establishment had a similar strategy behind their completely divergent rhetoric. They identified the rudimentary democratic experiment as a threat to their political agenda. Strategically thus in the first stage of their people's war, Maoists remained soft on the monarchy and hard on the party political machinery. This strategy obviously undermined the party political apparatus. It was hoped that soon the monarchy would take the center stage of the polity. This would result in a clearly defined polarization between the monarchy representing the military bureaucratic apparatus of the state and Maoists seemingly representing a coalition of subaltern classes. There would hardly be any middle group such as the Nepali Congress and CPN (UM-L) to compete for the loyalty of the masses. New developments in international politics and bizarre twists in national politics indeed further pushed political events in that direction.

THE CHANGED NATIONAL AND INTERNATIONAL POLITICAL CLIMATE AND NEW STRATEGIES

The so-called people's war entered a new phase in 2001. The politics of coercion took precedence over the politics of consent, with the assassination of King Birendra on 1 June. The new monarch Gyanendra lacked the widespread acceptance of his brother Birendra. Lingering doubts about his role in this tumultuous period among certain segments of the public cast a shadow over his succession. His lack of popularity was matched by his determination to restore royal authority even at the expense of constitutional mechanisms of governance. He also believed that firm military measures were required to suppress the Maoist insurgency through direct military operations.[51]

The situation became more distressing with increased insurgent activity in the countryside on the one hand and growing instability and internecine quarrels among politicians on the other. This process was further complicated when the law enforcement wings of the state police and army failed to cooperate with each other. The complexity of the situation became evident when the CPN (M) also stepped up their insurgent activities in 2004; for example, between 6 and 13 July 2004 they attacked a series of police outposts in Lamjung, Nuwakot, Ramechhap, Gulmi Dailekh, and Holeri. While the Maoists intensified their political offensive, the military strangely enough refrained from extending their support to beleaguered police forces at Holeri. By maintaining their aloofness the army signaled to the civilian political administration that they would not be dictated to by civilian administration. Facing such a situation of open defiance of civilian authority by army leaders, the Prime Minister Koirala had no other alternative but to resign, which he did on 19 July 2002. His position had already been shaken by his failure to provide adequate explanation of the royal tragedy. He was replaced by his rival within the Nepali Congress, Sher Bahadur Deuba.[52]

The Deuba administration raised hopes of reconciliation. He proposed talks with the Maoists. The latter also indicated their readiness to enter into talks, hoping to take advantage of Deuba's rather soft approaches. On 23 July 2002 the dialogue was opened. But the agreement to hold talks did not imply that a peaceful solution was imminent. Belying such expectations in September 2001, the CPN (Maoist) announced that it had formed a People's Liberation Army as the military wing of the movement.[53] The Maoists were following the classic strategy of pressure and compromise and pressure.

In the wake of changed political circumstances after the death of King Birendra and the appointment of Sher Bahadur Deuba, the Maoists calculated that they could further consolidate their position by entering into talks with the government. From the Maoist perspective talks were also a public relations exercise. The talks provided them with political prestige and enhanced their position—from being seen as desperados to the officially recognized counter-political force at par with government. They also entered the talks to persuade the wider civil society and international community of their supposed willingness to open a dialogue with the government. It is possible that they had hoped to secure an interim government that would supervise the election of a constituent assembly. It was clear that any Maoist participation in elections would be in their favor as they had a formidable political presence in vast areas of rural Nepal. They could then demand integration of the People's Liberation Army with the Royal Nepalese Army (RNA). The result would have been a Maoist victory. Such a program would have constituted a classic strategy of translating their moral and political capital into a hegemonic political capital through the use of coercion and persuasion. This strategy could be guessed from the Maoist modus operandi during the negotiation.

The Maoists nominated three members to negotiate with the government. Their delegation was headed by Baburam Bhattarai, the chairman of the United People's Front. He was assisted by two high-ranking aides while the government sent five delegates. In mid-September the Maoists tabled their irreducible demand lists: an interim government, a constituent assembly, a new constitution, and the institutionalization of a republic.[54] From the government side, it became clear that the civilian political regime was not in a position to compromise on the issue of a republic and constituent assembly. The palace establishment backed by the army would not tolerate such a radical step. Leaders of political parties were also ambivalent on the issue at that time. By the third round of talks on 13 November, the Maoists secured the release of sixty-eight political prisoners and the government also agreed to rescind security regulations. In return, the Maoists backed down from their demand for the establishment of a republic.

As talks dragged on, new tensions may have surfaced among grassroots-level Maoist leaders, the military wing of the movement, and the peace negotiators. It is possible that the commissars found it difficult to convince the peasant and youth supporters of the need for talks without tangible gains that would satisfy an ideological and moral *raison d'être* of the movement. There were rumors that the commander of the Maoist military forces, Ram Bahadur Thapa, was opposed to the continuation of the talks. In other words, the rank and file could and did intervene in shaping the movement's direction.[55] The Maoists did not constitute a homogenous and monolithic party machine. They had to satisfy the moral and psychological needs of their cadres and various constituents of the movement. Finally, on 21 November, Prachanda called for the suspension of the talks. On 23 November, Maoists attacked government forces in twenty out of the seventy-five district headquarters. Apart from the escalating of military confrontation, Maoists also formed a thirty-seven-member United People's Revolutionary Council to administer areas under their control. Thus the politics of consensus-building reached a dead end.[56]

If the Maoists lacked the political will to compromise, the fractious political elites were unable to reach a consensus. Maoists opted for an easier solution: continuing armed insurrection. The government also sought to organize a counteroffensive. Sher Bahadur Deuba, frustrated by the Maoists' turn around, ordered the mobilization of the RNA and presumably as a precondition for such a military operation, the army compelled him to declare a state of emergency, suspending civil rights.[57] From a ceremonial army often visible during parades and UN peacekeeping missions, the RNA increasingly became involved in a civil war with a pervasive presence in every aspect of the decision-making process.[58] Thus with the collapse of peace talks the political climate in Nepal altered radically. This marked the beginning of a new process of politics whereby monarchical regimes and Maoists aimed at exercising military options. The world situation also provided a new backdrop for military hostilities.

The Maoists were also apprehensive of radical changes in the world situation. After 11 September 2001 the Nepali government pledged its support to the U.S. government in their new policy of struggle against "terrorism worldwide."[59] As the Nepali government was looking for outside support for their counterinsurgency efforts, they found a qualified endorsement from India. Soon Indian government officials were dubbing the Communist Party of

Nepal (Maoist) a terrorist outfit, and offering support to the government of Nepal in its struggle against Maoists.[60]

The Maoists were aware of these international developments. They were developing new strategies in response to the rapid transformation of the international political climate. In June 2001 they moved to establish a new umbrella organization—CCOMPSA (Coordination Committee of Maoist Parties and Organizations of South Asia). This new political outfit included many marginal Maoist organizations in other parts of South Asia.[61]

The formation of this organization represented a careful attempt by Maoists to develop international allies and to overcome their political isolation as well as to send a signal to the Indian ruling authorities of their ability to foment trouble in India. A vast region constituting almost a corridor extended from Nepal's border through troubled caste-conflict-ridden districts of North Bihar, *adivasi*-dominated thickly wooded areas of Jharkhand, West Bengal, hill regions of Orissa and Dandakarayna of Chattisgarh to the long-standing Communist stronghold of Telengana in the heart of Andhra Pradesh. While extending their activities to the neighboring regions they also sought to consolidate their activities within the country.

International attention on Nepal actually increased with the visit of Secretary of State Colin Powell in January 2002—the first visit in thirty years of such a high-ranking official of the U.S. government.[62] Encouraged by growing U.S. interests Sher Bahadur Deuba visited Washington in May 2002 and requested U.S. assistance to defeat the Maoist insurgency during his meeting with President Bush. A similar request was made to the European leaders when Deuba visited Europe. Soon the U.S. government had allocated about twenty-two million dollars and sent military experts to provide training to Nepali officers in counterinsurgency operations. The United States continued its support to the Nepali government in the following years. In 2003 Nepal received a total of 31.65 million dollars. In 2004 the amount was increased to forty-five million dollars, and as of November 2005, about forty-four million dollars have been set aside for Nepal, with nearly one-third of the allocation earmarked for security-related activities.[63] The flow of international assistance and continued military operations under the stricter laws of emergency rule actually provided new confidence to the palace officials that they could stage a return to power. Indeed, as political parties prepared for a reform of the constitution, in May 2002, Sher Bahadur Deuba opted to continue the emergency measures. When his own party revolted against the idea, he dissolved the parliament. This plunged the party into crisis. Koirala, as the president of the party, sought clarification for his move. Deuba passed an ordinance that enabled him to extend the emergency regime and the suspension of the parliament. The monarchical state no longer possessed even the facade of popular support or constitutional legitimacy.

As a consequence of such moves, conflicts escalated in rural areas with renewed counterinsurgency offensives. Politicians continued to talk about seeking a popular mandate through election. This would have restored the formal process of popular consultation and avoided a constitutional imbroglio because of the absence of parliament, which alone could extend the emergency regime. The crises deepened when Maoist attacks on 10 and 11 September 2002 made it clear that the election commission would not be able to hold elections in the country. Yet under constitutional provisions the prime minister either had to hold elections or restore parliament. On 29 September the prime minister informed the king of his inability to hold further elections. A few days later, the king dismissed Deuba for this inability.[64] This meant an end to the constitutional process and even an attempt to establish ideological legitimacy or popular consultation. The monarch now sought to return to the days of pre-1990.

The monarch's inclination towards a *panchayat* regime became clear with the appointment of Lokendra Bahadur Chand as the new prime minister—Chand was a palace loyalist who had earlier served three times as prime minister in the 1980s and the 1990s under the royal *panchayat* regime.[65] While the political doldrums continued in Kathmandu and politics remained highly volatile, the insurgency slowly turned into a full-fledged civil war with royal forces stepping up counterinsurgency measures. To prove their potency against such concerted attacks by royal forces, the CPN (M) organized a nationwide general strike on 11–13 November 2002. The strike paralyzed Kathmandu valley. More damaging for the government was the assassination of Armed Police Force Chief Krishna Mohan Shrestha and his wife in Kathmandu on 26 January 2003.[66]

These incidents took place despite the government's best efforts to suppress the Maoists with international assistance. International support resulted in Interpol issuing "red corner" alert notices against eight top-level Maoist leaders, including the supremo Prachanda (Pushpa Kamal Dahal) and Baburam Bhattarai, chief ideologue and political wing leader, on 12 August 2002.[67] In December 2002, the American Assistant Secretary of State for South Asian Affairs, Christina Rocca assured the Nepali government of the United States' commitment to support it against the Maoists.[68] The royal government had overcome initial cautious criticism by the British and the Indian governments. However, the growing political impasse within the country, confrontations between political parties and the palace-appointed administration, and escalating violence committed by both sides, alarmed the United States, the UK, and India, the three main supporters of the royal government. While their support strengthened the hand of the royal government, donor countries also exerted pressure for a diplomatic solution.

Peace initiatives resumed in January 2003. Surprisingly, three days after the assassination of the police chief, the Maoists announced a truce. The government revoked the terrorist label and withdrew the "bounty on the heads" of chief insurgents. The government notified Interpol to remove "red corner" notices against Maoist leaders and even agreed to release high profile detainees. The security forces were instructed to suspend their offensives against the Maoists. It became clear that the Planning Minister Nayaran Singh Pun had been negotiating with the Maoists for several weeks. However, the talks recommenced in a politically charged environment. Both Koirala, the leader of the Congress Party, and Madhav Nepal, the leader of the CPN (UM-L), described the talks as an attempt to sideline the political parties.[69] The talks, however, continued. In the first round of peace talks, on 27 April, the Maoists put forward a thirty-five-point agenda including most of the demands that had been discussed during the previous peace talks. The second round of talks was held on May 9.

While talks continued, the volatility of high politics in Nepal involving party political actors and the crown continued. While negotiations took place on issues concerning restrictions on Army movements and the release of Maoist leaders from prison, the prime minister of the caretaker government, Lokendra Bahadur Chand, resigned. On 5 June, the king appointed another palace loyalist, Surya Bahadur Thapa, from Rashtriya Prajatantra Party (RPP), again a former prime minister from *panchayat* days, as the second caretaker prime minister. The talks continued in the midst of agitation by political parties and dismissals and reappointment of prime ministers.[70] This obviously reflected a new political reality in Nepal, aptly captured by Maoist leader Baburam Bhattarai during his press conference on 30 March 2003 when he claimed that there were actually two states in Nepal representing two armies and two cultures, and described the current ceasefire as a strategic equilibrium between two forces. Surprisingly, in a separate statement, government negotiator and Minister for Physical Planning and Works, Narayan Sing Pun, admitted that there existed two state powers in Nepal.[71]

Both these statements referred to the actual sidelining of political parties and constitutional mechanisms of government in Nepal. The Maoist insurgency and the royal coup and counterinsurgency measures had effectively ended even the most rudimentary experiments with democracy. Despite the announcement of talks both sides remained willing to settle their issues through military confrontation.

In these circumstances the third phase of the talks began on 17 August 2003. Though both sides submitted their agendas and the government admitted the possibility of a round table conference to form an all-party government—but not a constituent assembly—tensions simmered on. The Maoists maintained that the constituent assembly was the most important precondition for their dialogue. When news arrived about the RNA's attack of 17 August on Maoist insurgents in which nineteen Maoists perished, the latter hardened their stand on the demand for a republic and expressed their anger at the turn of events. Finally, on 28 August the talks were suspended (see chapter 1).

The peace process had thus failed to yield positive results. Mutual distrust prevailed in both camps and neither side reached consensus on any issues. Indeed, both sides used the talks as a period of respite in the middle of war. Maoists allegedly used the ceasefire to smuggle arms and recruit cadres while the government sought to equip the RNA with modern artillery imported from Western countries. The ceasefire was again an instance of negotiation of temporary truce in order to gain ultimate victory. After the talks failed, the government had no other option but to attempt to suppress the Maoists militarily. However, the RNA lacked sufficient trained personnel to obtain a ready military victory. The Maoists also did not have the ability to dislodge the government from power through mass insurrection in towns and prolonged guerilla warfare in rural areas. Indeed, the Maoists began losing popularity. The military solution thus involved a long-term ruthless war on both sides with increasing death and destruction.

From the royal government's perspective, the political parties constituted a major headache. They did not offer a clear solution, sought to impose their own political agendas, and stood in the way of full-scale counterinsurgency measures unless military operations served their political purpose. More importantly, five major political parties continued to oppose the king's use of Article 127, through which he acquired executive powers from the government. They demanded restoration of the parliament. The king on his part showed no interest in reinstating the dissolved parliament. However, international pressure was applied to the royal government to include political parties in counterinsurgency measures. Finally, after a prolonged street-level agitation and lobbying, political parties regained power when the king reappointed Sher Bahadur Deuba as the prime minister of Nepal on 2 June 2004. Deuba further expanded his cabinet of ministers on 5 July 2004. He sought to develop a united front as his cabinet comprised twelve ministers from his own party, the Nepali Congress Democratic NC (D), eleven from the Communist Party of Nepal-Unified Marxist Leninist (CPN-UML), five from the Rastriya Prajantantra Party (RPP), and one from the Nepal Sadbhavana Party (NSP); two ministers were the king's nominees. Significantly, Deuba did not include anyone from the Koirala faction of the Nepali Congress.[72]

The new ministers did not have a democratic mandate to govern the country. Internal feuds among Nepali politicians were proverbial. Despite military operations the Maoists remained strong enough to hold on to their rural bases. It was clear that both the monarch and the army were keen on a direct monarchical control over the system in order to intensify counterinsurgency operations. Such counterinsurgency measures required the suspension of democratic rights granted in the constitution. In these circumstances, in January 2005 the monarch again made an impossible request to Deuba to hold elections in the country. Deuba made some favorable noises in favor of holding elections but many of his cabinet members expressed doubts. On 1 February the king dramatically suspended the Deuba government, arrested major political leaders, and even suspended important constitutional provisions such as freedom of expression. Censorship was imposed on the newspapers, wireless telephone connections were blocked by the government, and many politicians were arrested without charge. The coup further escalated the conflict.

The coup also created a new political alignment in the country. The king and the military bureaucratic apparatus continued to exercise a stranglehold on power and Maoists and political parties sought to develop an understanding among themselves. Indeed, at the end of August 2005 there took place a meeting between leaders of the Nepali Congress and the CPN (UM-L). After the meeting the two parties decided to abandon their allegiance to the constitutional monarchy. In response to this development, Prachanda, the leader of the Communist Party of Nepal (Maoist), announced a unilateral ceasefire on 3 September 2005. In an interview with the BBC, the general secretary of the CPN-UML, Madhav Kumar Nepal, said an alliance with the Maoists would only be possible if they declared their commitment to a multiparty system.[73] However, the political situation remained fluid as political parties continued to demand the restoration of the parliament elected in 1999. This was obviously not to the liking of the Maoist leader, who realized that if the monarch accepted this demand, it would open the door for negotiation between the king and political parties. In such a situation the Maoists would not gain any political mileage. Rather, they would remain isolated.

Politics in Nepal from 2003, soon after the collapse of the talks with the Maoists onward, had witnessed intense militarization. Counterinsurgency operations had provided military leaders with access to larger funds, new weapons, and the ability to recruit more soldiers. The absence of constitutional safeguards had enabled them to operate with impunity in decimating supposed insurgents. The result was an increasing death toll, forced migration from rural areas, and redirection of development funds toward counterinsurgency operations.

CONCLUSION

What emerges from our discussion above is that the post-1991 formal democracy in Nepal opened up the political system and raised expectations of the population for an inclusive state structure. However, it failed to address effectively the concerns of those people on the margins. Politicians soon became engaged in a battle for power. In a transitional political situation without any stable institutional structure and hegemonic ideology to guide their action, politicians indulged in the shortcut of accessing power through coercion. Within every political party, different political players pursued their own agendas to secure control over the political system. Political actors indulged in coercion and systematic discrimination against their opponents. They sought to incorporate within their networks local political entrepreneurs and elites who were associated with the *panchayat* regime.

This obviously antagonized ethnic minorities, rural poor, women, and Dalits who were politicized with the opening up of the system and the flourishing of diverse political and social movements. Ethnic, political, economic, and gender marginalization against the background of a radical rhetoric of egalitarianism produced an explosive situation. It was in these circumstances that a small faction of Maoist groups, who felt excluded from the political system, launched an armed insurgency. In a situation where the state constituted a brittle institutional edifice, and against a background where democratization had politicized the marginal population but failed to produce radical transformation, these groups had sought to build up a new structure that initially provided some tangible gains to the rural poor and registered a positive presence in the popular consciousness. They sought to build up a counter-coalition of rural social classes and establish political hegemony from below.

Political elites failed to recognize the threat from the Maoists. They could not formulate a clear and effective solution to the Maoist insurrection. While democratic leaders had a clear policy toward the Maoists and responded as the situation unfolded, King Birendra took a calculated risk in enabling Maoists to continue with their operations which further destabilized the party political structure. The Maoists actually used the situation to further their project of building the edifice of a one-party state and a coalition of the marginalized from below. Selective targeted politically motivated acts of violence became a political weapon in their hands.

Continued political violence enabled the palace establishment to intervene further. Soon after the royal massacre of 2001, a new hard-line king took steps to restore the monarchical regime to power. This led to a process of militarization of the Nepali polity. Both the king and the Maoists confronted each other through violent extra-constitutional means. Nepal experienced a classic retrograde step of dismantling the institutional edifice of a rudimentary democracy and returning to extra positional violent confrontation and militarization of the polity.

With counterinsurgency measures becoming the political *raison d'être* of the regime, it was clear that it had now evolved into a situation of dominance without hegemony for the tottering monarchical state. This does not mean that Maoists have established a permanent ideological hegemony over the peasantry. The consciousness of the marginalized is neither static nor mortgaged to a particular brand of violent politics. Rather, it evolves in relation to the changing reality of social contradictions. Thus the possibility of a new resistance to the projects of Maoist commissars remained a real possibility should the party step beyond the evolving nature of peasant consciousness. Indeed, as reports of extortion and abduction increased in rural areas, it seemed that the Maoist charm was wearing thin.

NOTES

1. See the website of Election Commission of Nepal http://www.election-commission.org.np/ (22 May 2005).

2. For details concerning the conflicts within United Front and the split among Maoists, please see Dipak Thapa and Bandita Sijapati, *A Kingdom Under Siege: Nepal's Maoist Insurgency, 1996–2004* (New York: Zed Books, 2004): 43–45.

3. This penchant with ideological purity is reflected in the words of Pushpa Kumar Dahal, the leader of the Maoists when he stated, "My main thrust is that I hate revisionism. I seriously hate revisionism and I never compromise with revisionism. I fought and fought again with revisionism and the party's correct line is based on the process of fighting revisionism. I hate revisionism and I seriously hate revisionism." "Red Flag Flying on the Roof of the World," Li Onesto, *Revolutionary Worker* 1043, 20 February 2000, http://rwor.org/a/v21/1040-049/1043/interv.htm (28 May 2005).

4. For a contemporary perspective of fighting, see Werner Levi, "Political Rivalries in Nepal," *Far Eastern Survey* 23, no. 7 (July 1954): 102–7. See for details the first chapter.

5. See for details: CPN-NML, "History, First Congress," http://www.cpnuml.org/1congress.html (28 August 2005).

6. Anirudha Gupta, *Politics in Nepal: A Study of Post Rana Political Development and Party Politics* (Bombay: Allied, 1964): 203–9.

7. T. Louise Brown, *The Challenge to Democracy in Nepal: A Political History* (London: New York: Routledge, 1996): 33–41.

8. Deepak Thapa, "Radicalism and the Emergence of the Maoists," in *Himalayan People's War: Nepal's Maoist Rebellion*, ed. Michael Hutt (Bloomington: Indian University Press, 2004).

9. For details see CPN (UM-L), "Jhapa Struggle and Development of ML Mainstream," http://www.cpnuml.org/jhapa.html (29 August 2005). Also interview with Jhalanath Khanal member standing committee, CPN (UM-L), Kathmandu, 6 July 2006.

10. Interview with Jhalanath Khanal, member standing committee, CPN (UM-L), Kathmandu, 6 July 2006.

11. See: About CPN (UM-L), "Polarization and Integration," http://www.cpnuml.org/about/polarisation.htm (22 May 2005).

12. Interview with Jhalanath Khanal, member standing committee, CPN (UM-L), Kathmandu, 6 July 2006.

13. For details, see Thapa, "Radicalism," 32.

14. Revolutionary Worker, "Celebrate the 20th Anniversary of the Revolutionary International Movement," no. 1238, 1 May 2004, http://iwoi.oig/a/1238/rimedit.htm and "Revolutionary International Movement," http://cpnm.org/new/RIM/rim_index.htm (21 June 2005).

15. See for details Thapa, "Radicalism," 33.

16. See Nepal Election Commission Report, "Fact and Figure in Elections in Nepal," http://www.election-commission.org.np/ (8 June 2005).

17. Depak Thapa and Bandita Sijapati, *A Kingdom Under Siege*, 43.

18. Mahendra Lowte, *Towards a Democratic Nepal: Inclusive Political Institutions for a Multicultural Society* (New Delhi: Sage, 2005).

19. Brachet-Marquez, "Explaining Sociopolitical Change in Latin America," in *Latin American Research Review* 3 (1992): 91–122.

20. The torture committed by police throughout the counterinsurgency operation starting from the Congress period to the monarchical era was confirmed by various eyewitness accounts. For example, Subel Bhandari, a young journalist who is stridently critical of Maoists, described to one of the authors how police raped and murdered a young woman, suspected to be a Maoist in Rolpa. Interview with Subel Bhandari, Kathmandu, 19 June 2006.

21. CPNM, "One Year of People's War in Nepal—A Review," *Worker*, no. 3, February 1997, http://www.cpnm.org/worker/issue3/oneyear_pw.htm#THE%20SEC-OND%20PLAN:%20Planned%20Development%20of%20Guerrilla%20Warfare (6 July 2005).

22. Anne de Sales (translated by David Gellner), "The Kham Magar Country, Nepal: Between Ethnic Claims and Maoism," in *European Bulletin of Himalayan Research* 19, republished in *Understanding the Maoist Movement of Nepal*, ed. Deepak Thapa (Kathmandu: Martin Chautari, 2003), 59–88.

23. Interview with Dr. Baburam Bhattrai, *The Independent* V, no. 41, 13–19 December 1995.

24. See for details of this analysis Anne de Sales (translated by David Gellner), "The Kham Magar Country," 59–88.

25. Li Onesto, *Revolutionary Worker* 1043, 20 February 2000, http://rwor.org/a/v21/1040-049/1043/interv.htm (28 May 2005), reprinted in A. Karki and D. Seddon, *The People's War in Nepal: Left Perspectives* (Delhi: Adroit Publisher, 2003): 84.

26. "The Letter of Dr. Baburam Bhattarai on the Palace Massacre in Nepal," *Monthly Review* 53, no. 2, http://www.monthlyreview.org/0601letter.htm (20 May 2005).

27. Karan Pradyumnya and Hiroshi Ishi called Nepali bureaucracy a "feudal bureaucrat." See Karan Pradyumnya and Hiroshi Ishi, *A Himalayan Kingdom in Transition* (Tokyo: United Nations University Press, 1996).

28. K. R. Adhikary, "The Fruits of Panchayat Development," in *Himalayan Research Bulletin* XV, no. 2 (1995): 19.

29. K. R. Adhikary, "The Fruits of Panchayat," 19.

30. Arjun Guneratne, "Modernization, the State, and the Construction of a Tharu Identity in Nepal," *The Journal of Asian Studies* 57, no. 3 (August 1998): 749–73, and

Many Tongues, One People: The Making of Tharu Identity in Nepal (Ithaca: Cornell University Press, 2002).

31. This description is based on the article of Tatsuro Fujikura, "Emancipation of Kamaiyas: Development, Social Movement, and Youth Activism in Post-Jana Andolan Nepal," *Himalayan Research Bulletin* XXI, no. 1 (2001).

32. UNDP, *Nepal Human Development Report 2004, Empowerment and Poverty Reduction* (Kathmandu: UNDP, 2004): 10–18.

33. See for details: D. R. Dahal, Y. B. Gurung, B. Acharya, K. Hemchuri, and D. Swarnakar, "Nepal Dalit Strategy Report: Situational Analysis of Dalits in Nepal," (May 2002), Prepared for National Planning Commission, His Majesty's Government Nepal, http://www.nepalDalitinfo.20m.com/archives/Analysis2002.pdf (22 April 2005).

34. CPNM, "The Historic Initiation and After," *The Worker*, no. 2, June 1996, http://www.cpnm.org/worker/issue2/w2_1p.htm (6 August 2005).

35. See: "One Year of People's War In Nepal—A Review," *The Worker*, no. 3, February 1997, http://www.cpnm.org/worker/issue3/oneyear_pw.htm (6 July 2005).

36. Maoists put such plans in clear military phraseology, which amply makes clear their goals. We quote:

The basic objective of the Second Plan was to develop guerrilla warfare in a planned manner so as to prepare grounds to convert specific areas into guerrilla Zones in the near future. For this the emphasis would be on creating radicalized (or militarized) mass base in specific areas and upgrading & expanding the fighting capability of the armed detachments. Accordingly, broad categorization and identification of Principal Zones, Secondary Zones and Propaganda Zones were made and the forces and activities were sought to be channelized and centralized in keeping with the envisaged roles of different zones. As earlier a short period of preparation would precede the launching of the Second Plan, and by the very objective and nature of the Plan it would not commence on a fixed date but would follow an approximate time frame.

37. Stephen L. Mikesell, "The Maoist Movement and the Threat to Democracy in Nepal," *Himalayan Research Bulletin* XXI, 1 (2001).

38. Charles Haviland, "Meeting Nepal's Maoists," *BBC News*, 12 April 2005, http://news.bbc.co.uk/2/hi/south_asia/4434197.stm (13 April 2005).

39. Sudheer Sharma, "The Maoist Movement: An Evolutionary Perspective," in *Understanding the Maoist Movement in Nepal*, ed. Deepak Thapa (Kathmandu: Martin Chautari, 2003): 361–80.

40. Suman Pradhan, "Tales from Rolpa: A 10-Day Trek Across the Maoist Heartland," *Kantipur on line*, 20 June 2005.

41. Robert Garsony, "Sowing the Wind: History and Dynamics of Maoist Revolt in Nepal's Rapti Hills," Consultancy Reports to Mercy Corps International. See for detailed discussion of the report: "Discussion Forum International Resources Group," no. 15, p. 4, March 2004, http://www.irgltd.com/Resources/Discussion_Forum/DF15_Nepal_Maoist_Revolt-03-04.pdf (28 April 2005).

42. See for details: Shobha Goutam, Amrita Banskota, and Rita Manchanda, "Where There Are No Men: Women in the Maoist Insurgency in Nepal," in *Understanding the Maoist Movement of Nepal*, ed. Deepak Thapa (Kathmandu: Martin Chautari, 2003): 93–124.43. Pradhan, "Tales from Rolpa."

44. Pankaj Mishra, "The People's War," *London Review of Books* 27, no. 12 (23 June 2005).

45. Li Onesto, *Dispatches from the People's War in Nepal* (London: Pluto Press, 2005): 28.

46. South Asia Terrorism Portal, "Nepal Terrorist Groups Communist Party of Nepal Maoist," http://www.satp.org/satporgtp/countries/nepal/terroristoutfits/index.html# (23 May 2005).

47. See: Keshab Poudel, "Noble Monarch," *Spotlight* 23, no. 46 (4–10 June 2004).

48. "The Letter of Dr. Baburam Bhattarai on the Palace Massacre in Nepal," *Monthly Review* 53, no. 2, http://www.monthlyreview.org/0601letter.htm (25 May 2005).

49. See for details: Maoist-sponsored website, http://www.insof.org/politics/130701_interview_baburam.html (12 April 2005).

50. Mohan Bikram Singh, "The Royal Palace Massacre and the Maoists Pro-King Political Line," *Nepal Samachar Patra*, 15 June 2001; A. Karki and David Seddon, eds., *The People's War in Nepal: Left Perspectives* (New Delhi: Adroit Publishers 2003): 315–74.

51. King Gyanendra, "It's a Question of Survival," *Time Asia*, 18 April 2005.

52. Rita Manchanda, "Emergency and a Crisis," *Frontline* 19, no. 5 (2–15 March 2002).

53. Onesto, "Dispatches," xv.

54. Onesto, "Dispatches," xiv.

55. Rita Manchanda, "Himalayan Thunder," *Frontline* 18, no. 25 (8–21 December 2001).

56. Onesto, "Disptaches," xv.

57. Rita Manchanda, "Uneasy Peace in Kathmandu," *Frontline* 19, no.1 (5–18 January 2002).

58. A. K. Mehta, *The Royal Nepal Army—Meeting the Maoist Challenge* (New Delhi: Rupa, 2005).

59. See for details of Nepali calculation behind such declaration: "Nepal: Row Over U.S. Support," *BBC News*, 26 September 2001, http://news.bbc.co.uk/1/hi/world/south_asia/1564467.stm (29 May 2005).

60. For Indian involvement in Nepal, see: Conn Hallinan, "Nepal—Cleaning up the Mess," *Asia Times*, http://www.atimes.com/atimes/South_Asia/GB17Df05.html (30 May 2005).

61. Members of Coordination Committee of Maoist Parties and Organizations of South Asia (CCOMPSA) are: from India—Communist Party of India (Marxist-Leninist) (People's War), Maoist Communist Centre (MCC), Revolutionary Communist Centre of India (MLM), Revolutionary Communist Centre of India (Maoist), Communist Party of India (ML) (Nakshalbari); from Bangladesh—Purba Bangla Sarbahara Party (CC), Purba Bangla Sarbahara Party (Maoist Punarghathan Kendra), Bangladesh Samyabadi Party (ML); and from Sri Lanka—Communist Party of Ceylon (Maoist). [Source: CPN (Maoist) website: http://cpnm.org/new/ccomposa/ccomposa_index.htm (10 July 2005).]

62. For details of Powell's speech, see: Keshab Poudel, "Enduring Importance," in *Spotlight* 21, no. 27, 25–31 January 2002.

63. Ramtanu Maitra, "U.S. Jittery over Nepal," *Asia Times on Line*, http://www .atimes.com/atimes/South_Asia/GC16Df01.html (19 June 2005).

64. Rita Manchanda, "The King's Coup," *Frontline* 19, no. 21 (12–15 October 2002).

65. Rita Manchanda, "Unending Crisis," *Frontline* 19, no. 23 (9–22 November 2002).

66. *The Rising Nepal*, Kathmandau, "Chief of Armed Police Force Shot Dead," 27 January 2003.

67. See for details: "Red Corner Alert Notice Against Prominent Maoists: Royal Nepal Army," http://www.rna.mil.np/cio/wanted.php (11 June 2005).

68. See: Statement of Christina B. Rocca, Assistant Secretary of State for South Asian Affairs, Remarks to the American Enterprise Institute, Washington, DC, 10 October 2002, "Deepening U.S. Engagement in South Asia," http://www.state.gov/p/ sa/rls/rm/14296.htm (9 June 2005).

69. Rita Manchanda, "Talks and Fears," *Frontline* 20, no. 7 (29 March–11 April 2003).

70. Rita Manchanda, "Nepal's Challenges," *Frontline* 20, no. 12 (7–20 June 2003).

71. Ghanashyam Ojha, "Two State Powers in Nepal, Admits Pun," *The Kathmandu Post*, 31 March 2003, http://www.nepalnews.com.np/contents/englishdaily/ ktmpost/2003/mar/mar31/index.htm# (17 May, 2005).

72. For details of the Composition of the Government by Sher Bahadur Deuba, see: *Government of Nepal's Directory on line*, http://www.nepalhomepage.com/ politics/cabinet/cabinet.html (26 June 2005).

73. See: Rabindra Mishra, "Nepal Maoists Seek to Isolate King," *BBC News*, 4 September 2005, http://news.bbc.co.uk/1/hi/world/south_asia/4212988.stm (2 October 2005).

5

Popular Uprising 2006

Successful popular uprisings are usually the result of a combination of the failure of the incumbent regime to gauge popular sentiment and the opposition's ability to seize the moment. While discontent with the policies of the government and/or economic hardship create an environment for unrest, they are not sufficient to trigger an uprising that brings people of all walks of life together in opposition to the regime. This critical point is often produced by the regime's miscalculation or misreading of the popular opinion. But it turns out to be the critical point only when the opposition succeeds in taking advantage of the regime's miscalculation. Whether the opposition political forces will be able to seize the moment is dependent not only on their intent, but a fortuitous combination of organization and spontaneity. Organization, i.e., to call upon the people, to encourage them to join the demonstrations, and to have a plan, can be done by political parties, but spontaneity, by definition, cannot be planned or predicted. That entirely depends on the people. The popular uprising that shook Nepal for nineteen days in April 2006 bears testimony to this. In this chapter we demonstrate that three elements—the miscalculation of the palace, the successful organization of the mainstream political parties in conjunction with the Maoists, and the spontaneity of the common people—were at the heart of the democracy movement in April 2006.

ROYAL MISCALCULATION

The crises discussed in the previous chapters had been pushing the country toward the brink of a disaster for quite some time, but what accentuated the process was the royal coup of February 2005. The royal coup was premised on the palace's understanding that the Nepali people were frustrated by the inability of the political leaders to deliver and perturbed by the growing strength of the Maoists. Therefore, they concluded, a semblance of order would be enough to satisfy the people, even at the expense of their democratic rights. But the royal coup, in essence, was the second step in a two-step process of dismantling democratic institutions and returning to the absolute monarchy of the 1960s. The first step was taken in October 2002 when the parliament was disbanded and the elected government was deposed. Since then, the palace and its handpicked governments have not performed differently from their pre-October 2002 "political" counterparts. Yet the palace establishment assumed that further encroachment into the political rights of the people would be tolerated because of the tainted past of the political regimes and the politicians. More than two years of the king's direct rule not only failed to deliver tangible results in terms of reducing the violence or creating a better economic prospect, but also presided over the dismantling of the democratic institutions created after the democracy movement in 1990.

The coup was followed by a crackdown on the members of the political opposition, media, and all other potential sources of dissent. While the king initially faced condemnation from the international community, the rigor gradually subsided as Indian policy lacked clarity and the United States' support for the restoration of democracy was lukewarm at best. Additionally, China continued its quiet support for the palace without any reference to the changed circumstances.[1] This gave the palace a sense of relief, but it was evident that the coup had isolated the king from his traditional allies. The initial protests organized by opposition parties dissipated without making any dent in the authoritarian measures adopted, strengthening the perception of the palace that no major challenge was on the horizon. The immediate aftermath of the coup was that it pushed some of the erstwhile supporters of monarchy to become republicanist. Congress central committee member Krishna Prasad Sitaula's comment on 8 February that his party is "even ready to join hands with the Maoists to put an end to the monarchy" is a case in point.[2] Oblivious to these political developments, especially the emerging understanding between the seven-party alliance and the Maoists (see appendix 3), and the growing popularity of the demand for a republic, the palace continued with its plan to move backwards and return to a variant of *panchayat*-era political arrangements. With this view in mind the palace and its handpicked government under the leadership of Tulsi Giri planned the municipal elections in early February 2006. The opposition political parties' attempt to stage a mass demonstration in Kathmandu on 20 January 2006 failed when the government preempted the move and arrested the leaders en masse.

The turning point, however, came on 6 February 2006. Although it had been apparent for quite some time that the government's plan to hold the municipal elections was doomed to fail, as all opposition parties had decided to boycott the election, the popular support for the opposition's plan became clear as the day progressed. With 20 percent voter turnout[3] (most of whom were government officials, members of the military, police, and other law enforcing agencies), the message was loud and clear: the attempt to legitimize direct royal rule had been crushed. Everything from this point on was downhill for the palace and the regime.

The last set of events began on 6 April with the beginning of a four-day countrywide general strike combined with demonstrations all over the country called by the Seven-Party Alliance (SPA) and supported by the Maoists. The initial response of the general populace was somewhat reserved, but as news of killings of demonstrators by the army began to come in, the mood started to change and participation began to swell. While the heavy-handedness of the army, the imposition of a curfew, the gradual collapse of the civil administration, encirclement of the capital by demonstrators from the rural areas, and loss of morale among royal supporters, including members of the cabinet, helped to foster a sense of imminent victory for the political activists, the palace was hoping that popular enthusiasm would diminish over time and that it could ride out the storm. Instead, the original plan for a four-day strike continued for weeks. It was a miscalculation of royal proportions. The zero-sum game strategy adopted by the palace since 2002 and particularly since February 2005 had backfired. A last-ditch effort to salvage the sinking ship came on 21 April: the king offered to return executive power to the political parties and asked the SPA to nominate a candidate for prime minister.[4] It was too little and too late, and merely added fuel to the fire. Three days later the king capitulated: "cognizant of the spirit of the ongoing people's movement as well as to resolve the ongoing violent conflict and other problems facing the country according to the road map of the agitating seven-party alliance,"[5] the king finally declared the restoration of parliament.

ORGANIZING THE UPRISING

Support for Nepali politicians among the general populace was on the wane in 2002 when the king disbanded parliament and fired the Deuba government. Their actions between October 2002 and February 2005 had not been of a character to inspire the people to join them in restoring political parties to power. Yet, the April 2006 uprising demonstrates that the people had heeded their call to challenge the monarchy. What made the change of heart possible? The Nepali people decided to give the political parties another chance because they were looking for a peaceful way out of the crisis. Over the years, particularly between 2002 and 2006, it became clear that a military solution to the Maoist insurgency was impossible, and that, taking advantage of the situation, the palace was hell-bent on driving the nation backwards. The emergence of the seven-party alliance, and their understanding with the Maoists in November 2005 gave the people hope.

As for the mainstream political parties, the royal coup of February 2005 made it necessary that they change their course. The parties were prompt in realizing the need. Subsequently came the actions. The first among these new realizations was that the palace was more interested in marginalizing the constitutional political parties than the Maoist insurgency. The measures taken after the royal coup in February were clear enough to show that the prime targets of the palace were the political parties. Secondly, the opposition political parties also understood that they were in danger of losing touch with their constituencies. A further continuation of the situation might make them irrelevant to Nepali politics in the future. Thirdly, although never openly acknowledged, it was evident to them that their previous policies for dealing with the Maoists had not worked.[6] These realizations prompted the political parties to act fast.

On 8 May 2005, the leaders of seven political parties—the Nepali Congress, CPN (UM-L), Nepali Congress Democratic, Jan Morcha, Nepal Workers' and Peasant Party, Nepal Sadbhavana Party (Anandi Devi faction), and United Left Front formed a seven-party alliance. Barring the Nepali Congress and Terai-based Sadbhavana Party, this alliance was primarily composed of various parliamentary Marxist groups. Their "joint declaration for a United Effort to Resolve the National Crisis" became a landmark manifesto for the restoration of democracy in Nepal. The new manifesto unequivocally stressed the issue of the revival of parliament as their goal. The parliamentary parties also appealed to the Maoists to open a dialogue and join the mainstream political process. They demanded that the Maoists affirm their faith in democracy and civil society. The Maoists responded positively to this overture and requested the seven parties to enter into a dialogue with them. When members of the Nepali civil society also insisted on an agreement and the Indian authority threw its weight in favor of this undertaking, it became easier for the political parties to go ahead.

The process was not free from internal strife within the political parties, however. The Nepali Congress, for example, faced radical challenges within its own party. Gagan Thapa, reputedly a young Turk of the Nepali Congress, initiated a new move toward radicalization of the party's political agenda. The Nepali Congress developed a new political program. It openly declared its commitment toward framing a new constitution by an elected constituent assembly. This position obviously removed their differences with Maoist leaders at a fundamental level. The Congress also announced its pledge to constitutional reforms in order to create a state responsive to the people's demands, even organizing a referendum for basic constitutional provisions. The party did not want to commit itself openly to a republic, but definitely sought to provide safeguards against the monarchy and called for an inclusive democracy that would uphold the supremacy of parliament. In the words of Laxman Basnet, the powerful leader of the Nepal National Trade Union Congress, affiliated to the Congress Party, the monarchy had become irrelevant to the people and could survive only as a ceremonial institution.[7] However, the Nepali Congress Party's younger cadres and intellectual sympathizers committed themselves openly to the idea of a republic. Subel Bhandari, a young activist journalist and a supporter of Gagan Thapa, captured the mood of the younger generation by simply stating that the Maoists had been around for ten years and "their [the Maoists'] challenge" to democracy could be resolved easily, but the monarchy had been present for two hundred and fifty years, and had to be removed for the sake of democracy.[8] Although the leadership of the Nepali Congress was divided on committing to a republic, they were united and ready to act against monarchy.

For the Maoists, the adoption of a strategy to join multiparty politics came after more than two years of intra-party debate. The October 2005 plenum recognized that they had achieved their primary goals, but also acknowledged that it was time to move out of the cold. It is no secret that support in the rural areas, trumpeted by the Maoists, is far from spontaneous. They have been criticized for blatant violations of human rights and the patience of the common people has been wearing thin.

The twelve-point understanding between the Maoists and the SPA was reached against this backdrop of widespread dissatisfaction. Kanak Mani Dixit has rightly noted:

> This has stemmed from [the Maoists'] willingness to submit to geopolitical reality, as well as the dawning realization [sic] that state power cannot be attained militarily. For this reason, and their evident willingness to finally abandon arms, the political parties have created space for them in the national mainstream.[9]

Whatever the motives were, both the SPA and the Maoists should be credited for their pragmatism. The understanding was cemented when an identical statement was issued by the SPA leaders and the Maoist supremo Prachanda on 19 March.

It was against this background that a four-day strike was called in early April. The Maoists called for blockade of the district headquarters, mobilized their supporters in rural areas, and sent some of their unarmed cadres to the capital ahead of the strikes. They led some of the demonstrations organized under the banner of the mainstream political parties and highlighted the demand for a republic. Simultaneously, the leaders of the mainstream political parties evaded the arrests,[10] toured some parts of the country, and organized their supporters in Kathmandu to participate in street agitations. These actions galvanized public support.

SPONTANEITY

A great deal of planning and organization were necessary for the uprising, but it was the groundswell of support among the common people and the participation of members of the civil society that provided the strength and momentum to the uprising making it truly a *Jana Andolon*. Observers of the events noted the unprecedented participation of people who had no affiliation with any political parties or organizations. A report of the International Crisis Group states:

> There were at least four categories of participation: (i) organizers [*sic*] and instigators (mainstream party, Maoist, or independent); (ii) active participants—those on the streets, chanting slogans, marching; (iii) indirect participants—onlookers and hangers-on, those giving water or other help to demonstrators; and (iv) silent supporters, who may have stayed at home but supported in other ways; for example, the large sums raised very quickly, but in multiple small donations, for injured protestors' medical relief were a sign of the depth of public support. Youth and students were prominent, many not from political backgrounds.[11]

Popular participation was far more widespread and spontaneous than the first popular uprising of 1990, according to journalists and participants. For many, participation proved to be a life-changing experience. This remained a major issue of public discussion even three months after the uprising.[12] An important feature of the participation was that while these demonstrators were angry, particularly over the killings of civilians, it was rather hope that drew them to the street. The participation of members of the civil society had played a major role in bringing non-partisan people to the streets. Among civil society organizations the "Citizen's Movement for Democracy and Peace" was highly active. This organization came into being in August 2005 under the auspices of the former finance minister Dr. Devendra Raj Pandey, independent Marxist critic and writer Khagendra Sangrauolo, professor and Marxist intellectual Pitambar Sharma, and noted human rights activists Krishna Pahadi and Professor Krishna Khanal. Devendra Raj Pandey, deeply frustrated with the political parties' token resistance after the royal coup, issued a call for a meeting for democracy and peace at the end of August 2005 with a group of like-minded citizens. This meeting attracted a large audience; political leaders also attended it as part of the audience. The meeting heralded a new mode of resistance whereby musicians performed, artists exhibited their pictures, and poets recited poems.[13] The idea was to convey a new message that this was a movement not for political power but for an open dialogue for democracy and peace. Such a claim by a stalwart of civil society obviously provided a new dimension to the movement and appealed primarily to the urban constituents who had a more cynical attitude toward politics. Given that these members of professional organizations and human rights groups had no political ambitions and no tainted past, the common people came forward to help them in as many ways as possible.

CONCLUSION

The preceding discussion on the events of the April 2006 uprising have shown that since the royal coup of February 2005, the palace had miscalculated the popular mood and remained oblivious to the political developments that brought the mainstream political parties, the Maoists, and the members of civil society to one platform against the king's direct rule. Additionally, the palace assumed that, as on previous occasions, street agitations could be tamed through repression. Instead, new political realities and the popular support for a change through peaceful means triumphed. What began as a movement with a narrow goal, the restoration of the House of Representatives, became a broader movement for democracy, peace, and a challenge to the patrimonial monarchical state structure. This was a vindication of the political strength of the opposition parties, including the Maoists, and the people's willingness to give the political parties an opportunity. But most importantly it was a victory of hope over despair.

NOTES

1. Official Chinese comment on the Nepal situation came in February 2006 when Chinese Foreign Ministry spokesman Kong Quan said that that China was "fairly concerned" about the political situation in Nepal and appealed to all parties to "narrow their differences through dialogue."

2. International Crisis Group (ICG), "Nepal: Responding to the Royal Coup," *Asia Policy Briefing* 36 (24 February 2005): 2.

3. In previous elections the participation had been more than 60 percent. 66 percent of voters cast their votes in parliamentary elections in 1999 and 62 percent voted in the municipal elections of 1997.

4. "Nepal King Yields to Protestors," *BBC News*, 21 April 2006, http://news.bbc.co.uk/2/hi/south_asia/4931000.stm (22 April 2006).

5. Text of Gyanendra's speech, 24 April 2006, http://news.bbc.co.uk/2/hi/south_asia/4940876.stm (24 April 2006).

6. Based on interviews with leaders of various political parties in Kathmandu in July 2006.

7. Interview with Laxman Basnet, Kathmandu, 7 July 2006.

8. Interview with Subel Bhandari, Kathmandu, 5 July 2006.

9. Kanka Mani Dixit, "Nepal: The Fuzzy Logic of Maoist Transformation," *Open Democracy*, http://www.opendemocracy.net/content/articles/PDF/3671.pdf (1 July 2006).

10. The opposition political parties called for street agitations in January 2006. But the government preempted the move by arresting the leaders before the agitations began. This foiled their plan. In April the leaders went into hiding before declaring the program. Some moved to rural areas.

11. ICG, "Nepal: from People Power to Peace?" *Asia Report* 115 (10 May 2006): 6.

12. During the visit of one of the authors in July 2006, many came forward to tell their stories of participation.

13. Interview with Devendra Raj Pandey, Kathmandu, 4 July 2006.

6

Problems and Prospects

To say that Nepal stands at a crossroads today is both a cliché and an understatement. Characterization of the present situation as a critical juncture and the description of the April 2006 popular uprising as a watershed in the history of Nepal may sound like exaggerations. But they all are true. Ironically, they are also reminiscent of two earlier times—April 1990 and January 1951; on both occasions Nepalis thought that a democratic Nepal was within reach only to see their dreams shattered, and the old state and the ancient régime returned with new repressive powers. The nation also saw the return of the politics of status quo, clientelism, and exclusion. In Latin the expression would be: *Eadem Mutato Resurgo* (Although changed, I rise again the same).

However, it is different this time. Unlike on previous occasions, the crises are deeper, the challenges are greater, and the stakes are higher. As we have demonstrated throughout the book, at the center of the crises lies the Nepali state—the effectiveness of which is questionable, not only on the basis of its capacity to deliver and transform the society, but also on the grounds of legitimacy. This is not to exonerate the Nepali politicians whose narrow social and ethnic base, myopic visions, and pursuance of vested interests have contributed to an unending crisis leading to state failure. The economic impediments and ecology have played a role as much as the ethnic composition of the country. A combination of the structural and conjunctural factors has been at work. This has deepened the crisis to the extent that a solution cannot be postponed any longer. Economic woes—stemming from natural causes, collapsing rural government services, price-hikes, and lack of donor confidence—are making the life of common people harsher and demand immediate attention. The culture of violence, militarization of the society, and norms of impunity have proliferated throughout the society and now pose a threat to the social equilibrium. These problems are rooted in politics but no longer limited within the political realm, and cannot be overlooked. Indeed, the Nepali state has managed to pull itself off from the brink of a total collapse, but resumption of violence, insurgency, and governmental meltdown may push the state back in that direction. Mindful of the post-9/11 global environment, we can say with confidence that a failed state located between two nuclear powers in a region peppered with insurgencies does not bode well for the nation and region.

The differences between the previous popular uprisings and the post-April 2006 Nepal not only point to the urgency of the situation, but also to the responsibilities and challenges the politicians face in charting a new course for the nation. Some of these challenges are immediate, while others are long-term in nature. In any case, the road to a stable and secure Nepal is long and arduous. The journey will require patience, ingenuity, wisdom, and persistence from all the parties involved in the process. The inescapable point of departure is the acknowledgement that the Nepali state, characterized by its patrimonial nature and repressive feature, has failed and the transformation of the Nepali state is well overdue. In some ways the commitment to this has been made in the eight-point declaration of 16 June 2006 where it set the objective to "bring about a forward-looking restructuring of the state . . . to resolve the class-based, racial, regional, and gender-based problems" (see appendix 4).

The political processes of the last decade and the events of 2006 have clearly identified the actors who would play pivotal roles: the mainstream political parties (either as an alliance or as separate entities), the Maoists, the civil society, and the palace and its beneficiaries. Any political move that keeps any of these forces out of the equation is heading for failure.

CHALLENGES AHEAD

The most immediate challenge is to maintain the understanding among the members of the SPA, and between the alliance and the Maoists. The mainstream political parties and their leaders do not enjoy the unremitting and everlasting support of the Nepali people. Previously the leaders have squandered their opportunity. The people of Nepal appear willing to give them another chance. But time is against them and patience may be thin on the part of the people; as such, the leaders will have to avoid any signs of partisan wrangling and deliver what is expected of them—a peaceful process leading to an election of the constituent assembly. The understanding between the alliance and the Maoists is fragile at best. Therefore, it needs to be handled with utmost care. The understanding reached in November 2005 and reaffirmed in June 2006 has produced two unambiguous documents, but that does not mean that their future is sealed together. The fragility of this understanding became obvious in the discussions in regard to the "management of arms" and the role of the United Nations in overseeing the process. Fortunately, both parties agreed in early August 2006 that Maoist forces and their weapons will be confined within designated cantonment areas under UN supervision during the election process. Similarly, the Nepali army will remain in its barracks and its weapons will not be "used for or against any side." The agreement reflected significant compromises on both sides, given the prime minister's earlier insistence that the rebel forces be first decommissioned before elections to an assembly were held and Maoist leaders' refusal to any such decommissioning before the polls. The responsibility of maintaining the understanding does not fall on the shoulders of the SPA leaders alone; the Maoist leaders too will have to act responsibly. If there is one distinct characteristic of the April 2006 uprising, that is the non-violence on the part of the pro-democracy activists. The Maoist leadership should not forget the fact that the uprising came about when they joined the unarmed people in their struggle for a democracy, not the other way round. Therefore, the expressed desire of the Nepali people is "a non-violent society where historical ills are tackled through discourses and political evolution rather than through atavistic violence."[1]

Having a functioning government during the period leading up to the election is a significant challenge for the political leaders. Although much won't be expected from the interim government, routine economic activities, continuation of developmental efforts, and ensuring a stable law and order situation are key to the survival of the government and its acceptability to the international community. The slow economic growth of the previous year is likely to constrain government efforts, but the government should not allow economic woes to derail the entire political process. Perhaps these would be easier to resolve than the issue of law and order. As of August 2006, more than four months after the uprising and the declaration of ceasefire, incidents of abduction, extortion, and killings by the Maoists were being reported in the press. For example, on 11 August the local press reported that four Dalit youths had been abducted by the Maoists in Baglung.[2] On 27 June, the UN Office of the High Commissioner for Human Rights in Nepal said that Maoists were responsible for the deaths of nine people in the first two months of the ceasefire. Similarly, extortion by the Maoists continued with the approval of the central leaders. Baburam Bhattarai, in a meeting with the business community in Kathmandu on 9 August, said that his party's donation and "taxation" drive was a transitional arrangement to raise resources to take care of its militia and urged the business community to bear with it until the political problem is solved. He insisted that, in the absence of budgetary support from the government, they had no option but to "raise money from donations."[3]

All eyes will be on Nepal in coming days to see whether the political parties and the interim government are making the right moves toward organizing the constituent assembly election, particularly ensuring an environment that allows participation without intimidation. A vast area of rural Nepal is under the control of the Maoist guerrillas. The question is whether the people in these areas will have the opportunity to listen to what political parties have to offer before going to the polls. There is no doubt that the central leaders will promise access, but it is the ground-level activists with arms at their disposal who will be the deciding factors. It will take more than promises and announcements from the party leaders to ensure a free and fair election. This will be a crucial test of Maoists' readiness to operate in a multiparty political environment, and their attitude toward dissent. Intimidation may not necessarily be directly related to politics, but continuation of violence and human rights violations are sufficient to scare off potential voters. Also important is ensuring that the political opponents will not be persecuted at a later date—whether by the Maoists or any other groups.

The role of the Maoists leading up to the election is closely related to a larger issue: the transformation of a rebel force into a political entity that feels comfortable in open politics. Simply stated, "the Maoist cadres need to undergo a rapid process of 'politicization' [sic] so that they learn to function in open society, without resorting to the threat of pointed muzzle."[4] This is a difficult task for the both the Maoist leaders and their foot soldiers. But this is not unprecedented, and such transformation does not require abandoning overall aims. The party's decision in the October 2005 plenum to join multiparty politics followed by the understanding with the SPA indicates that this is not a tactical move, but a reorientation of political strategy. In any event, they are not exactly alien to open politics; they emerged from mainstream politics in 1996. The political parties' willingness to create a space for them was both recognition of this change and their inability to bring changes in Nepali politics. If the political parties and the civil society want the transformation to take place, they have to lend a helping hand.

The power of the monarch has been significantly curtailed after the restoration of the parliament. This has also brought the question of the future of the monarchy to the fore. The public sentiment against the king was high and support for republicanism had been on the rise during and after the April 2006 uprising. But the future of the monarchy is a crucial and sensitive issue, and this will dominate Nepali politics until the new constitution is written. It can be said without any hesitation that Nepali society is now more polarized on the question of the fate of the monarchy as an institution than ever before. While the question "will Nepal retain a ceremonial monarchy or will it become a republic?" is being debated at all levels of the society, it is necessary to keep the palace under watch. As one of the Nepali youth leaders, Gagan Thapa, rightly noted, "it might be tempting to conclude that King Gyanendra is already history but the palace has definitely bought time for itself, a commodity that is more useful than legal provisions."[5] It is naïve to expect that the king and the powerful networks around him would accept a defeat and be thrown into oblivion so easily. Instead, the king, and to a great extent the army, would be looking for signs of weakness in the constitution writing process and acrimony among the political parties, and exploit those to their benefit. It should be of no surprise if the palace makes a move through its proxies, for example the Rashtriya Prajatantra Party (RPP) and Rashtriya Janashakti Party (RJP), in the political arena. Projecting the monarchy as a symbol of national unity would be the easiest slogan of the supporters of the palace to unite around. Any slip on this issue may derail the democratic process. The prime minister and Congress leader Girija Prasad Koirala's comment that the "king should also be given a space in democracy"[6] represents such moments when the schism within parties may open an opportunity for the palace to intervene.

The issue of religion may be thrust to the center of the debate to shore up support for the monarchy. Swami Dhruba—a Kathmandu-based Hindu preacher—insists that the deletion of Hinduism from the Nepali constitution was a very wrong decision on the part of the reinstated House. He warned, "We will not remain silent and continue to expose the policy of appeasement."[7] The Indian opposition Bharatiya Janata Party (BJP) may play a role in fueling this sentiment and the government needs to be proactive in this regard.

An interim constitution to govern the country and to hold the election is in place, but the difficulties associated with framing a permanent constitution are yet to be tackled. The constitution, like the process through which it will be written, will have to be inclusive, people-driven, and endorsed by the people. How will the new constitution redress the centuries of oppression and exclusion of ethnic groups, women, and the marginal population? Will a federal structure help to bring about equity among various regions? How will the new state institutions be built to reflect the social diversity? These questions represent some of the core issues of building a new state. But are the Nepali political leaders ready to build a new state? It is only their deeds that can answer the question.

While building a new Nepal is primarily a political process and therefore the responsibility falls on the shoulders of the politicians, the civil society has to play a pivotal role. The members of civil society have demonstrated that they are capable of playing their parts. After the royal coup in February

2005, the Citizen's Movement for Democracy and Peace (CMDP) and the press were at the forefront of the resistance and bore the brunt of repression. Equally important was their role as go-betweens to forge a unity between the SPA and the Maoists. Finally, they were at the forefront of the April 2006 uprising and the participation of members of the civil society galvanized the movement. The success of April 2006 was testimony to their appeal to the common people. Under new circumstances, the civil society will have to act as the conscience of the nation and remain vigilant to keep the politicians on track.

THE ROLE OF THE INTERNATIONAL COMMUNITY

The democratization of Nepal and the transformation of the Nepali state is entirely an endogenous process—it is for the people of Nepal to decide in which direction they want to take their country. But that is not to say that the international community has no role to play. The geographical location of the country matched with its dependence on foreign aid expose it to international vagaries and policies of various powerful countries. Unfortunately, the role of the international community, not only after the royal coup of 2005 but also during the crisis in April 2006, was not favorable to the pro-democracy movement.[8] But it is expected that the international community has learned from their mistakes and will make serious efforts to contribute to the democratization processes. Their roles can be broadly divided into four: 1) avoid making hasty judgments on political issues; 2) do not resume military aid to the Nepali army; 3) continue, and if possible increase, developmental support; and 4) support the peace process.

The fragile political process requires the space to work out solutions. The most important issue, as we discussed before, would be the future of the monarchy. There is a growing fear that the United States and/or China will try to protect the monarchy as an institution, at least in a ceremonial role. For the United States, the central argument could be that the monarchy will act as a neutralizing force against the Maoists' influence. The U.S. policy not to recognize the interim government if the Maoists join before renouncing violence is fueling the suspicion that the United States is trying to restore the monarchy. Such policies would harm the process and may turn out to be counter-productive. Despite commonly held suspicions about India's intentions, India has a significant role in the process. India's role in brokering an agreement between the Maoists and the opposition parties in 2005 has improved its standing in the eyes of Nepalis, but whether India is ready to accept a Nepal without the monarchy is yet to be made clear. In addition, the Indian opposition party—the Bharatiya Janata Party (BJP)—opposes any moves against the monarchy and has criticized the parliament's decision to declare Nepal a secular state.[9]

Increased military assistance from the United States to the Royal Nepalese Army (RNA) under the pretext of the "global war on terror" since 11 September 2001 has contributed to grave human rights violations and bolstered the king's hope that a military solution to the crisis is possible.[10] But the United States was not alone in providing the weapons; the United Kingdom and India have been the principal sources of weapons to the Nepali government for quite some time. Most of these supplies were supposedly halted after the royal coup. But press reports suggested that China and Pakistan either provided or offered to provide weapons. There was a major increase in security-related expenses in 2005. According to Finance Minister Ram Sharan Mahat, the government spent the equivalent of U.S. $261 million on security in 2005 compared with U.S. $164 million in 2001. Nevertheless, with a ceasefire in place and a peace process in progress, there cannot be any justifications for a continuing supply of arms.

The donors were seriously concerned with the pace of development works in the days running up to the April uprising. But the peace process should allow them to resume their work and to reach previously inaccessible areas. The reinvigoration of the development works will be the first signal to the people in the rural areas that it is no longer business-as-usual. An important element of the new development strategy should be inclusiveness.

Finally, the peace process will require support from the United Nations at various levels—from monitoring the ceasefire to the rehabilitation of the former combatants. Support from the international community should be forthcoming whenever the parties involved ask for help.

STATE FAILURE: BEYOND NEPAL

Underscoring the need for a better appreciation of state failure, Bilgin and Morton noted that "the conditions that allow for state failure to occur are almost never investigated."[11] Cognizant of this lacuna, we have attempted to fill in this void through this case study of Nepal. The historical development of the Nepali state and its relationship to the society has been examined employing the structural-historical approach. For the strength of this approach lies in combining not only the structural aspects of the society, but also the functional elements of the institution and the roles of individuals, because "state failures are man-made, not merely accidental nor—fundamentally—caused by geographical, environmental, or external factors."[12] Borrowing from Bilgin and Morton we can say that this study has analyzed "socio-economic conjuncture within which such 'failure' emerges." It is our understanding that it is precisely owing to the lack of this perspective that the international community has a dismal track record in responding to state failure.[13] Instead of trying to reorient the policy-making machinery to respond early to growing problems, the international community waits until "the situation becomes acute enough to threaten the world beyond their boundaries."[14] Stated simply, state failures receive little attention unless there is a spillover effect, although it is well known that that state failure "directly affects" the domestic situation while it only "contributes to" external instability.[15]

The state failure in Nepal is yet to have a spillover effect causing regional instability, and to date, the likelihood of Nepal becoming a hotbed of militancy or breeding ground for transnational terrorists is slim. But as this study has demonstrated Nepal offers lessons in understanding state failure, the relevance and implications of which stretch far beyond the boundaries of Nepal.

NOTES

1. Kanak Mani Dixit, "Nepal: The Fuzzy Logic of Maoist Transformation," *Open Democracy*, 2006, http://www.opendemocracy.net/content/articles/PDF/3671.pdf (1 July 2006).

2. Lal Prasad Sharma, "Maoist Abducts Four, Thrash One," *eKantipur*, 2006, http://www.kantipuronline.com/kolnews.php?&nid=82440 (12 August 2006).

3. "Bear with Donations for Some Time," *Kathmandu Post*, 2006, http://www.southasianmedia.net/cnn.cfm?id=316045&category=Economy&Country=NEPAL (10 August 2006).

4. Dixit, "Nepal: The Fuzzy Logic."

5. "People's Movement Defines Nepal," *BBC News*, 2 June 2006, http://news.bbc.co.uk/2/hi/south_asia/5033512.stm (15 June 2006).

6. "King Should Be Given Space: PM," *Nepal Post* (7 August 2006): 1.

7. "'Secular Nepal' Finds Itself in the Eye of Controversy," *Nepalnews.com*, 24 May 2006, http://www.nepalnews.com/archive/2006/others/feature/may/news_feature07.php (14 August 2006).

8. For detailed discussion on the role of the foreign diplomats in Kathmandu during the April 2006 uprising, see: ICG, "Nepal: From People Power to Peace?" *Asia Report* 115 (10 May 2006): 11–13 and 19–20.

9. "BJP Rues Nepal's Switch from Hindu to Secular State," *Times of India* (20 May 2006): 1.

10. U.S. military assistance to Nepal increased dramatically after 2001; in mid-2001, the U.S. administration anticipated spending some $225,000 the following fiscal year (October 2001–September 2002) on the military training of Nepali troops and did not plan to provide any financing (via grants and loans) for military purchases by Nepal. After 9/11, the United States added $20 million in a supplemental allocation. In fiscal 2003, Nepal received $3.15 million from the Foreign

Military Funding program and $500,000 under another program. For fiscal 2004, the U.S. administration asked Congress for $10.6 million financing. The justification offered is interesting: "FMF in Nepal will help its government cope with a brutal insurgency, restore enough stability to permit elections, and prevent the countryside from becoming a haven for al Qaeda and other terrorist groups." Farooq Sulehria, "Nepal: A Royal Coup," *Green Left Weekly* (16 February 2005).

11. Pinar Bilgin and Adam David Morton, "From 'Rouge' to 'Failed' States?' The Fallacy of Short-Termism," *Politics* 23, no. 3 (2004): 174.

12. Robert Rotberg, "The New Nature of Nation-State Failure." *The Washington Quarterly* 25, no. 3 (2002): 93.

13. David Carment, "Assessing State Failure: Implications for Theory and Policy," *Third World Quarterly* 24, no. 3 (2003): 408.

14. Bilgin and Morton, "From 'Rouge,'" 171.

15. Chester A. Corcker, "Engaging Failing States," *Foreign Affairs*, (September/October 2003): 34–37.

Appendix 1

Nepal: The Fundamentals

A mountainous and landlocked country in South Asia, Nepal is located between the two most populous countries of the world, India to the east, south, and west, and China to the north. The total area of the country is 147,181 sq. km. The northern range (Himalayas) is covered with snow all year round, while the southern area (Terai) is of alluvial soil and consists of dense forests. The country is divided into three ecological belts: mountain, hill, and Terai, accommodating 7.3, 44.3, and 48.4 percent of the population respectively. The hills are located in the central region. The total population of Nepal is estimated at twenty-seven million (the last census in 2001 recorded the number at 23.07 million). Per capita annual income is U.S. $230.[1] While agriculture constitutes the backbone of the country's economy—providing employment to 81 percent of the total population—only 20 percent of the land area is cultivable and land ownership is highly skewed. "The bottom 40 percent of households owns only 9 percent of the total agricultural land, while the top 6 percent occupies more than 33 percent."[2]

Nepal has fourteen *anchals*, or zones, and seventy-five *jillas*, or districts, which are grouped under five development regions (eastern, central, western, mid-western, and far western). About 86 percent of the population lives in the rural areas. Nepali society is ethnically diverse. The Nepal government officially recognizes fifty-nine Janajati (nationalities) groups, which is a contentious issue. The census data of 2001 lists people belonging to 102 caste/ethnic groups. Together, indigenous people comprise 37.2 percent of the population; the largest among them are the Maar (7.1 percent), the Tharu (6.7 percent), and the Tamang (5.6 percent). There are at least ninety-two different languages, and ten different religions in Nepal. The recently conducted second Nepal Living Standard Survey (NLSS) report

183

2003/2004 has revealed that the absolute poverty level in Nepal has declined by 11 percent as compared to the NLSS-I, which had indicated that 42 percent of people were living under the absolute poverty line in 1995/1996. Adult literacy rate is 48.6 percent. Life expectancy at birth is 61.6 years. The annual population growth rate between 1975 and 2003 was 2.3 percent.[3]

NOTES

1. World Bank, *World Development Report 2004* (New York: Oxford University Press, 2004). A recent unofficial estimate puts the amount at U.S. $271.

2. SAAPE (South Asia Alliance for Poverty Eradication), *Poverty in South Asia 2003: Civil Society Perspectives* (Kathmandu: SAAPE, 2003): 126.

3. UNDP, *Human Development Report 2003* (New York: Oxford University Press, 2003).

Appendix 2

Memorandum from UNPF to the Prime Minister

[Note: Baburam Bhattarai, the leader of the UNPF, the political wing of the Communist Party, submitted a forty-point memorandum to the Prime Minister Sher Bahadur Deuba on 4 February 1996. Following is the reproduction of the memorandum.]

Right Honourable Prime Minister
Prime Minister's Office
Singha Darbar, Kathmandu
Sub: Memorandum

Sir,

It has been six years since the autocratic monarchical partyless Panchayat system was ended by the 1990 People's Movement and a constitutional monarchical multiparty parliamentary system established. During this period state control has been exercised by a tripartite interim government, a single-party government of the Nepali Congress, a minority government of UML and a present Nepali Congress-RPP-Sadbhavana coalition. That, instead of making progress, the situation of the country and the people is going downhill is evident from the fact that Nepal has slid to being the second poorest country in the world; people living below the absolute poverty line has gone up to 71 percent; the number of unemployed has reached more than 10 percent while the number of people who are semi-employed or in disguised employment has crossed 60 percent; the country is on the verge of bankruptcy due to rising foreign loans and deficit trade; economic and cultural encroachment within the country by foreign, and especially Indian, expansionists is increasing by the day; the gap between the rich and the poor and between towns and villages is growing wider. On the other hand, parliamentary parties that have formed the government by various means have shown that they are more interested in remaining in power with the blessings of foreign imperialist and expansionist masters than in the welfare of the country and the people. This is clear from their blindly adopting so-called privatisation and liberalisation to fulfil the interests of all imperialists and from the recent "national consensus" reached in handing over the rights over Nepal's water resources to Indian expansionists. Since 6 April 1992, the United People's Front has been involved in various struggles to fulfil relevant demands related to nationalism, democracy and livelihood, either by itself or with others. But rather than fulfil those demands, the governments formed at different times have violently suppressed the agitators and taken the lives of hundreds; the most recent example of this is the armed police operation in Rolpa a few months back. In this context, we would like to once again present to the current coalition government demands related to nationalism, democracy and livelihood, which have been raised in the past and many of which have become relevant in the present context.

OUR DEMANDS

Concerning nationality

- All discriminatory treaties, including the 1950 Nepal-India Treaty, should be abrogated.
- The so-called Integrated Mahakali Treaty concluded on 29 January 1996 should be repealed immediately, as it is designed to conceal the disastrous Tanakpur Treaty and allows Indian imperialist monopoly over Nepal's water resources.
- The open border between Nepal and India should be regulated, controlled and systematised. All vehicles with Indian license plates should be banned from Nepal.
- The Gorkha Recruitment Centres should be closed. Nepali citizens should be provided dignified employment in the country.
- Nepali workers should be given priority in different sectors. A "work permit" system should be strictly implemented if foreign workers are required in the country.
- The domination of foreign capital in Nepali industries, business and finance should be stopped.
- An appropriate customs policy should be devised and implemented so that economic development helps the nation become self-reliant.

- The invasion of imperialist and colonial culture should be banned. Vulgar Hindi films, videos and magazines should be immediately outlawed.
- The invasion of colonial and imperial elements in the name of NGOs and INGOs should be stopped.

Concerning people's democracy

- A new constitution should be drafted by representatives elected for the establishment of a people's democratic system.
- All special privileges of the king and the royal family should be abolished.
- The army, the police and the bureaucracy should be completely under people's control.
- All repressive acts, including the Security Act, should be repealed.
- Everyone arrested extra-judicially for political reasons or revenge in Rukum, Rolpa, Jajarkot, Gorkha, Kabhrc, Sindhupalchowk. Sindhuli, Dhanusa, Ramechhap, and so on, should be immediately released. All false cases should be immediately withdrawn.
- The operation of armed police, repression and state-sponsored terror should be immediately stopped.
- The whereabouts of citizens who disappeared in police custody at different times, namely Dilip Chaudhary, Bhuwan Thapa Magar, Prabhakar Subedi and others, should be investigated and those responsible brought to justice. The families of victims should be duly compensated.
- All those killed during the People's Movement should be declared martyrs. The families of the martyrs and those injured and deformed should be duly compensated, and the murderers brought to justice.
- Nepal should be declared a secular nation.
- Patriarchal exploitation and discrimination against women should be stopped. Daughters should be allowed access to paternal property.
- All racial exploitation and suppression should be stopped. Where ethnic communities are in the majority, they should be allowed to form their own autonomous governments.
- Discrimination against downtrodden and backward people should be stopped. The system of untouchability should be eliminated.
- All languages and dialects should be given equal opportunities to prosper. The right to education in the mother tongue up to higher levels should be guaranteed.
- The right to expression and freedom of press and publication should be guaranteed. The government mass media should be completely autonomous.

- Academic and professional freedom of scholars, writers, artists and cultural workers should be guaranteed.
- Regional discrimination between the hills and the Terai should be eliminated. Backward areas should be given regional autonomy. Rural and urban areas should be treated at par.
- Local bodies should be empowered and appropriately equipped.

Concerning livelihood

- Land should belong to "tenants." Land under the control of the feudal system should be confiscated and distributed to the landless and the homeless.
- The property of middlemen and comprador capitalists should be confiscated and nationalised. Capital lying unproductive should be invested to promote industrialisation.
- Employment should be guaranteed for all. Until such time as employment can be arranged, an unemployment allowance should be provided.
- A minimum wage for workers in industries, agriculture and so on should be fixed and strictly implemented.
- The homeless should be rehabilitated. No one should be "relocated" until alternative infrastructure is guaranteed.
- Poor farmers should be exempt from loan repayments. Loans taken by small farmers from the Agricultural Development Bank should be written off. Appropriate provisions should be made to provide loans for small farmers.
- Fertiliser and seeds should be easily available and at a cheap rate. Farmers should be provided with appropriate prices and markets for their produce.
- People in flood and drought-affected areas should be provided with appropriate relief materials.
- Free and scientific health services and education should be available to all. The commercialisation of education should be stopped.
- Inflation should be checked. Wages should be increased proportionate to inflation. Essential goods should be cheaply and easily available to everyone.
- Drinking water, roads and electricity should be provided to all villagers.
- Domestic and cottage industries should be protected and promoted.
- Corruption, smuggling, black marketing, bribery, and the practices of middlemen and so on should be eliminated.
- Orphans, the disabled, the elderly and children should be duly honoured and protected.

We would like to request the present coalition government to immediately initiate steps to fulfil these demands which are inextricably linked with the Nepali nation and the life of the people. If there are no positive indications towards this from the government by 17 February 1996, we would like to inform you that we will be forced to adopt the path of armed struggle against the existing state power.

Thank you.

Dr. Baburam Bhattarai
Chairman
Central Committee, United People's Front, Nepal

Source: Deepak Thapa, ed., *Understanding the Maoist Movement of Nepal* (Kathmandu, Martin Chautari, 2003): 391.

Appendix 3

Unofficial Translation of the Letter of Understanding between the Seven-Party Coalition and the Communist Party of Nepal

[Agreed in November 2005]

The long struggle between absolute monarchy and democracy in Nepal has now reached a very grave and new turn. Establishing peace by resolving the ten-year-old armed conflict through a forward-looking political outlet has become the need of today. Therefore, implementing the concept of absolute democracy through a forward-looking restructuring of the state has become an inevitable need to solve the problems related to class, caste, gender, region, etc., of all sectors including political, economic, social, and cultural, bringing autocratic monarchy to an end and establishing absolute democracy. We make public that, against this existing backdrop and reference in the country, the following understanding has been reached between the seven parliamentary parties and the CPN (Maoist) through different methods of talks.

POINTS OF UNDERSTANDING

1. Today, democracy, peace, prosperity, social advancement, and a free and sovereign Nepal is the chief wish of all Nepalese. We completely agree that autocratic monarchy is the main hurdle in (realizing) this. It is our clear view that without establishing absolute democracy by ending autocratic monarchy, there is no possibility of peace, progress, and prosperity in the country. Therefore, an understanding has been reached to establish absolute democracy by ending autocratic monarchy, with all forces against the autocratic monarchy centralizing their assault against autocratic monarchy from their respective positions, thereby creating a nationwide storm of democratic protests.

191

2. The seven agitating parties are fully committed to the fact that only by establishing absolute democracy through the restoration of the parliament with the force of agitation, forming an all-party government with complete authority, holding elections to a constituent assembly through dialogue and understanding with the Maoists, can the existing conflict in the country be resolved and sovereignty and state power completely transferred to the people. It is the view and commitment of the CPN (Maoist) that the above mentioned goal can be achieved by holding a national political conference of the agitating democratic forces, and through its decision, forming an interim government to hold constituent assembly elections. An understanding has been reached between the agitating seven parties and the CPN (Maoist) to continue dialogue on this procedural work-list and find a common understanding. It has been agreed that the force of people's movement is the only alternative to achieve this.

3. Today, the country has demanded the establishment of permanent peace along with a positive solution to the armed conflict. Therefore, we are committed to ending autocratic monarchy and the existing armed conflict, and establishing permanent peace in the country through constituent assembly elections and forward-looking political outlet. The CPN (Maoist) expresses its commitment to move along the new peaceful political stream through this process. In this very context, an understanding has been reached to keep, during the holding of constituent assembly elections after ending autocratic monarchy, the armed Maoist force and the royal army under the supervision of the United Nations or any other reliable international supervision, to conclude the elections in a free and fair manner, and accept the result of the elections. We expect reliable international mediation even during the dialogue process.

4. Expressing clearly and making public institutional commitment to the democratic norms and values like the competitive multi-party system of governance, civil liberties, human rights, the concept of the rule of law, fundamental rights, etc., the CPN (Maoist) has expressed commitment to move forward its activities accordingly.

5. The CPN (Maoist) has expressed its commitment to create an environment allowing the political activists of other democratic parties displaced during the course of the armed conflict to return to their former localities and live there with dignity, return their home, land, and property seized in an unjust manner, and carry out their activities without let or hindrance.

6. Undertaking self-criticism and self-evaluation of past mistakes, the CPN (Maoist) has expressed commitment not to repeat such mistakes in future.

7. The seven political parties, undertaking self-evaluation, have expressed commitment not to repeat the mistakes of the past which were committed while in parliament and in government.
8. In the context of moving the peace process forward, commitment has been expressed to fully respect the norms and values of human rights and press freedom and move ahead accordingly.
9. As the announcement of municipal polls pushed forward with the ill-motive of deluding the people and the international community and giving continuity to the autocratic and illegitimate rule of the king, and the talk of elections to parliament are a crafty ploy, we announce to actively boycott them and call upon the general public to make such elections a failure.
10. The people and their representative political parties are the real guardians of nationality. Therefore, we are firmly committed to protecting the independence, sovereignty, geographical integrity of the country and national unity. Based on the principle of peaceful coexistence, it is our common obligation to maintain friendly relations with all countries of the world and good-neighbor relationships with neighboring countries, especially India and China. But we request the patriotic masses to be cautious against the false attempt by the king and (his) loyalists to prolong his autocratic and illegitimate rule and delude the patriotic people by projecting the illusory "Mandale" nationalism and questioning the patriotism of the political parties, and appeal to the international powers and the people to support, in every possible way, the democratic movement against autocratic monarchy in Nepal.
11. We call upon the civil society, professional organizations, various wings of parties, people of all communities and regions, press, and intellectuals to actively participate in the peaceful movement launched on the basis of these understandings centered on democracy, peace, prosperity, forward-looking social change, and the country's independence, sovereignty, and pride.
12. Regarding the inappropriate conducts that took place between the parties in the past, a common commitment has been expressed to investigate any objection raised by any party over such incidents, take action if found guilty, and to make the action public. An understanding has been reached to settle any problem emerging between the parties through peaceful dialogue at the concerned level or at the leadership level.

Source: "12-Point Understanding Between Parties and Maoists," *eKantipur .com*, 22 November 2005, http://www.kantipuronline.com/kolnews.php ?&nid=57858 (12 April 2006).

Appendix 4

Unofficial Translation of the Eight-Point Agreement between SPA and the CPN (M)

[Note: On 16 June 2006 the seven-party alliance (SPA) and the CPN (M) reached an Eight-Point Agreement setting out the conditions for immediate and fair elections to a Constituent Assembly.]

Below is the unofficial translation of the agreement:

1. Effectively and honestly implement the twelve-point understanding reached between the SPA and Maoists in November last year and the twenty-five-point Ceasefire Code of Conduct signed between the SPA government and CPN (Maoist) on 26 May this year.
2. Commitment to democratic norms and values including competitive multi-party system, civic liberties, fundamental rights, human rights, press freedom, and the concept of rule of law and carry out each other's activities in a peaceful manner.
3. Request the United Nations to help in the monitoring and management of the armies and arms of both government and Maoist sides for a free and fair election to the constituent assembly.
4. Guarantee the democratic rights achieved through the 1990 Popular Movement and the recent historic People's Movement; draft an interim constitution based on the twelve-point understanding and the ceasefire Code of Conduct; form an interim government accordingly; announce the dates for constituent assembly elections; dissolve the House of Representatives through consensus after making alternative arrangement; dissolve the people's governments of CPN (Maoist).
5. Decide issues of national interests having long-term effects through consensus.

6. Guarantee the fundamental right of the Nepali people to participate in the constituent assembly elections without any fear, influence, threat, and violence. Invite international observation and monitoring during the elections as per the need.

7. Bring about a forward-looking restructuring of the state so as to resolve the class-based, racial, regional, and gender-based problems through constituent assembly elections. Transform the ceasefire between the Nepal Government and CPN (Maoist) into permanent peace by focusing on democracy, peace, prosperity, forward-looking change and the country's independence, sovereignty, and pride, and express commitment to resolve the problem through talks.

8. The government and Maoist talk teams have been directed to accomplish all tasks related to above-mentioned points without any delay.

Source: "Nepal—July 2006," *Analytical Monthly Review*, 20 July 2006, http://mrzine.monthlyreview.org/amr200706.html (4 August 2006).

Bibliography

Adhikari, Jagannath. "Farmers' Rights to Land: A Crucial Dimension on Livelihood Security." *South Asia Partnership Canada,* 2004. http://action.web.ca/home/sap/nepal_resources.shtml?x=69984 (6 August 2006).

Adhikary, K. R. "The Fruits of Panchayat Development." *Himalayan Research Bulletin* XV, no. 2 (March 1996): 19.

Ali, Daud. *Courtly Culture and Political Life in Early Medieval India.* Cambridge: Cambridge University Press, 2004.

Aryal, Gorkhana Raj, and Ghan Shyam Awasthi. "Agrarian Reform and Access to Land Resource in Nepal: Present Status and Future Perspective Action." CERAI: Center for Rural Studies and International Agriculture, n.d. http://www.cerai.es/fmra/archivo/nepal.pdf (28 July 2006).

Asian Development Bank. "Nepal: Public Finance Management Assessment." ADB Strategy and Assessment Program. Mimeo, Manila: ADB, December 2005.

Banerjee, Sumanta. *India's Simmering Revolution: The Naxalite Uprising.* London: Zed, 1984.

Baral, Lok Raj. *Nepal's Politics of Referendum: A Study of Groups, Personalities and Trends.* New Delhi: Vikas, 1983.

———, ed. *Nepal: Parties and Parliament.* Delhi: Adroit, 2003.

Barchet-Marquez, Viviane. "Explaining Sociopolitical Change in Latin America." *Latin American Research Review* 27, no. 3 (1992): 91–122.

Bastola, Tunga, and Radhakrishna G. C. "A Perspective on Population Census 2001." *Population Monograph* 1. Kathmandu: Central Bureau of Statistics Report, Government of Nepal Central Bureau of Statistics Report, 2005.

Bayly, C. A. *Indian Society and the Making of the British Empire.* Cambridge: Cambridge University Press, 1988.

BBC News. "Nepal: Row Over U.S. Support," 2001. http://news.bbc.co.uk/1/hi/world/south_asia/1564467.stm (29 May 2005).

BBC News. "People's Movement Defines Nepal," 2006. http://news.bbc.co.uk/2/hi/ south_asia/5033512.stm (15 June 2006).

Bhattachan, Krishna B. "Possible Ethnic Revolution or Insurgency in a Predatory Hindu State." In *Domestic Conflict and Crisis of Governability in Nepal*, edited by Dhruba Kumar, 135–63. Kathmandu: Center for Nepal and Asian Studies, 2000.

Bhurtel, Jugal, and Saleem H. Ali. "The Green Roots of Red Rebellion: Environmental Degradation and the Rise of the Maoist Movement in Nepal." www.uvm .edu/~shali/Maoist.pdf (29 September 2005).

Bilgin, Pinar, and Adam Morton D. "From 'Rouge' to 'Failed' States? The Fallacy of Short-Termism." *Politics* 23, no. 3 (2004): 169–80.

Bista, D. B. *Fatalism and Development: Nepal's Struggle for Modernization*. Calcutta: Orient Longman, 1991.

Bøås, Morten, and Kathleen Jennings. "Insecurity and Development: The Rhetoric of the Failed State." *European Journal of Development Research* 17, no. 5 (September 2005): 385–95.

Bratton, Michael, and Nicolas van de Walle. "Neo-Patrimonial Regimes and Political Transitions in Africa." *World Politics* 46, no. 4 (July 1994): 453–89.

Brown, Louise T. *The Challenge to Democracy in Nepal: A Political History*. London and New York: Routledge, 1996.

Burghart, Richard. "The Formation of the Concept of Nation-State in Nepal." *The Journal of Asian Studies* 44, no. 1 (November 1984): 101–25.

——. "The Political Culture of Panchayat Democracy." In *Nepal in the Nineties: Version of the Past, Visions of the Future*, edited by Michael Hutt, 1–13. New Delhi: Oxford University Press, 1994.

Bush, George W. "The National Security Strategy of the United States of America," September 2002. http://www.whitehouse.gov/nsc/nss.html (22 January 2003).

Cameron, Mary M. *On the Edge of the Auspicious: Gender and Caste in Nepal*. Urbana and Chicago: University of Illinois Press, 1998.

Carment, David. "Assessing State Failure: Implications for Theory and Policy." *Third World Quarterly* 24, no. 3 (2003): 407–27.

Center for Strategic and International Studies (CSIS) and the Association of the US Army (AUSA). *Play to Win: Bi-partisan Commission on Post-Conflict Reconstruction* Washington, DC: CSIS, and Arlington: AUSA, 2003.

Chandra, Kanchan. *Why Ethnic Parties Succeed: Patronage and Ethnic Headcounts in India*. Cambridge: Cambridge University Press, 2004.

Colombo Plan. *The Columbia Electronic Encyclopedia*. © 1994, 2000–2005, on Infoplease. http://www.infoplease.com/ce6/history/A0812916.html (20 August 2006).

Communist Party of Nepal (CPNM). "One Year of People's War in Nepal—A Review." *Worker* 3, February 1997. http://www.cpnm.org/worker/issue3/oneyear_pw .htm#THE%20SECOND%20PLAN:%20Planned%20Development%20of%20 Guerrilla%20Warfare (6 July 2005).

Communist Party of Nepal (CPN-UML). "History, First Congress." http://www .cpnuml.org/1congress.html (28 August 2005).

——. "Jhapa Struggle and Development of ML Mainstream." http://www.cpnuml .org/jhapa.html (29 August 2005).

——. "Polarization and Integration." http://www.cpnuml.org/about/polarisation .htm (22 May 2005).

——. "The Historic Initiation and After." *The Worker*, no. 2, June 1996. http://www.cpnm.org/worker/issue2/w2_1p.htm (6 August 2005).

Corcker, Chester A. "Engaging Failing States." *Foreign Affairs* 82, no. 5 (September/October 2003): 34–37.

Dahal, D. R., Y. B. Gurung, B. Acharya, K. Hemchuri, and D. Swarnakar. "Nepal Dalit Strategy Report: Situational Analysis of Dalits in Nepal." Prepared for National Planning Commission, His Majesty's Government Nepal (May 2002). http://www.nepaldalitinfo.20m.com/archives/Analysis2002.pdf (22 April 2005).

Dahal, Ram Kumar. *Constitutional and Political Development in Nepal*. Kathmandu: Ratna Pushtak Bhandar, 2001.

Dearth, Douglas H. "Failed States: an International Conundrum." *Defense Intelligence Journal* 5, no. 2 (1996): 119–30.

De Sales, Anne. Translated by David Gellner. "The Kham Magar Country, Nepal: Between Ethnic Claims and Maoism." In *European Bulletin of Himalayan Research* 19, edited by Deepak Thapa, 59–88. Kathmandu: Martin Chautari, 2003.

Devkota, Surendra R. "The Politics of Poverty in Nepal: Structural Analysis of Socioeconomic Development from the Past Five Decades." *Heidelberg Papers in South Asian and Comparative Politics*. Working Paper no. 25. Heidelberg: South Asia Institute, Department of Political Science, University of Heidelberg, February 2005.

Dhakal, Dhanendra Purush. *Jana Andolan 2046 (Mass Movement 1990)*. Kathmandu: Bhupendra Purush Dhakal, 1992.

Dirks, N. B. *The Hollow Crown: Ethnohistory of an Indian Kingdom*. Cambridge: Cambridge University Press, 1987.

Dixit, Shanta. "Nepal Education in Crisis." *Harvard South Asian Journal* 3, no. 1 (2005). http://www.harvardsaa.org/saj/news.php?nID=7&pgID=1 (12 August 2006).

Dorff, Robert. "Failed States after 9/11: What Did We Know and What Have We Learned." *International Studies Perspectives* 6, no. 1 (2005): 20–34.

Evans, Peter. *Embedded Autonomy: States and Industrial Transformation*. Princeton: Princeton University Press, 1995.

Fujikura, Tatsuro. "Emancipation of Kamaiyas: Development, Social Movement, and Youth Activism in Post-Jana Andolan Nepal." *Himalayan Research Bulletin* XXI, no. 1 (March 2002): 29–35.

Fukuyama, Francis. "Nation Building 101." *Atlantic Monthly*, 2004. http://www.theatlantic.com/doc/200401/fukuyama (25 January 2005).

Garsony, Robert. "Sowing the Wind: History and Dynamics of Maoist Revolt in Nepal's Rapti Hills." Consultancy Reports to Mercy Corps International, March 2004. http://www.irgltd.com/Resources/Discussion_Forum/DF15_Nepal_Maoist_Revolt-03-04.pdf (28 April 2005).

Garver, John W. "China-India Rivalry in Nepal: The Clash over Chinese Arms Sales." *Asian Survey* 31, no. 10 (October 1991): 956–75.

Gayley, Holly. "Gyanendra's Test Nepal's Monarchy in the Era of Democracy." *Harvard Asia Quarterly* VI, no. 1, Winter 2002. http://www.asiaquarterly.com/content/view/113/ (April 24 2005).

Geertz, Clifford. *Negara: Theatre State in Nineteenth Century Bali*. Princeton: Princeton University Press, 1982.

Gellner, David N. "Introduction." In *Nationalism and Ethnicity in a Hindu Kingdom: The Politics of Culture in Contemporary Nepal*, edited by David Gellner, N. Joanna

Pfaff-Czarnecka, and John Whelpton, 3–32. Amsterdam: Hardwood Academic Publishers, 1997.

Gellner, David N. "Introduction: Transformations of the Nepalese State." In *Resistance and the State: Nepalese Experience*, edited by David Gellner, 1–30. New Delhi: Social Science Press, 2002.

Goodwill, Merrill. "Bureaucracy and Bureaucrats: Some Themes Drawn from the Nepal Experience." *Asian Survey* 15, no. 10 (October 1975): 892–95.

Goutam, Shobha, Amrita Banskota, and Rita Manchanda. "Where There Are No Men: Women in the Maoist Insurgency in Nepal." In *Understanding the Maoist Movement of Nepal*, edited by Deepak Thapa, 93–124. Kathmandu: Martin Chautari, 2003.

Gramsci, Antonio. *Selections from Prison Notebooks.* New York: International General, 1971.

Guha, Ranajit. *Dominance without Hegemony: History and Power in Colonial India.* Cambridge, MA: Harvard University Press, 1998.

Guneratne, Arjun. "Modernization, the State, and the Construction of a Tharu Identity in Nepal." *The Journal of Asian Studies* 57, no. 3 (August 1998): 749–73.

Guneratne, Arjun. *Many Tongues, One People: The Making of Tharu Identity in Nepal.* Ithaca, NY: Cornell University Press, 2002.

Gupta, Anirudha. *Politics in Nepal: A Study of Post Rana Political Development and Party Politics.* Bombay: Allied, 1964.

Gurung, Harka. *Nepal: Social Demography and Expressions.* Kathmandu: New Era, 1998.

——. *Social Demography Nepal Census 2001.* Lalitpur: Himal Books (Second Edition), 2005.

——. "The Sociology of Elections in Nepal, 1959 to 1981." *Asian Survey* 22, no. 3 (March 1982): 304–14.

Hacchethu, Krishna. "Political Parties and the State." In *Resistance and the State: Nepalese Experience*, edited by D. Gellner, 133–77. New Delhi: Social Science Press, 2002.

——. *Party Building in Nepal: Organization, Leadership and People, a Comparative Study of the Nepali Congress and the Communist Party of Nepal (Unified Marxist-Leninist).* Kathmandu: Mandala Book Point, 2002.

Hallinan, Conn. "Nepal—Cleaning up the Mess." *Asia Times*, 17 February 2005. http://www.atimes.com/atimes/South_Asia/GB17Df05.html (30 May 2005).

Hangen, Susan. "The Emergence of a Mongol Race in Nepal." *Anthropology News* 47, no. 2 (February 2006): 12. http://www.aaanet.org/press/an/hangen.html (31 August 2006).

Haviland, Charles. "Meeting Nepal's Maoists." *BBC News*, 12 April 2005, http://news.bbc.co.uk/2/hi/south_asia/4434197.stm (13 April 2005).

Helman, Gerald and Steven Ratner. "Saving Failed States." *Foreign Policy* 89 (Winter 1993): 3–20.

Höfer, András. *The Caste Hierarchy and the State in Nepal—A Study of the Muluki Ain of 1854.* Innsbruck: Universitatsverlag Wagner, 1979.

Hoftun, Martin. "The Dynamics and Chronology of the 1990 Revolution." In *Nepal in the Nineties: Version of the Past, Visions of the Future*, edited by Michael Hutt, 14–27. New Delhi: Oxford University Press, 2002.

Hoftun, Martin, William Raeper, and John Whelpton. *People, Politics an Ideology: Democracy and Social Change in Nepal*. Kathmandu: Mandala Book Point, 1999.

Home-Dixon, T. "On the Threshold: Environmental Changes as Causes of Acute Conflict." *International Security* 16, no. 2 (Fall 1991). 76–116.

Hutt, Michael. "Introduction." In *Himalayan People's War: Nepal's Maoist Rebellion*, edited by Michael Hutt, 1–20. Bloomington, Indiana University Press, 2004.

International Crisis Group. "Nepal: From People Power to Peace?" *Asia Report*, no.115 (10 May 2006): 11–13, 19–20.

Interview with Jhalanath Khanal, member standing committee, CPN (UM-L), Kathmandu, 6 July 2006.

Jamison, T., and Marlaine E. Lockheed. "Participation in Schooling: Determinants and Learning Outcomes." *Economic Development and Cultural Change* 35, no. 2 (January 1987): 279–306.

Joshi, B., and L. F. Rose. *Democratic Innovations in Nepal. A Case Study of Political Acculturation*. Berkeley: University of California Press, 1966.

Joshi, Sushma. "Goodwill Hunting." *Madhesi*, 31 July 2006. https://madhesi .wordpress.com/2006/07/31/goodwill-hunting/ (2 September 2006).

Kaplan, Robert D. "The Coming Anarchy." *Atlantic Monthly* 273, no. 2 (February 1994): 44–76.

Kathmandu Post. "Bear with Donations for Some Time," 2006. http://www .southasianmedia.net/cnn.cfm?id=316045&category=Economy&Country=NEPAL (10 August 2006).

Khadka, Naryan. "Crisis in Nepal's Partyless Panchayat System: The Case for More Democracy." *Pacific Affairs* 59, no 3 (Autumn 1986): 429–54.

———. "Foreign Aid to Nepal: Donor Motivations in the Post-Cold War Period." *Asian Survey* 37, no. 11 (November 1997): 1044–61.

———. "Nepal's Stagnant Economy: The Panchayat Legacy." *Asian Survey* 31, no. 8 (August 1991): 694–711.

———. "U.S. Aid to Nepal in the Cold War Period: Lessons for the Future." *Pacific Affairs* 73, no. 1 (Spring 2000): 77–95.

Khan, Mushtaq H. "State Failure in Developing Countries and Strategies of Institutional Reform." Paper presented at the Annual Bank Conference on Development Economies, Oslo, 24–26 June 2002.

Kimyu, Peter. "Development Policy in Kenya: Which Way Forward?" *Wajibu* 15, no. 2 (1999). http://web.peacelink.it/wajibu/7_issue/p1.html (1 September 2005).

King Ganayndra. "It's a Question of Survival." *Time Asia*, 2005. http://www.time .com/time/asia/2005/nepal/int_ganendra.html (25 April 2005).

Kumar, Dhruba. "Managing Nepal's India Policy?" *Asian Survey* 30, no. 7 (July 1990): 697–710.

Lawoti, Mahendra. "Centralizing Politics and the Growth of the Maoist Insurgency in Nepal." *Himalaya* 13, no. 1 (2003): 49–58.

———. "Inclusive Democratic Institutions in Nepal." *Himal Assocation, Kathmandu*. Summary of a conference paper, "The Agenda of Transformation: Inclusion in Nepali Democracy", organized by Social Science Baha, 24–26 April 2003, Birendra International Convention Centre, Kathmandu.

———. *Towards a Democratic Nepal: Inclusive Political Institutions for a Multicultural Society*. New Delhi: Sage, 2005.

Lecomte-Tilouine, Marie. "The History of the Messianic and Rebel King Lakhan Thapa: Utopia and Ideology among Magars." In *Resistance and the State: Nepalese Experience*, edited by D. Gellner, 244–78. New Delhi: Social Science Press, 2002.

Lemarchand, René. "Patterns of State Collapse and Reconstruction in Central Africa: Reflections on the Crisis in the Great Lakes Region." *afrika spectrum* 32, no. 2, (1997): 173–93.

Levi, Werner. "Government and Politics of Nepal: I." *Far Eastern Review* 21, no. 18 (December 1952): 190.

———. "Political Rivalries in Nepal." *Far Eastern Survey* 23, no. 7 (July 1954): 102–7.

Levine, Nancy. "Caste, State, and Ethnic Boundaries in Nepal." *Journal of Asian Studies* 46, no. 1 (1987): 71–78.

Library of Congress, Nepal Education, n.d. http://countrystudies.us/nepal/34.htm (12 August 2006).

———, Nepal, n.d. http://www.country-data.com/cgi-bin/query/r-9115.html (20 August 2006).

Logan, Marty. "NEPAL: A Nod to Indigenous People." *Interpress Service News Agency*, 31 August 2006. http://www.ipsnews.net/news.asp?idnews=34495 (31 August 2006).

Maitra, Ramtanu. "U.S. Jittery over Nepal." *Asia Times on Line*, 16 March 2005. http://www.atimes.com/atimes/South_Asia/GC16Df01.html (19 June 2005).

Manchanda, Rita. "Himalayan Thunder." *Frontline* 18, no. 25 (December 2001). http://www.hinduonnet.com/fline/fl1825/18250490.htm (15 March 2006).

———. "Talks and Fears" *Frontline* 20, no. 7 (March 2003). http://www.hinduonnet.com/fline/fl2007/stories/20030411000406200.htm (15 March 2005).

———. "The King's Coup." *Frontline* 19, no. 21 (October 2002). http://www.frontlineonnet.com/fl1921/stories/20021025006712800.htm (21 April 2005).

———. "Uneasy Peace in Kathmandu." *Frontline* 19, no. 1 (January 2002). http://www.hinduonnet.com/fline/fl1901/19010590.htm (21 April 2005).

———. "Unending Crisis." *Frontline* 19, no. 23 (November 2002). http://www.hinduonnet.com/fline/fl1901/19010590.htm (22 April 2005).

———. "Emergency and a Crisis." *Frontline* 19, no. 5 (March 2002). http://www.hinduonnet.com/fline/fl1905/19050500.htm (23 April 2005).

Mann, Michael. "The Autonomous Power of the State." In *States in History*, edited by John A. Hall, 109–36. Oxford: Basil Blackwell, 1986.

Marks, Thomas A. *Insurgency in Nepal*. Carlisle, PA: U.S. Army College Strategic Studies Institute, 2003.

Marshall, P. J. *East Indian Fortunes: the British in Bengal in the Eighteenth Century*. Oxford: Clarendon Press, 1976.

Matthew, Richard and Bishnu Raj Upreti. "Environmental Stress and Demographic Change in Nepal: Underlying Conditions Contributing to a Decade of Insurgency." In *Environmental Change and Security Program Report* 11, 29–39. Washington, DC: The Woodrow Wilson Center for International Scholars, 2005.

Mehtam, A. K. *The Royal Nepal Army—Meeting the Maoist Challenge*. New Delhi: Rupa, 2005.

Meillassoux, C. "Are There Castes in India?" *Economy and Society* 2, no. 1 (1973): 89–111.

Mikesell, Stephen L. "The Maoist Movement and the Threat to Democracy in Nepal." *Himalayan Research Bulletin* XXI, 1 (2001).

Mishra, Pankaj. "The People's War." *London Review of Books* 27, no. 12 (June 2005): 20–23.

Monthly Review. "The Letter of Dr. Baburam Bhattarai on the Palace Massacre in Nepal." 53, no. 2. http://www.monthlyreview.org/0601letter.htm (25 May 2005).

Mukherjee, Ramkrishna. *The Rise and Fall of the East India Company: A Sociological Appraisal.* New York: Monthly Review Press, 1974.

Muni, S. D. "Chinese Arms Pour into Nepal." *Times of India,* 1 September 1988.

Murshed, Mansoob S. and Scott Gates. "Spatial-Horizontal Inequality and the Maoist Insurgency in Nepal." *DFID of the UK,* 2003. www.worldbank.org/research/inequality/June18Papers/NepalConflict.pdf (2 October 2005).

National Planning Commission (NPC). *The Tenth Plan (Poverty Reduction Strategy Plan) 2002–2007.* Kathmandu: NPC, 2003.

Nepalnews.com. "'Secular Nepal' Finds Itself in the Eye of Controversy." *Nepalnews.com,* 2006. http://www.nepalnews.com/archive/2006/others/feature/may/news_feature07.php (14 August 2006).

Nepal Post. "King Should Be Given Space: PM." 7 August 2006.

Nguyen, Ming. "The Question of 'State Failure.'" *JRS Occasional Paper* 8 (March 2005).

Ojha, Ghanashyam. "Two State Powers in Nepal, Admits Pun." *The Kathmandu Post* (2003). http://www.nepalnews.com.np/contents/englishdaily/ktmpost/2003/mar/mar31/index.htm#2 (17 May 2005).

Olson, Mancur. "Dictatorship, Democracy, and Development." *American Political Science Review* 87, no. 3 (1993): 567–76.

———. *Power and Prosperity.* New York: Basic Books, 2000.

Onesto, Li. *Dispatches from the People's War in Nepal.* London: Pluto Press, 2005.

———. *Revolutionary Worker* 1043, 20 February 2000. http://rwor.org/a/v21/1040-049/1043/interv.htm (28 May 2005).

Pandey, Tulsi Ram, Surendra Mishra, Damber Chemjong, Sanjeev Pokhrel, and Nabain Rawal. "Forms and Patterns of Social Discrimination in Nepal: A Report." UNESCO Series of Monographs and Working Paper no. 8, Lalitpur 2006. http://unesdoc.unesco.org/images/0014/001460/146086e.pdf#search=%22Mahendra%20Lawati%20Nepal%20Book%22 (28 August 2006).

Pantha, Ritu, and Bharat Raj Sharma. "Population Size, Growth and Distribution." *Population Monograph* 1. Kathmandu: Central Bureau of Statistics Report, Government of Nepal Central Bureau of Statistics Report, 2002.

Pfaff-Czarnecka, Joanna. "Debating the State of the Nation: Ethnicization of Politics in Nepal—A Position Paper." In *Ethnic Futures: The State and Identity Politics in Asia,* edited by Joanna Pfaff-Czarnecka, Darini Rajasigham-Senanayeke, Ashis Nandy, and Edmund Terrace Gomez, 41–98. New Delhi: Sage Publications, 1999.

Piers Blakie, John Cameron, and David Seddon, eds. *Nepal in Crisis: Growth and Stagnation at the Periphery.* Oxford: Clarendon Press, 1980.

Pigg, Stacy Leigh. "Inventing Social Categories through Place: Social Representations and Development in Nepal." *Comparative Studies in Society and History* 34, no. 3 (July 1992): 419–513.

Poudel, Keshab. "Enduring Importance." *Spotlight* 21, no. 27 (January 2002): 1.

——. "Noble Monarch." *Spotlight* 23, no. 46 (June 2004): 4.

Pradhan, K. *The Gorkha Conquests: The Process and Consequences of the Unification of Nepal with Particular References to Eastern Nepal.* Calcutta: Oxford University Press, 1991.

Pradhan, Suman. "Tales from Rolpa: a 10-Day Trek Across the Maoist Heartland." *Kantipur on line* (June 2005).

——. "Terai on a Slow Burn." *Madhesi*, 21 August 2006. https://madhesi.word press.com/2006/08/21/tarai-on-a-slow-burn/ (2 September 2006).

Pradyumnya, Karan, and Hiroshi Ishi. *A Himalayan Kingdom in Transition.* Tokyo: United Nations University Press, 1996.

Rabindra, Mishra. "Nepal Maoists Seek to Isolate King." *BBC News* (2005). http://news.bbc.co.uk/1/hi/world/south_asia/4212988.stm (2 October 2005).

Rajendra Mahto. "Nepal's Terai People Neglected." 4 August 2006. https://madhesi .wordpress.com/2006/08/04/nepals-terai-people-neglected/ (3 September 2006).

Rana, N. R. L. *The Anglo Gorkha War 1814-1816.* Kathmandu: NRL Rana, 1970.

Regmi, M. C. *A Study of Nepali Economic History 1768-1846.* New Delhi: Manjushree Publishing House, 1971.

——. *An Economic History of Nepal, 1846-1951.* Varanasi: Nath, 1988.

——. "Recent Land Reform Programs in Nepal." *Asian Survey* 1, no. 7 (September 1961): 32-37.

Reuschmeyer, Dietrich, and Peter Evans. "Transnational Linkages and the Economic Role of the State: an Analysis of Developing and Industrial States in the Post World War II Period." In *Bringing the State Back In*, edited by Peter Evans, Dietrich Reuschmeyer, and Theda Skocpol, 192-226. Cambridge: Cambridge University Press, 1986.

Revolutionary Worker. "Celebrate the 20th Anniversary of the Revolutionary International Movement." no. 1238, 1 May 2004. http://rwor.org/a/1238/rimedit.htm and "Revolutionary International Movement." http://cpnm.org/new/RIM/rim_ index.htm (21 June 2005).

Riaz, Ali. *Unfolding State: The Transformation of Bangladesh.* Ontario: de Sitters Publications, 2005.

Rocca, Christina B. "Deepening U.S. Engagement in South Asia." 2005. http://www.state.gov/p/sa/rls/rm/14296.htm (9 June 2005).

Rose, L. E. *Nepal: A Strategy for Survival.* Berkeley: University of California Press, 1971.

Rose, L. E., and E. Fisher. *The Politics of Nepal: Persistence and Change in an Asian Monarchy.* Ithaca, NY: Cornell University Press, 1970.

Rose, L. E., and Roger Dial. "Can a Ministate Find True Happiness in a World Dominated by Protagonist Powers? [The] Nepal Case." *Protagonists, Power, and the Third World: Essays on the Changing International System, Annals of the American Academy of Political and Social Science* 386 (November 1969): 89-101.

Rotberg, Fiona. "Nepal: Environmental Scarcity and State Failure." 2006. http://www.worldsecuritynetwork.com/showArticle3.cfm?article_id=12984 (31 July 2006).

Rotberg, Robert I. "Failed States, Collapsed States, Weak States: Causes and Indicators." *State Failure and State Weakness in a Time of Terror*, edited by Robert I. Rotberg. Washington, DC: Brookings Institution Press, 2003.

———. "The Failure and Collapse of Nation States: Breakdown, Prevention and Repair" *When States Fail: Causes and Consequences,* ed. Robert Rotberg. Princeton: Princeton University Press, 2004, 3.

———. "The New Nature of Nation-State Failure." *The Washington Quarterly* 25, no. 3, (2002): 93.

Royal Nepal Army. "Red Corner Alert Notice Against Prominent Maoists." Kathmandu: Royal Nepal Army. http://www.rna.mil.np/cio/wanted.php (11 June 2005).

Schloss, Aran. "Stages of Development and Uses of Planning." *Asian Survey* 23, no. 10 (October 1983): 1115-27.

Schwarz, Rolf. "State Formation Processes in Rentier States: The Middle Eastern Case." Paper presented at the fifth Pan-European Conference on International Relations, ECPR Standing Group on International Relations, Hague, 9-11 September 2004.

Seddon, D. *Nepal : A State of Poverty.* New Delhi: Vikas, 1987.

Seddon, D., P. Blaikie, and J. Cameron. *Nepal in Crisis: Growth and Stagnation at the Periphery.* New Delhi: Oxford University Press, 1980.

Shah, Sukhdev. "Developing an Economy—Nepal's Experience." *Asian Survey* XXI, no. 10 (October 1981): 1060-79.

Shaha, R. *Modern Nepal: A Political History 1769-1955. Volume 1 (1769-1885).* New Delhi: Manohar, 1990.

Shanin, Teodor. "Class, State and Revolutions: Substitutes and Realities." In *Introduction to the Sociology of the "Developing Societies,"* edited by Hamza Alavi and Teodor Shanin, 308-31. New York: Monthly Review Press, 1982.

Sharma, Hari. "Political Conflict in Nepal and Quest for Autonomy." *Calcutta Research Group Seminar,* July 2005.

Sharma, Lal Prasad. "Maoist Abducts Four, Thrash One." *eKantipur,* 2006. http://www.kantipuronline.com/kolnews.php?&nid=82440 (12 August 2006).

Sharma, Shiva, and Bijendra Basnyat. "Nepal: Bonded Labor among Child Workers of Kamayia System: A Rapid Assessment." International Labor Organization, International Labor Program on the Elimination of Child Labor, 2001. http://www.ilo.org/public/english/standards/ipec/simpoc/nepal/rap/bonded.pdf (15 July 2006).

Sharma, Sudheer. "The Maoist Movement: An Evolutionary Perspective." In *Understanding the Maoist Movement in Nepal,* edited by Deepak Thapa, 361-80. Kathmandu: Martin Chautari, 2003.

Singh, Mohan Bikram. "The Royal Palace Massacre and the Maoists Pro-King Political Line." In *The People's War in Nepal: Left Perspectives,* edited by A. Karki and David Seddon, 315-74. New Delhi: Adroit Publishers, 2003.

Singh, Nirvikar. "Cultural Conflicts in India: Punjab and Kashmir." In *The Myth of Ethnic Conflict,* edited by Ronnie Lipschutz and Beverly Crawford, 352-60. Berkley, CA: University of Berkley Press, 1999.

Smith, T. B. "Nepal's Political System in Transition." In *Political Participation and Change in South Asia: The Context of Nepal,* edited by M. Dharamdasani, 29-30. Varanasi: Shalimar, 1984.

Sob, Durga. "Dalit Women: The Triple Oppression of Dalit Women." *Asian Human Rights Commission, Human Rights Solidarity* 11, no. 8, August 2001. http://www.ahrchk.net/hrsolid/mainfile.php/2001vol11no08/1169/ (2 September 2006).

South Asia Alliance for Poverty Eradication (SAAPE). *Poverty in South Asia 2003: Civil Society Perspectives*. Kathmandu: SAAPE, 2003.

South Asia Terrorism Portal. "Nepal Terrorist Groups—Communist Party of Nepal Maoist," n.d. http://www.satp.org/satporgtp/countries/nepal/terroristoutfits/index.html# (23 May 2005).

Srestha, Anit. "Dalits in Nepal: Story of Discrimination." *Asia Pacific News* 30, 2002. http://www.hurights.or.jp/asia-pacific/no_30/04.htm (31 August 2006).

Srestha, Nanda R. *Landlessness and Migration in Nepal*. Boulder: Westview Press, 1990.

Stahl, Rachel and Michael Stahl. "The Failed and Failing State and the Bush Administration: Paradoxes and Perils." Paper prepared for the workshop on "Failed and Failing States," Florence, Italy, 10–14 April 2001. http://www.cdi.org/issues/failedstates/Bush.htm (10 March 2004).

Thapa, Deepak. "Radicalism and the Emergence of Maoists." In *Himalayan People's War: Nepal's Maoist Rebellion*, edited by Michael Hutt, 21–37. Bloomington: Indiana University Press, 2004.

Thapa, Deepak, and Bandita Sijapati. *A Kingdom Under Siege: Nepal's Maoist Insurgency, 1996–2004*. New York: Zed Books, 2004.

Thapliyal, Sangeeta. "Contesting Mutual Security: India—Nepal Relations." *Observer Research Foundation Analysis*. New Delhi: ORF, 2005.

The Election Commission of Nepal. http://www.election-commission.org.np/ (22 May 2005).

The Election Commission Report. "Fact and Figure in Elections in Nepal." http://www.election-commission.org.np/ (8 June 2005).

The Independent. Interview with Dr. Baburam Bhattrai, vol. V, no. 41, December 1995.

The Rising Nepal, Kathmandau. "Chief of Armed Police Force Shot Dead." 2003. www.nepalnews.com.np/contents/englishdaily/trn/2003/jan/jan27/index1.htm (14 February 2005).

Theis, Cameron. "State Building, Interstate and Intrastate Rivalry: A Study of Post-Colonial Developing Country Extractive Efforts, 1974–1993." Paper presented at the annual meeting of the International Studies Association, New Orleans, March 2002.

Tilly, Charles. *Coercion, Capital and European States, AD 990–1990*. Oxford: Basil Blackwell, 1990.

———. "Entanglements of European City States." In *Cities and the Rise of the State in Europe, AD 1000–1800*, edited by Charles Tilly, 1–27. Boulder, CO: Westview, 1994.

———. "Reflections on the History of European State-Making." In *The Formation of National States in Western Europe*, edited by Charles Tilly, 3–84. Princeton, NJ: Princeton University Press, 1975.

———. "War Making and State Making as Organized Crime." In *Bringing the State Back In*, edited by Peter Evans, Dietrich Reuschmeyer, and Theda Skocpol, 169–91. Cambridge: Cambridge University Press, 1985.

Times of India. "BJP Rues Nepal's Switch from Hindu to Secular State." 20 May 2006.

UNDP. *Nepal Human Development Report 2004: Empowerment and Poverty Reduction*. Kathmandu: UNDP, 2004.

Weber, Max. *The Theory of Social and Economic Organization*, edited by Talcott Parsons. London: Collier-Macmillan Ltd, 1947.

Weekly Telegraph (Kathmandu) Editorial. "Failed State?" 19 February 2004. http://www.nepalnews.com.np/contents/englishweekly/telegraph/2004/feb/feb18/editorial.htm (14 January 2006).

Werner, Levi. "Government and Politics in Nepal: II." *Far Eastern Survey* 22, no. 1 (January 1953): 5–10.

Whelpton, John. *A History of Nepal*. Cambridge: Cambridge University Press, 2005.

Wolf, Stefan. "State Failure in a Regional Context." 2005. www.stefanwolff.com/working-papers/state-failure.pdf (25 March 2006).

World Bank. "Poverty in Nepal at the Turn of the Twenty-First Century." Report no: 18639-NEP. Washington, DC: The World Bank, 1998.

———. *World Development Report (2000/2001): Attacking Poverty*. (Washington, DC: World Bank, 2001).

World Health Organization (WHO). "Nepal and Family Planning: An Overview." *World Health Organization Report*, 2001. http://w3.whosea.org/LinkFiles/Family_Planning_Fact_Sheets_nepal.pdf (12 August 2006).

Index

About the Authors

Ali Riaz is professor and chair of the Department of Politics and Government at Illinois State University. He has previously taught at Claflin University in South Carolina, Lincoln University in the United Kingdom, and Dhaka University in Bangladesh. He worked as broadcast journalist in the British Broadcasting Corporation (BBC) in London for five years. Riaz has served as consultant to various national and international organizations. Ali Riaz earned his Ph.D. from the University of Hawaii and received the Dean's Award for Outstanding Scholarship in 2004, the Outstanding College Researcher Award in 2005 at Illinois State University, and the 2006 Pi Sigma Alpha Teaching Award. He has to his credit more than ten books in Bengali and four in English. His publications include *God Willing: The Politics of Islamism in Bangladesh* (2004) and *Unfolding State: The Transformation of Bangladesh* (2005).

Subho Basu is associate professor in the Department of History at Maxwell School of Citizenship and Public Affairs, Syracuse University. After completing his Ph.D. at Cambridge University, UK, he was Smuts Hinduja Fellow at the Centre of South Asian Studies, University of Cambridge, and was also elected a fellow of Wolfson College at Cambridge University. In years following, he taught at the College of St. Mark and St. John, Plymouth, School of Oriental and African Studies, University of London, and Illinois State University. He coedited with Suranjan Das *Electoral Politics in South Asia* and has widely published on labor history and contemporary Indian politics. Recently, he has published his monograph *Does Class Matter?* His other works include a coedited volume with Crispin Bates, *Rethinking Indian Political Institutions* (2006).

Made in the USA
Lexington, KY
18 June 2013